The
Sauces
& Salsas
Cookbook

The
Sauces
& Salsas
Cookbook

Christine France

LORENZ BOOKS

This edition is published by Lorenz Books
Lorenz Books is an imprint of Anness Publishing Ltd
Hermes House, 88–89 Blackfriars Road, London SE1 8HA
tel. 020 7401 2077; fax 020 7633 9499
www.lorenzbooks.com; info@anness.com
© Anness Publishing Ltd 2004

UK agent: The Manning Partnership Ltd
tel. 01225 478444; fax 01225 478440; sales@manning-partnership.co.uk

UK distributor: Grantham Book Services Ltd
tel. 01476 541080; fax 01476 541061; orders@gbs.tbs-ltd.co.uk

North American agent/distributor: National Book Network
tel. 301 459 3366; fax 301 429 5746; www.nbnbooks.com

Australian agent/distributor: Pan Macmillan Australia
tel. 1300 135 113; fax 1300 135 103; customer.service@macmillan.com.au

New Zealand agent/distributor: David Bateman Ltd
tel. (09) 415 7664; fax (09) 415 8892

A CIP catalogue record for this book is available from the British Library.

Publisher: Joanna Lorenz
Managing Editor: Linda Fraser
Editor: Joy Wotton
Jacket and Text Design: Chloe Steers
Typesetting: Jonathan Harley
Illustrations: Angela Wood

1 3 5 7 9 10 8 6 4 2 1

NOTES
Bracketed terms are intended for American readers.
For all recipes quantities are given in both metric and imperial measures and,
where appropriate, measures are also given in standard cups and spoons. Follow
one set, but not a mixture, because they are not interchangeable. Standard spoon
and cup measures are level. 1 tsp = 5ml, 1 tbsp = 15ml, 1 cup = 250ml/8fl oz.
Australian standard tablespoons are 20ml. Australian readers should use 3 tsp in
place of 1 tbsp for measuring small quantities of gelatine, flour, salt etc.
Medium (US large) eggs are used unless otherwise stated.

CONTENTS

INTRODUCTION

Sauce-making has gained itself a reputation for being a difficult art, but in fact, most sauces are simplicity itself and can be made in a matter of minutes. True, there are some classic sauces whose preparation takes a little time and a degree of skill, but the techniques are easily learned and you don't have to be a fully trained chef to achieve success. However, such is the reputation of sauces that your guests may think you are a professional.

Once you've mastered a few basic methods and simple techniques, you'll find the myth is dispelled and you'll have a collection of sauce recipes always to hand, ready to add a touch of individuality to your cooking, whether for everyday family meals or the most sophisticated dinner parties. Even if you lack the time or skills to cook elaborate dishes, sauces will add originality to your cooking, an extra finishing touch to the dish and transform even the plainest foods into something special.

Sauces can play many different roles in cookery, involving a variety of dishes and almost every occasion and course. A sauce may be used to complement a dish, adding a touch of piquancy, balancing flavours, or simply enhancing the appearance. Others are used to tenderize or moisten foods before and during cooking, or to bind ingredients together. Some are integral to a dish, while others are served on the side and diners can choose how much or how little they wish to add. Served in the form of a tasty dip or relish, they can give an added dimension to an endless selection of snacks or party dishes for the buffet table.

This book brings together a comprehensive collection of sauces, salsas, dips, relishes, marinades and dressings, from classics to modern ideas, which build to make an invaluable reference and source of creative ideas in your kitchen.

General Reference

Whether you are a novice cook who wants to add interest and new flavours to weekday meals, or an expert who would like to broaden your culinary repertoire, understanding the basics of sauce-making will provide a firm foundation for a lifetime of creative cooking. Many sauce-making ingredients, such as flour, eggs and fat, are basics in every kitchen. But adding just a few other well-chosen ingredients will provide you with a store cupboard (pantry) from which to make an extensive range of interesting and flavourful accompaniments to meals.

Sauce-making doesn't require any specialist equipment, and much of what you already own will be sufficient – a selection of pans, bowls, whisks, ladles, sieves, weighing scales and measuring jugs (cups) will guarantee that the correct equipment is always to hand. Nevertheless, it's worth having a look at the guide to especially useful kitchen tools for some expert advice.

The following pages provide a brief explanation of the science behind a successful sauce – which flours to use for a smooth texture, which fats and oils add the best flavour, how much and what type of liquid to use and how to infuse (steep) flavours. All the basic methods of sauce-making are included, from a classic white sauce to a rich roux, whether you want sweet or savoury, hot or cold sauces. There is advice on preparation techniques, from clarifying butter to melting chocolate, suggestions for adapting and modifying basic sauces to suit different kinds of dishes, and plenty of hints and tips to help you produce the best results every time.

FLOURS

There is a wide range of flours and thickening agents on the market, all of them widely available. It is important to select the right product, since the choice of flour used for a sauce will determine not only the cooking method to be used, but the final texture and flavour of the finished sauce. These general guidelines should help remove any mystique or confusion involved.

PLAIN WHITE FLOUR

Also known as all-purpose flour, this is the standard choice for making roux-based sauces and gravies. Its fine, smooth texture combines easily with melted fat or, more rarely, hot oil for a sauce with a roux base, so that when heated, the starch grains burst and cook, thickening the sauce liquid.

White flour usually contains 70–75 per cent of the wheatgrain. Most of the bran and wheatgerm have been removed during the process of milling, leaving it almost pure white, so it is excellent for thickening white sauces. White flour is chemically bleached, making it pale in colour and therefore more suitable for white sauces than unbleached, stoneground flours. As a general rule, it is simply labelled plain or all-purpose flour, and the word "white" does not appear anywhere on the label.

SELF-RAISING, STRONG AND SOFT FLOURS

These are flours designed for specific baking uses, not for sauces, but they could be used in an emergency if you run out of plain flour. Self-raising (self-rising) flour has chemical agents added during milling that react with heat to make cake mixtures rise during cooking. Strong flour has a higher proportion of gluten, making it most suitable for bread-making. Soft flours have a lower gluten content, and are designed for cakes and pastries, but they also make a good thickener for smooth sauces.

WHOLEMEAL, WHEATMEAL AND BROWN FLOURS

These flours contain more of the bran and wheatgerm, giving them a coarse texture and darker colour. They are not usually chosen for making sauces, but if you don't mind the texture and colour, there's no reason why you shouldn't use them, and they will add a little fibre to your diet.

SAUCE FLOUR

This flour has been recently introduced, and has a lower protein level than ordinary wheat flour, so that sauces made with it are less likely to go lumpy. It is designed specifically for making cooked white sauces and gravies. It is also a good choice for making healthier sauces, since it is suitable for those made by the all-in-one or blending method, in which no fat is used.

CORNFLOUR

Also known as cornstarch, this fine ground maize (cornmeal) flour is gluten-free. It is light and smooth-textured, producing velvety, lump-free sauces, usually made by the blending method. When first added to a clear liquid it gives a cloudy appearance, but on heating, the sauce becomes almost clear. This makes it a popular choice for Chinese sauces, and its smooth texture makes it ideal for using in sweet white sauces or those that are to be used for coating foods.

POTATO FLOUR

Also known as *farine de fécule*, potato flour is made from pure potato starch. It is very fine, smooth and bright white in colour. It makes a light, clear thickener for sauces without affecting the flavour. You will need to use slightly less potato flour than plain (all-purpose) flour for thickening. It is most suited to the blending method of sauce-making, and is often used in Chinese and Asian dishes and stir-fry sauces, so it is widely available from Asian stores.

ARROWROOT

This is a finely ground powder made from the root of a tropical tree. It is used in the same way as cornflour (cornstarch) and gives a smooth, clear appearance to sweet and savoury sauces without affecting either the colour or the flavour.

STORING FLOUR

Store flour in a cool, dark, dry, airy place, away from steam or damp. Place the flour into a clean container or a storage jar with a close-fitting lid, and always make sure you wash and dry the container thoroughly before refilling it. Check the "use by" dates, and use up the flour within the recommended pack date, or replace it. Don't add new flour to old in a storage jar.

Once opened, plain (all-purpose) white flour can be stored under the right conditions for up to six months, but wholemeal (whole-wheat) and brown flours have a higher fat content so these are best used within two months. Like all food, flour is best used while fresh. Make sure it is stored in dark, cool conditions; buy it in small quantities and plan to use it quickly rather than storing it indefinitely, when it will turn rancid.

CUSTARD POWDER

A useful store-cupboard (pantry) thickener for quick custard sauces, this is simply a coloured cornflour- (cornstarch-) based flour. For a quick custard, a similar result can be achieved by using a small amount of cornflour with a few drops of yellow food colouring and vanilla essence (extract). Make into a sauce with milk by the blending method and sweeten to taste.

FATS

Fats improve the flavour and texture of sauces. Those usually used are "yellow" fats, such as butter or oils. Many sauces, such as roux or beurre maniére, are made from a flour base. Hollandaise, mayonnaise and other classic emulsified sauces use melted butter or liquid oils, beaten with eggs to enrich and thicken. The same principle is used in reduced sauces and oil-based salad dressings.

BUTTER

A natural product made by churning cream, butter has an 80 per cent fat content. Butter is made in two basic types, sweetcream and lactic, and both are available salted, lightly salted or unsalted (sweet). The choice will depend on whether you are making a sweet or savoury sauce.

Clarified butter, ghee or concentrated butters will withstand higher temperatures and will not burn so easily.

MARGARINE

Soft (tub) margarines, made from a blend of vegetable oils and/or animal oils, have a soft, spreadable texture. Hard (packet) margarines have a firmer texture and are made from animal and vegetable fats. Both types have the same fat content as butter, and can be used as a direct substitute for butter in making sweet and savoury sauces. As the flavour is inferior to butter, margarines are best chosen for more robustly flavoured sauces.

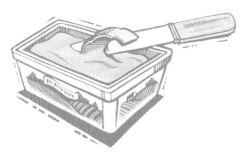

SPREADS

The extensive choice of different spreads on the market is confusing, to say the least, but as a general guide, unless they are labelled "low-fat", or "very low-fat", they are usually suitable for sauce-making. Beyond that, choice is very much a matter of personal preference.

Polyunsaturated vegetable oil spreads: Products described in this way are made either from a single vegetable oil or sunflower oil alone, or from a blend of different vegetable oils. They vary in fat content from 61 to 79 per cent.

Monounsaturated vegetable oil spreads: Made from olive oil or rapeseed (canola) oil, these spreads vary in fat content from 60 to 75 per cent.

Dairy spreads: These contain cream or buttermilk to retain a buttery flavour and smooth texture, while providing a lower-fat alternative to butter. The fat content varies between 61 and 75 per cent.

Reduced fat spreads: These are either made from vegetable oils alone or may also contain some dairy or animal fat. Their fat content is between 50 and 60 per cent.

Low-fat spreads and very low-fat spreads: These spreads, popular with the weight-conscious, contain less than 40 per cent fat, and are often as low as 25 per cent. They are not recommended for cooking, although they can be added to all-in-one method sauces.

OILS

These are fats that are liquid at room temperature, and are used in emulsion sauces, such as mayonnaise, or in salad dressings, usually balanced with vinegar or other acids, such as citrus juices. However, they can also be used as a direct replacement for butter or hard fats in roux or other flour-thickened sauces, with good results. With the exception of coconut oil and palm oil, they are mostly rich in unsaturated fat, which helps reduce cholesterol levels. The choice of individual oils for a particular sauce depends largely on flavour and personal taste.

Groundnut (peanut) oil: Made from peanuts, this is usually used where a mild flavour is required.

Sesame seed oil: Usually used for flavouring Asian sauces at the end of cooking, as it has an intense, rich flavour and burns easily when heated. However, it can be heated with care, or mixed half and half with another oil, such as groundnut (peanut).

Soya oil: A mild-flavoured oil which will withstand high temperatures, this keeps well and is economical to use.

Sunflower oil: A little more expensive to use than soya oil, this versatile, light-flavoured oil is good for sauces or dressings, as it does not mask other flavours.

Nut oils: Walnut and hazelnut oils are the most commonly used nut oils for dressings, lending their rich, distinctive flavours to salads. Use nut oils in moderation, perhaps combined with a milder oil, as the flavours can be strong.

OLIVE OILS

The characteristics and quality of olive oils vary and depend on variety, growing region and method of production. Many are blended, but the best quality oils are produced on individual estates. For most sauces, including mayonnaise, it's best to choose virgin or pure olive oil, and keep the more expensive extra virgin ones for salad dressings, or for drizzling directly over foods. It is more economical to buy olive oils in larger quantities.

Extra virgin first pressed or cold pressed olive oils: These oils are made from what is literally the first pressing of the olives, with no additional treatment, such as heat or blending. By law, these oils never have more than 1 per cent acidity, guaranteeing a fine flavour. They have a very distinctive flavour, as well as a pungent aroma. They are usually a deep green colour and are sometimes cloudy, although both of these factors vary according to the area where the oil has been produced.

Virgin olive oil: This is also cold pressed and unrefined, but has a higher acidity content than extra virgin oil, with a maximum level of 1 to 1.5 per cent.

Pure olive oil: This comes from the third or fourth pressing of the olives, and is usually blended. It has a maximum acid content of 2 per cent. It is widely used in cooking since it is not overpowering.

Light olive oil: This is from the last pressing of the fruit and has the lightest flavour.

THE STORE CUPBOARD

Awell-stocked store cupboard (pantry) makes every cook's life considerably easier and when it comes to sauce-making, it really does make sense. Just by making sure that you keep a few standard ingredients and flavourings in stock, you will always be able to whip up an impromptu sauce when the occasion demands, transforming a simple dish into something really special.

STOCK CUBES AND POWDERS
There is a wide choice of commercial stock (bouillon) cubes and powders on the market, and these vary in flavour and quality. Good-quality products make adequate substitutes for fresh stock, and are certainly very convenient to use. However, some brands tend to be quite salty, so allow for this when adding other seasonings. Follow the pack directions for quantities to use. Generally speaking, it is worth paying a little more for good-quality stock cubes or powder, and it is also worth looking for one that is made with natural ingredients, which are likely to impart a more natural flavour.

Many supermarkets also now sell ready-made cartons of basic fresh stocks in the chilled foods section, such as beef, chicken, fish and vegetable stock, and these are a good substitute for home-made if you're short of time to make your own. These usually have a better flavour than stock cubes or powder, but must be stored in the refrigerator rather than the store cupboard.

Bottled stocks are treated with ultra-high heat to preserve them, in the same way as UHT or longlife milk. This tends to affect the flavour adversely. However, they can be very convenient as they keep in the store cupboard for a very long time, but once opened should be kept in the refrigerator.

Canned consommé makes an excellent substitute for a good brown stock in rich savoury sauces, so is well worth keeping handy in the store cupboard. If you need a light stock, the colour of consommé may be too dark, but brands vary.

CANNED TOMATOES AND SAUCES
Since many of the plum tomatoes we buy out of season in this country are lacking in flavour, it's a safer bet to go for good-quality canned tomatoes in recipes, either whole or chopped. The best are from Italy, so check the label carefully. *Polpa di pomodoro* are finely chopped or crushed. Avoid those with added herbs or spices, which are best added fresh, according to the recipe.

COCONUT MILK AND CREAM

Coconut milk and cream are used widely in Asian dishes, particularly those based on spicy and curried sauces. They can be used rather like dairy products, for thickening, enriching and flavouring.

Coconut milk: *This is available in cans and longlife packs. It is similar in thickness to single (light) cream.*

Coconut cream: *This has the thickness of double (heavy) cream. Creamed coconut is solid and white; it is sold in blocks, so you can cut off just the amount you need and melt it into sauces.*

Crushed or creamed tomatoes: Sold as sugocasa, polpa and passata (bottled strained tomatoes), and usually packed in convenient jars or bottles, these are invaluable for sauces. Sugocasa and polpa have a chunky texture, and passata is sieved to a smooth purée.

Tomato purée (paste): This is concentrated, cooked tomato pulp in a strong, thick paste, and is sold in tubes or cans. The strength of different brands varies, so use with care or the flavour can overpower a sauce. Sun-dried tomato paste is a purée of sun-dried tomatoes with olive oil. It has a sweet, rich flavour, and is milder and less acid than ordinary tomato purée.

Tomato ketchup: Made from puréed tomatoes, vinegar, sugar and spices, there is more to this great favourite than shaking it on chips (French fries). It is invaluable for adding extra flavour to barbecue sauces and sauces made with meat.

COMMERCIAL SAUCES

The huge range of commercially-made flavouring sauces now available is a boon to the creative cook. Some of the most useful ones to keep in your store cupboard are:

Hot pepper sauces: Used in South American and Caribbean cooking, there are many versions of pepper sauce, the most famous being Tabasco. Use with caution, as they can be fiery. These sauces will pep up almost any savoury sauce, marinade or dressing.

COOK'S TIP
Chopped canned tomatoes are usually more expensive than whole ones, so you can save valuable pennies by simply chopping them yourself.

Mustards: Ready-made mustards are a blend of ground mustard seeds with flour and salt, often with wine, herbs and other spices. Dijon is often used for classic French sauces and for dressings such as vinaigrette and mayonnaise – it also helps to stabilize the emulsion. Bordeaux, also sometimes simply called "French mustard", is darker and stronger, but still smooth and good for adding to robust sauces. The other really well-known French mustard, Meaux, is grainy and quite spicy in flavour. Yellow English (hot) mustard is a good choice to give colour and bite to cheese sauce or to flavour rich gravies for meat. It is also widely available in powdered form. Milder German mustard is good for a barbecue sauce to serve with chops or sausages. Mild, creamy American mustard is squeezed on to hotdogs or burgers. Wholegrain mustard gives a pleasant texture, particularly to creamy savoury sauces and dressings, and is excellent in marinades for steak.

Oyster sauce: A thicker-textured, Chinese sauce made with the extract of real oysters, this adds a delicious sweet-savoury flavour to sauces for accompanying and marinades for meat, fish or vegetables.

Pesto: Commercially made pesto is sold in jars, either as the traditional green basil pesto, or as a red pesto made from sun-dried tomatoes. Use it just as it is as a replacement for fresh pesto sauce to stir into pasta, pepped up with a little freshly grated Parmesan cheese or an extra drizzle of olive oil. You can also add it by the spoonful to enrich and enhance the flavour of tomato sauces, salsas and dressings. Once the jar of pesto has been opened, it should be treated as a fresh sauce and stored in the refrigerator.

Soy sauce: Although this is traditionally used for Chinese and Japanese foods, there is no need to limit its use to Asian dishes. Use it to flavour and colour all kinds of savoury sauces, marinades and dressings. Light soy sauce is good in light, sweet-and-sour or stir-fry sauces for fish or vegetables, and the richer, sweeter dark soy sauce is best with rich meat sauces such as satays, or for barbecue sauces.

Thai fish sauce or *nam pla*: This is a classic Thai sauce made from fermented fish. It has a pungent flavour and is best in cooked sauces. It adds a richness to sauces for both meat and fish.

Worcestershire sauce: This classic English sauce has its origins in India. Its spicy, mellowed flavour enhances savoury sauces, marinades and dressings of any type.

VINEGARS

These are made from alcoholic bases of malt, wine, beer, cider, rice wine and sugar, and most of these can be used to enhance flavour in sauces or as emulsifiers. Red and white wine vinegars, and fruit vinegars, such as raspberry, are particularly useful for salad dressings. Fruit vinegars are also a good choice for making sauces with the pan juices after cooking duck breasts. Herb vinegars add extra flavour to salad dressings and mayonnaise. Tarragon vinegar is the best known and is widely used for making Béarnaise sauce, but other herb vinegars include rosemary, basil and thyme. Rice vinegars add authentic flavours to Asian sauces. Spanish sherry vinegar and Italian balsamic vinegar are smooth and mellow in flavour, having been aged in wooden casks, sometimes for as long as 20 years. Bear in mind that they have intense, powerful flavours and you may need only a few drops, which is just as well, as they are quite expensive. They are best used in dressings without the addition of strong, masking flavours, such as garlic.

SWEETENERS

Some savoury sauces and salad dressings, as well as dessert sauces require a touch of sweetening.

Honey: Clear honey is widely used in marinades and dressings for savoury dishes, especially in Chinese cooking and for meat intended for the barbecue. Generally speaking, blended honey is quite adequate for this purpose, as it is often combined with strongly-flavoured ingredients that would mask the subtle flavour of single-flower honeys. However, it is worth considering these more expensive varieties of honey for use in dessert sauces – an orange sauce, for example, might be enhanced by the use of orange blossom honey.

Syrup: Several syrups are used in sauce-making, including cane and corn, but the most popular and richest tasting is maple.

Sugar: Icing (confectioners') and caster (superfine) sugar are widely used in sweet sauces, while brown sugars, such as muscovado (molasses), can enhance the flavour and enrich the colour of savoury sauces and marinades, especially those for meat intended for the barbecue.

Herbs & Spices

Many sauce recipes call for herbs and/or spices to add both flavour and colour, and there's almost no end to the variety you can buy nowadays, especially in the larger supermarkets and good Asian food stores. Generally speaking, herbs are the leafy tops and stems and, sometimes, roots of an edible plant, and spices are from the berries, seeds, bark and roots.

Culinary Herbs

Fresh herbs are preferable to dried or frozen, as they have more flavour and colour. It's worth growing a few of the more useful common herbs yourself. Some herbs grown in pots on the kitchen windowsill will always be handy when you need to snip off a few sprigs. It is considerably cheaper, too, as supermarket fresh herbs, even the ones in pots, have a limited life and can be quite costly. A useful basic selection to grow at home would include parsley, chives, thyme, mint, oregano, sage, bay and dill.

When cooking with herbs, you don't need to be too precise. Treat the measurements quoted in recipes as a general guide, and add the herbs according to your personal preference.

Dried and Frozen Herbs

Dried herbs are useful for emergencies. Many of the delicate-leaved herbs, such as basil, coriander (cilantro) or chervil, do not dry successfully, but the ones that are worth buying dried are thyme, rosemary, parsley, mint, oregano, tarragon and dill. Store dried herbs in airtight containers in a cool place away from light, and use them quickly as their flavour is soon lost.

Frozen herbs, such as parsley, chives and coriander, retain more of the flavour of fresh herbs and can be very useful and convenient – they can be added to a sauce or dressing straight from the freezer.

Salt and Pepper

Good-quality sea salt has a more intense flavour than "table" or "cooking" salt. Strong black peppercorns, mild white and very mild green are all worth storing. Green peppercorns, whether preserved in brine, freeze-dried or dehydrated, are often used in flavoured butters to serve with grilled (broiled) steak and in sauces that go with rich meats, such as pork and duck. The slightly resinous-tasting pink peppercorns are not true peppercorns.

Spices

Keep a good store of spices in the kitchen. A useful selection includes whole nutmeg, cinnamon sticks, vanilla pods (beans), coriander seeds, cumin seeds and curry paste (pastes keep for much longer than powders and often have a better flavour).

Cinnamon sticks: These have a sweet, spicy flavour and are widely used in sweet sauces and chutneys. They can either be crushed, although this is quite difficult, or used whole and then removed and discarded at the end of cooking.

Coriander: These seeds are used in chutneys and have a warm, mild sweet flavour. They feature in Indian, South-east Asian and Moroccan dishes.

Cumin: A key ingredient in chutneys and curries and widely used in Mexican, Middle Eastern and Indian sauces, these seeds have a strong and slightly bitter taste.

Curry paste: This is sold in a range of strengths and flavours. It keeps for much longer than curry powder.

Vanilla pods: Infuse (steep) these dried pods (beans) in milk or cream for sweet sauces and custards. Store in a jar of caster (superfine) sugar to make vanilla sugar.

Whole nutmeg: Freshly grated whole nutmeg is much better than the ground variety, which quickly loses its flavour, even when stored carefully.

DAIRY PRODUCTS

The number of sauces, especially traditional and classic ones, based on dairy products is enormous, so it is worth taking the time to understand the many different products available. You may be aiming for a rich and creamy sauce, or perhaps you would prefer a lighter, healthier alternative. The following descriptions should help you choose precisely the right ingredients.

MILK

The choice of milk for sauces depends upon the richness desired – for a rich flavour and creamy texture, choose full-fat (whole) milk, but if you're watching fat levels and looking for a lighter sauce, it is better to go for skimmed or semi-skimmed (low-fat).

Pasteurized: Most milk sold these days has been pasteurized (i.e. heat-treated) to destroy harmful bacteria. This should keep for up to 5 days under refrigeration.

Homogenized: This has been processed to distribute the fat globules evenly throughout the milk. It has the same keeping quality as ordinary milk.

Sterilized: This is homogenized, bottled and heat-treated for 20 minutes, so that it keeps without refrigeration until it is opened.

UHT: This milk is homogenized, then heat-treated to high temperatures. It has a slightly caramelized flavour, but is useful as a standby as it keeps unopened for about a year without refrigeration.

Condensed: This sweetened milk, sold in cans, has been reduced and concentrated through boiling. It is useful for rich dessert sauces. Lower-fat versions are available.

Evaporated (Unsweetened condensed): Unsweetened milk that has had some of the water removed by evaporation, this type of milk has a concentrated flavour and is slightly caramelized. It is available either in cans or longlife packs and there are also lighter-fat versions.

Goat's milk: Many people who are allergic to cow's milk can tolerate goat's milk, which may be used as a substitute. It has a similar flavour, but is slightly sharper and more digestible.

CREAM

All kinds of cream can be used to enrich and thicken both sweet and savoury sauces, both hot and cold.

Single (light) cream: This cream has a fat content of 18 per cent, which is too low for whipping. It will not withstand boiling without splitting, but can be stirred into sauces at the end of cooking.

Sour cream: This is single cream with an added souring culture, which sharpens the flavour and thickens the texture.

Double (heavy) cream: The fat content is 48 per cent. The cream almost doubles in bulk when whipped. It is especially good in hot sauces because it can withstand boiling without separating.

Whipping cream: This has 35 per cent fat, and whips up to a light texture, or can be stirred into sauces after cooking.

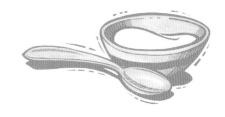

CRÈME FRAÎCHE

This has a mild, tangy flavour similar to that of sour cream, which makes it great for both sweet and savoury sauces. With a fat content of around 40 per cent, it is more stable than sour cream when heated. You can also buy a half-fat version, which can be successfully added to hot sauces.

YOGURT

This is a good lighter replacement for cream in many sweet and savoury sauces, and can be used as a substitute to add a lighter tang to all kinds of uncooked sauces. For cooked sauces, yogurt should be stabilized first with cornflour (cornstarch).

Greek (US strained plain) yogurt: This may be made from either cow's or sheep's milk. It is richer in flavour and texture than most yogurts, but still only has a fat content of around 8–10 per cent, so it makes a light substitute for cream in sauces.

Low-fat yogurt: It is the use of semi-skimmed (low-fat) milk that makes this yogurt low-fat. Very low-fat yogurt is made with skimmed milk. Both types have quite a sharp, tangy flavour.

EGGS

The freshness of eggs is easier to check nowadays, as most are individually marked with a date stamp on the shell. Fresh eggs should store well for two weeks, providing that the shell is not damaged or dirty. Egg shells are porous, so they are best stored away from strong-smelling foods. Before use, eggs should be left at room temperature for about 30 minutes.

CHEESE

Many hard cheeses can be grated and melted into sauces. Their fine flavour complements pasta sauces or a creamy white sauce to pour over vegetables. Always grate them freshly when needed and never use ready-grated Parmesan, as the flavour is soon lost. Once you've added cheese to a sauce, heat it gently without boiling.

Soft, fresh cheeses such as ricotta or mascarpone are also used to enrich a wide range of sauces and dips, from tomato sauces to fruit purées or custards. Ricotta is light in texture and mild in flavour, and makes a good base for dips, instead of yogurt, or can be melted into hot sauces.

Sauce-making Equipment

Making sauces requires very little in the way of specialist equipment, but a carefully selected set of basic equipment will help make tasks such as boiling, whisking and straining much easier. You may even find that most of these items are already in your kitchen. Shop around for those you still need, as quality varies enormously and it's worth buying the best you can afford.

Pans

The rule here is to choose the right pan for the job, which means that your pans do not necessarily have to be a matching set. Some pans may be suitable for more than one task, but you will need a variety of sizes and types. Look for solid, heavy pans that are stable when empty, and have tight-fitting lids and firmly riveted handles. Buying good-quality pans is an investment, as they will last for years, but cheap, thin pans will not only wear out quickly, but will conduct heat unevenly and cause burnt patches. A good selection would be:

- Milk pan with high sides and a lip. This may be non-stick, but it is not essential.
- Three pans with lids, ranging in size from about 1 litre/1¾ pints/4 cups to 7 litres/1⅔ pints/30 cups. They should be deep and straight-sided to minimize evaporation.
- Sauté pan with deep, straight sides.

- Double boiler – a useful pan for making delicate creams and custards and melting ingredients such as chocolate. If you don't have one, improvise with a heatproof bowl placed over a pan of hot water.

Materials for Pans

Stainless steel: This is attractive and hard-wearing, and providing they have a thick base with aluminium or copper, the pans will conduct heat evenly and efficiently.

Anodized aluminium: Light and easy to clean, this conducts the heat well and does not corrode. The metal reacts when in contact with acid and alkaline, so food should not be left to stand too long.

Copper: These pans are expensive but conduct heat very efficiently and are attractive and durable. Choose pans with a stainless steel lining, which is harder-wearing than tin.

Enamelled cast iron: This is heavy but conducts the heat well, evenly and slowly. These pans retain the heat for a long time, and are hard-wearing and durable.

Measuring Jug

Choose a solid jug (cup) marked clearly with standard measurements. Heatproof glass is ideal, as it is easy to see the liquid level and can take boiling liquids, yet the handle remains cool as it is a poor conductor of heat. Stainless steel jugs are attractive and hard-wearing.

MEASURING SPOONS

A set of clearly marked, standard measuring spoons is crucial for accurate measuring of small amounts of sauce ingredients. Spoon measurements given in recipes are always level – overfill the spoon, then scrape off the excess with a knife.

WOODEN SPOONS

A good assortment of wooden spoons is essential, and it is a good idea to keep them for individual uses. For example, you might reserve one for spicy sauces, one for creams and custards and so on; then there is no risk of flavour transfer. A good selection includes a wooden spoon, a wooden corner spoon with an edge to reach into the corners of pans, and a flat-edged wooden spatula, for efficient stirring without scratching the pan.

LADLES

Available in various sizes, ladles are useful for spooning and pouring sauces over foods. Some smaller ones have a useful lip for precise pouring. Stainless steel ladles are best. A slotted stainless steel draining spoon is invaluable for skimming and removing small pieces of ingredients from sauces.

WHISKS

Balloon whisks and spiral sauce whisks are the most efficient for blending sauce ingredients or whisking dressings, and it is useful to have two different sizes. Choose ones with a comfortable grip.

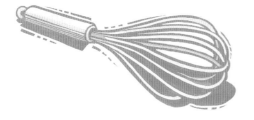

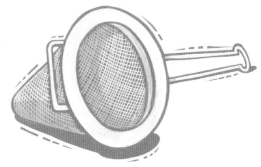

SIEVE AND CHINOIS

A fine-meshed stainless steel sieve is essential for sauce-making, and it can also be very useful to have a chinois, a cone-shaped sieve that is used for straining and puréeing a range of ingredients.

ELECTRICAL EQUIPMENT

Although not essential for making sauces, a blender, food processor, hand blender or whisk can take much of the hard work out of many sauces and dressings. All kinds of textures can be achieved from the very smooth to the slightly rough. Hand-held electric blenders are perhaps more versatile and convenient than larger machines for sauces, as they can be used to blend or purée ingredients directly in a pan or jug (pitcher), and are easy to clean by simply swishing in hot soapy water after use. A hand-held electric whisk is also invaluable for quick and easy beating and whisking.

MAKING BASIC STOCKS

A good home-made stock is simple to make and adds a rich flavour to all kinds of savoury sauces. Stock cubes and bouillon powder won't match the flavour, but they can be very useful for enriching a stock that lacks flavour: heat it until boiling, then stir in a stock cube or 5ml/1 tsp bouillon powder until dissolved. Each recipe below makes approximately 1 litre/1¾ pints/4 cups.

BEEF STOCK

675g/1½ lb shin of beef, diced
1 large onion, chopped
1 large carrot, chopped
1 celery stick, chopped
bouquet garni
6 black peppercorns
2.5ml/½ tsp sea salt
1.75 litres/3 pints/7½ cups water

1 Place all the ingredients in a large pan and gradually bring to the boil.

2 Cover the pan and simmer for 4 hours, skimming occasionally to remove the skum. Strain the stock and leave to cool.

FISH STOCK

1kg/2¼lb white fish bones and trimmings
1 large onion, sliced
1 large carrot, sliced
1 celery stick, sliced
bouquet garni
6 white peppercorns
2.5ml/½ tsp sea salt
150ml/¼ pint/⅔ cup dry white wine
1 litre/1¾ pints/4 cups water

1 Place all the ingredients in a large pan and gradually bring to the boil.

2 Skim any scum from the surface, cover and simmer for 20 minutes. Strain the stock and leave to cool.

CHICKEN STOCK

1 chicken carcass and chicken giblets
1 leek, chopped
1 celery stick, chopped
bouquet garni
5ml/1tsp white peppercorns
2.5ml/½ tsp sea salt
1.75 litres/3 pints/7½ cups water

1 Break up the carcass, place in a pan with the remaining ingredients. Bring to the boil.

2 Reduce the heat, cover and simmer gently for about 2½ hours, skimming occasionally to remove scum. Strain the stock and cool.

VEGETABLE STOCK

500g/1¼lb chopped mixed vegetables
(e.g. onions, carrots, celery, leeks)
bouquet garni
6 black peppercorns
2.5ml/½ tsp sea salt
1 litre/1¾ pints/4 cups water

1 Place the ingredients in a pan and bring the pan to the boil.

2 Skim any scum from the surface, then cover the pan and simmer gently for 30 minutes. Strain and leave to cool.

KEEPING STOCK CLEAR

Excess fat should always be removed from the liquid since this not only improves the look and taste of the stock but will also help to keep the stock clear.

1 Trim any fat from the meat or bones before adding to the stock pan, as this can create a cloudy stock.

2 Keep the heat at a low simmer, and skim off any scum from time to time as it gathers on the surface during cooking. Most vegetables can be added to stock for flavour, but potatoes will tend to break down and make the stock cloudy, so it is best to avoid using these vegetables.

3 Strain the cooked stock through a sieve lined with muslin (cheesecloth), and avoid pressing the solids, as this may spoil the stock's clarity.

FREEZING STOCK

Stock will keep for up to one week in the refrigerator, and it freezes well. To freeze stock in convenient portions to add to sauces, pour into ice-cube trays. The frozen cubes can be kept in bags, ready for use.

COOK'S TIPS

- *Use salt sparingly at the beginning of cooking – if you are going to reduce the stock it will become much more salty.*
- *To make a brown stock from beef or veal bones, roast the bones in a hot oven for 40 minutes. Add the vegetables halfway through the roasting time. Deglaze the pan with a little water and simmer the bones and vegetables as usual.*
- *To make a stock with a concentrated flavour, simmer the stock until reduced by half. Continue to reduce the stock until it will coat the back of a spoon. At its most concentrated it will set as a solid jelly and give you a quick and easy way to add rich flavour to sauces.*

REMOVING FAT FROM STOCK

1 Let the stock stand until the fat settles on the surface, then skim off and discard as much fat as possible with a large, shallow spoon.

2 To absorb even more grease, blot the surface with several layers of kitchen paper. Then, drop in a few ice cubes. The fat will set around the ice so it can be simply spooned off.

FLOUR-BASED SAUCES

The standard way to adjust the consistency of a sauce is to thicken it with one of the many different available types of flour. There are three basic methods for doing this – blending, roux or all-in-one. Once you have mastered the basic skills of these methods, you will be able to produce any flour-thickened sauce without problems – and also without lumps.

Many of the classic white sauces are based on a "roux", which is simply a cooked mixture of flour and fat. The most basic white sauce uses milk, but by varying the liquid used, other well-known white sauces can be made. For a classic béchamel sauce, the milk is flavoured first by infusing (steeping) with vegetables and herbs. For velouté sauce, the milk is replaced by stock, giving the sauce a more opaque appearance, and the thickened sauce may be enriched with cream after cooking. Brown sauces or gravy are made by browning the roux, usually with onions, before adding stock or other liquid, such as wine.

BLENDING METHOD
Sauces which are thickened by the blending method are usually made with cornflour (cornstarch), arrowroot, potato flour or sauce flour. You will need about 45ml/ 3 tbsp cornflour or sauce flour to thicken 300ml/½ pint/1¼ cups liquid. Arrowroot or potato flour are slightly stronger, so use about 30ml/2 tbsp to 300ml/½ pint/ 1¼ cups liquid.

1 Place the flour in a bowl and add just enough liquid to make a thin paste. Heat the remaining liquid until almost boiling.

2 Stir a little of the liquid into the blended mixture. Whisk the mixture back into the pan, return to the heat and stir until boiling

MAKING A ROUX-BASED WHITE SAUCE
The trick to making a roux is to stir the pan over the whole of the base, and add the liquid gradually; it is a good idea to heat the milk or stock before adding to the roux as this helps avoid lumps.

1 Melt the butter in a pan, then add the flour. To prevent browning, cook on a low heat and stir for 1–2 minutes. Allow the mixture to bubble until it resembles a honeycomb in texture. It is important to cook well at this point, to allow the starch grains in the flour to swell and burst.

2 Remove the pan from the heat and gradually stir in the liquid. Return to the heat and stir until boiling and thickened. Reduce the heat and simmer, stirring constantly, for 2 minutes, until the sauce is thickened and smooth, then simmer gently for 2 minutes, stirring.

Making Beurre Manié

Literally translated as "kneaded butter", this is a mixture of flour and butter, which can be stirred into a hot sauce, poaching liquid or cooked dish such as a casserole or ragout to thicken the juices. It's a convenient way to adjust the consistency of a sauce or dish at the end of cooking, and is easy to control as you can add the exact amount required, adjusting as it thickens. The butter adds flavour and a glossy sheen to the finished sauce. Any leftover beurre manié can be stored in a covered jar in the refrigerator for about 2 weeks, ready to use in sauces, soups, stews or casseroles.

1 Place equal amounts of butter and flour in a bowl and knead together with your fingers or a wooden spoon to make a smooth paste.

2 Drop teaspoonfuls of the beurre manié paste into the simmering sauce, whisking thoroughly to incorporate each spoonful before adding the next, until the sauce is thickened and smooth, and the desired consistency is achieved.

Using an Egg Yolk Liaison

This is a simple way to lightly thicken hot milk or stock, cream or reduced poaching liquids, and is good for enriching savoury white or velouté sauces. Two egg yolks should be enough to enrich and thicken about 300ml/½ pint/1¼ cups liquid, depending on the recipe. A mixture of egg yolk and cream will have the same effect, but add it to the mixture when the pan is off the heat to avoid curdling.

Place two egg yolks in a small bowl and stir in 30ml/2 tbsp of the hot liquid or sauce. Stir the egg mixture into the remaining liquid or sauce and heat gently, stirring, without boiling.

Adding Flavourings to Flour-based Sauces

Once you've made your basic sauce, try some of these quick flavour additions to pep up the flavour and add variety:

- *Stir 50g/2oz/½ cup grated Cheddar or other strong cheese into a basic white sauce with 5ml/1 tsp wholegrain mustard and a generous dash of Worcestershire sauce.*
- *Wine livens up the flavour of most stock-based sauces – boil 60ml/4 tbsp red or white wine in a pan until well reduced, then stir the wine into the finished sauce with a grating of nutmeg or black pepper.*
- *Parsley, or any fresh herbs will infuse (steep) and change the flavour of a white sauce.*
- *Add chopped herbs a few minutes before the end of the cooking time.*

All-in-one Method

This method uses the same ingredients and proportions as the roux method, but the liquid added must be cold.

Place the flour, butter and cold liquid in the pan and whisk with a sauce whisk or balloon whisk over a medium heat until boiling. Stir over the heat for 2 minutes, until thickened and smooth.

Correcting a Lumpy Sauce

If your flour-thickened sauce has gone lumpy, don't despair – it can be corrected.

1 First, try whisking the sauce hard with a light wire whisk in the pan to smooth out the lumps, then reheat it gently, stirring constantly.

2 If the sauce is still not smooth, rub it through a fine sieve, pressing firmly with a wooden spoon. Return to the pan and reheat gently, stirring constantly.

3 Alternatively, pour the sauce into a food processor and process until smooth. Return to the pan and reheat gently, stirring constantly.

Keeping Sauces Hot

1 Pour the sauce into a heatproof bowl and place over a pan of gently simmering water.

2 To prevent a skin from forming, place a sheet of lightly oiled or wetted greaseproof (waxed) paper or non-stick baking paper (baking parchment) directly on to the surface of the sauce. Stir before serving.

Degreasing Sauces

Even after skimming any surplus fat from a finished hot sauce or gravy with a flat metal spoon, final traces of fat may still remain. These can be removed by dragging the flat surface of a piece of kitchen paper over the surface to absorb traces of grease.

Making a Roux-based Brown Sauce

A brown roux is the basis of many meat dish sauces. Onions or other vegetables are usually browned in the fat before the flour is added. The fat can be a mixture of butter and oil, or dripping. Butter alone is unsuitable for such sauces as it burns very easily at high temperatures. You should use about 30ml/2 tbsp fat and about 25g/1oz/¼ cup plain (all-purpose) flour for the roux to about 600ml/1 pint/2½ cups reduced brown stock. At the last moment before you serve the dish, stir in 15g/½oz/1 tbsp chilled butter to give the sauce a glossy finish.

1 Melt the fat and cook 1 small, finely chopped onion over a gentle heat until it is softened and golden brown. Sprinkle on the flour and stir with a wooden spoon until combined. Stir over a low heat for 4–5 minutes, until rich brown in colour.

2 Remove the pan from the heat and gradually stir in the liquid, which may be either hot or cold. Return to the heat and stir until boiling. Simmer gently, stirring, for a further 2 minutes, until the sauce is thick and smooth. The sauce may be strained to remove the onions at this stage if you like.

Adding Flavourings to a Brown Sauce

- *A handful of chopped fresh basil, chives or flat leaf parsley can be stirred into the sauce just before serving.*
- *For game or poultry, stir in a little curry paste and 2 crushed garlic cloves with the onion. Stir in chopped fresh coriander (cilantro) just before serving.*
- *Add coarsely grated orange rind and serve the sauce with duck or game.*

MAKING TRADITIONAL GRAVY

Good gravy should be smooth and glossy, never heavy and floury. Generally speaking, it's best to use the minimum of thickening, but this can be adjusted to your own taste. Providing that the meat has been roasted to a rich golden brown, the meat juices will have enough colour to colour the gravy. If the gravy is still too pale, then add a few drops of gravy browning and stir it in to darken it slightly.

1 To make a thickened gravy, use a skimmer to skim off all the fat except about 15ml/ 1 tbsp from the juices in the pan after the meat has been roasted. Gradually stir in about 15ml/1 tbsp plain (all-purpose) flour, carefully scraping up the sediment at the base of the pan and the meat juices.

2 Place the pan directly over the heat and stir the roux until it begins to bubble. Make sure that it does not burn. Cook it, stirring constantly, for 1–2 minutes, until the roux is brown and the flour cooked.

3 Gradually stir in the liquid, which may be either stock or vegetable water, until the gravy is of the thickness desired. Simmer for 2–3 minutes, stirring constantly, and adjust the seasoning to taste.

IDEAS FOR DEGLAZED SAUCES

Brandy and Peppercorn – deglaze the pan with brandy or sherry, stir in cream and coarsely ground black pepper. Serve with grilled (broiled) or fried steaks.

Red Wine and Cranberry – deglaze the pan with red wine and stir in cranberry sauce or jelly. Good with game or turkey.

Sauce Bercy – deglaze with dry white wine or vermouth, stir in a finely chopped shallot and sauté gently until soft. Add cream, lemon juice and chopped parsley. Excellent with fried or poached fish.

USING A DEGLAZED SAUCE

Deglazing means adding a small amount of liquid, such as stock, to the pan after roasting or pan-frying, to dilute the rich concentrated juices into a simple sauce. Spoon off the excess fat, and then scrape up the sediment from the base of the pan with a spoon as you stir in the liquid.

1 Tilt the pan and spoon off excess fat from the surface of the juices.

2 Stir in a few tablespoons of wine, stock or double (heavy) cream. Simmer over a medium heat, stirring and scraping up the sediment as the sauce boils. Boil rapidly to reduce the juices until syrupy, then pour over the food.

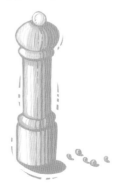

VEGETABLE SAUCES & SALSAS

Many sauces use vegetables for flavour, colour and texture, and there's no end to the healthy variations you can make with a few simple techniques. Puréed or chopped vegetables can be used to make both cooked sauces and fresh salsas. Vegetable sauces and salsas make fresh low-fat alternatives to more conventional sauces, and they are invariably very easy and quick to make.

BASIC TOMATO SAUCE

For the best flavour, use plum tomatoes. If using canned, make sure that they are not already flavoured with herbs. Peel fresh tomatoes before using. Fresh tomatoes rather than canned tomatoes can be used. Substitute about 500g/1¼lb tomatoes for each 400g/14oz can.

Makes about 450ml/¾ pint/scant 2 cups
15ml/1 tbsp olive oil
15g/½oz/1 tbsp butter
1 garlic clove, finely chopped
1 small onion, finely chopped
1 celery stick, finely chopped
400g/14oz can chopped tomatoes
handful of basil leaves
salt and ground black pepper

1 Heat the oil and butter in a heavy pan. When the oil starts to bubble, add the garlic, onion and celery. Sauté the ingredients gently over a low heat, stirring occasionally, for about 15–20 minutes, or until the onions are just beginning to colour.

2 Stir the chopped tomatoes into the sauce and bring to the boil. Cover and simmer the sauce gently for 10–15 minutes, stirring occasionally, until thick.

3 Tear or roughly chop the basil leaves and stir into the sauce. Adjust the seasoning with salt and pepper, and serve hot.

MAKING QUICK SALSA CRUDO

This is literally a "raw sauce" of vegetables or fruits, and it's easy to create your own combinations of flavours. A good basic start for a salsa crudo is chillies, (bell) peppers, onions and garlic.

1 Prepare the vegetables as necessary, then cut into small, even dice. Put all the diced ingredients into a bowl.

2 Add 15–30ml/1–2 tbsp olive oil, a squeeze of lime or lemon juice and finely chopped fresh herbs. Season to taste and toss well.

COOK'S TIP
A soffritto (Italian), or sofrito (Spanish), is the basis of many Mediterranean meat or tomato sauces. It consists of onion, garlic, green (bell) pepper and celery, sometimes with a little carrot or pancetta added. The finely chopped ingredients are sautéed slowly to soften and caramelize the flavours.

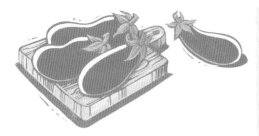

ROASTED VEGETABLE SAUCE

Serve roasted vegetable sauce with pork, ham, poultry or game. If you prefer a sauce with more texture, simply process for a shorter time.

Makes about 300ml/½ pint/1¼ cups
2 red or orange (bell) peppers
1 small onion
1 small aubergine (eggplant)
2 tomatoes, peeled
2 garlic cloves, unpeeled
30–45ml/2–3 tbsp olive oil
15ml/1 tbsp lemon juice

1 Cut the peppers, onion and aubergine in half, leaving the skins on, and, if necessary, remove any seeds and core. Place the vegetables cut side down on a baking sheet with the garlic cloves. Place under a very hot grill (broiler) or in a hot oven and cook until the skins are blackened and charred, and the flesh is tender.

2 Remove from the heat and leave until cool enough to handle, then peel off the skins from the peppers and onions.

3 Scoop the flesh from the aubergines, and squeeze the flesh from the garlic.

4 Place all the vegetables in a blender or food processor and process to a very smooth purée, adding oil and lemon juice to taste. If you prefer a very smooth sauce, rub the purée through a fine sieve.

TO PEEL TOMATOES

1 *Cut a small cross in the skins of the tomatoes. Bring a pan of water to the boil and add the tomatoes. Turn off the heat and leave for 30 seconds, then lift out carefully with a slotted spoon and place in a bowl of cold water. Using a small knife, peel off the skins.*
2 *Alternatively, place the tomato firmly on the prongs of a fork and hold in a gas flame until the skin blisters and splits. When the tomatoes are cool enough to handle, peel off the skins with a knife.*

THICKENING A VEGETABLE PURÉE

Stir in a handful of fresh breadcrumbs and process for a few seconds until the purée is the desired consistency.

CHARGRILLING VEGETABLES FOR PURÉES AND SAUCES

Many puréed sauces or salsas call for cooked or chargrilled vegetables. Chargrilling on a barbecue is the best way to get the finest flavour from many vegetables, such as red and green (bell) peppers, aubergines (eggplant), tomatoes, garlic and onions, retaining and caramelizing the flavourful juices and tenderizing the flesh. However, since this method is not always practical, the next best way is to roast the vegetables on a baking sheet under a grill (broiler).

SAVOURY BUTTER SAUCES

The simplest sauce of all is a melted butter sauce, flavoured with lemon juice or herbs – ideal to drizzle over a simply cooked piece of fish or vegetables. A more refined version of this is clarified butter sauce, while emulsions of butter with vinegar or other flavourings make deliciously rich beurre blanc or hollandaise sauce. Cold, flavoured butters can be shaped prettily for garnish.

BLENDER HOLLANDAISE

Hollandaise is a rich butter and egg sauce, which tastes like a hot mayonnaise. This quick method eliminates whisking by hand and uses a blender to incorporate the ingredients to a thick, smooth emulsion.

Makes 250ml/8fl oz/1 cup
60ml/4 tbsp white wine vinegar
6 peppercorns
1 bay leaf
3 egg yolks
175g/6oz/¾ cup clarified butter
salt and ground black pepper

1 Place the wine vinegar, peppercorns and bay leaf in a small pan and heat until boiling, then simmer to reduce to about 15ml/1 tbsp. Remove from the heat and discard the flavourings.

2 Place the egg yolks in the blender goblet and start the motor. Add the reduced white wine vinegar liquid through the feeder tube and blend for 10 seconds.

3 Heat the butter until hot. With the motor running, pour the butter through the feeder tube in a thin, steady stream until thick and smooth.

4 Adjust the seasoning to taste with salt and pepper, and serve warm with poached fish, eggs or vegetables.

Preventing Curdling

If hollandaise sauce is overheated, or if the butter is added too quickly, it may curdle. If this happens, remove it from the heat, drop an ice cube into the sauce, then beat hard until the cube melts and cools the sauce. Stand the pan in a bowl of iced water.

BEURRE BLANC

This is one of the simplest sauces. White wine and vinegar are reduced in volume to produce an intense flavour. Butter is whisked into the liquid to enrich and thicken it.

1 Place 45ml/3 tbsp each of white wine vinegar and dry white wine in a small pan with a finely chopped shallot. Bring to the boil and boil until reduced to 15ml/1 tbsp.

2 Cut the 225g/8oz/1 cup chilled unsalted (sweet) butter into small cubes. On a low heat, gradually whisk in the butter, piece by piece, allowing each piece to melt and be absorbed before adding the next. Season to taste and serve immediately.

How to Clarify Butter

Ideal for serving with vegetables such as asparagus or artichokes, clarified butter is butter that has been melted and has had all the salts, moisture and impurities removed, leaving it clear, with a rich, pure flavour. Clarified butter, called ghee in Indian cooking, keeps longer and can be heated to higher temperatures than ordinary butter without the risk of burning. It gives a mild flavour and a high gloss to sauces. There are two main methods:

Place the butter in a pan with an equal quantity of water. Heat until the butter melts. Remove from the heat and leave to cool until the butter sets. Carefully lift out the fat, leaving the water and solids behind.

Alternatively, melt the butter in a small pan over a very low heat, then skim off the froth with a slotted spoon. Pour the rest through a sieve lined with fine muslin (cheesecloth), to strain out the solids.

Making Savoury Butters

Flavoured butters can be shaped or piped decoratively to serve with grilled (broiled) steaks or poached or grilled fish. To make a herb-flavoured butter, finely chop your choice of fresh herbs. Beat the butter until softened then stir in the herbs to mix them in evenly.

Piping Butter

Using a star nozzle, pipe softened butter on to non-stick baking paper (baking parchment) and chill lightly.

Flavourings for Savoury Butters

- *Finely chopped herbs, e.g. chives, parsley, dill, mint, thyme or rosemary. Use one herb or a combination of your choice and add as much as the butter will comfortably absorb, or enough to achieve the desired flavour.*
- *Finely grated lemon, lime or orange rind and juice.*
- *Finely chopped canned anchovy fillets.*
- *Finely chopped gherkins or capers.*
- *Crushed, dried chillies or finely chopped fresh chillies.*
- *Crushed, fresh garlic cloves, or roasted garlic purée.*
- *Ground coriander seeds, curry spices or curry paste.*

Making Shaped Slices

To make butter slices, chill the softened herb butter lightly. With your hands, roll the butter into a long sausage-shape and wrap in non-stick baking parchment or clear film (plastic wrap). Chill and cut off slices of the butter as required.

Making Shaped Butters

To make shaped butter pats, chill the butter lightly, then roll it out gently between two sheets of non-stick baking parchment. Chill the butter until it is firm, and then remove the top sheet and stamp out decorative shapes with a small cutter.

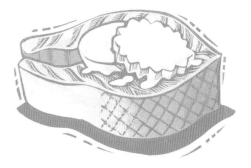

SAVOURY EGG SAUCES

The versatility of eggs comes in useful in all kinds of sauces, most commonly for thickening and enriching cooked sauces, or for holding an emulsion such as in mayonnaise. Keep spare egg yolks in the freezer, ready to enrich sauces whenever they are needed – stir in a pinch of salt or sugar before freezing to prevent them from thickening, and don't forget to label which is which.

MAYONNAISE

The texture of hand-whisked mayonnaise is unlike any other – smooth, glossy and rich,

Makes about 300ml/½ pint/1¼ cups
2 egg yolks
15ml/1 tbsp lemon juice
5ml/1 tsp Dijon mustard
300ml/½ pint/1¼ cups light olive oil
salt and ground black pepper

1 Place the egg yolks, lemon juice, mustard, salt and pepper in a bowl and beat the egg yolk mixture until smooth.

2 Pouring with one hand and whisking with the other, add the oil gradually, drop by drop, making sure that each drop is whisked in before adding more.

3 Once a thick emulsion has formed, the oil can be poured faster, in a fine, steady stream, and whisked until the mixture becomes smooth and thick. Adjust the seasoning.

Using a Food Processor for Mayonnaise

A food processor can speed up the at times laborious process of making mayonnaise. Use a whole egg instead of the egg yolks. It is easier to get a good emulsion and prevent the mayonnaise from curdling if all the ingredients are at room temperature.

Home-made mayonnaise is the perfect partner to delicately poached salmon or a chicken salad.

Process the egg and flavourings for a few seconds, then slowly pour in the oil through the feeder tube in a thin, steady stream with the motor running, until the mixture forms a smooth, creamy texture.

MAYONNAISE VARIATIONS

- *For Fresh Garlic Mayonnaise, crush 3–6 garlic cloves into the ingredients.*
- *For Spicy Mayonnaise, add to the basic recipe mixture 15ml/1 tbsp mustard, 7–15ml/½–1 tbsp Worcestershire sauce and a dash of Tabasco sauce.*
- *For Green Mayonnaise, combine 25g/ 1oz each parsley and watercress sprigs in a blender or food processor. Add 3–4 chopped spring onions (scallions) and 1 garlic clove. Blend until finely chopped. Add 120ml/4fl oz/½ cup mayonnaise and blend until smooth.*
- *For Blue Cheese Dressing, mix 225g/ 8oz crumbled Danish blue cheese into the mayonnaise.*

Sweet Egg Sauces

Sweet egg sauces include many rich and creamy techniques, from classic egg-based custards, with a variety of flavourings, to serve with winter puddings, to light and fluffy sabayon, which can be served as a delicious dessert on its own or as a luxurious sauce for gilded fruits. Don't forget traditional baked custard, which can be served hot or cold with a variety of tasty toppings.

Egg Custard Sauce

Crème anglaise is the traditional vanilla custard sauce made with eggs, a far cry from the quick custard powder versions so often used. As well as being served as a classic sauce, either hot or cold, *crème anglaise* is often used as the base for other sweet sauces, such as the *crème pâtissière* used to fill éclairs and profiteroles. It's frequently enriched with cream instead of milk, or flavoured with liqueurs for making special desserts.

The trick here is to be patient – the egg must be cooked slowly; if it's overheated, it will turn to scrambled egg, and there is nothing you can do with this other than throw it away.

Makes about 400ml/14fl oz/1⅔ cups
300ml/½ pint/1¼ cups milk
1 vanilla pod (bean)
3 egg yolks
15ml/1 tbsp caster (superfine) sugar

1 Heat the milk with the vanilla pod until just boiling, then remove from the heat. (To intensify the flavour split the pod lengthways before adding it to the pan.) Cover and leave to infuse (steep) for about 10 minutes, then strain into a clean pan.

2 Beat the eggs and sugar together lightly in a bowl. Pour the milk on to the eggs, whisking constantly.

3 Pour into the pan and stir until the custard thickens just enough to lightly coat the back of a wooden spoon. Remove from the heat and immediately pour into a jug (pitcher) to prevent overcooking.

Preventing Curdling

Remove the egg custard from the heat and plunge the base of the pan into cold water. Whisk in 5ml/1 tsp cornflour (cornstarch) until smooth, then reheat.

Sabayon Sauce

1 Whisk 1 egg yolk and 15ml/1 tbsp caster (superfine) sugar per portion in a bowl over a pan of simmering water. Whisk in 30ml/2 tbsp sweet white wine, liqueur or fruit juice, for each egg yolk. Whisk the sauce over a constant heat until frothy.

2 Whisk until the sauce holds a trail on top of the mixture. Serve immediately or whisk until cool.

DESSERT SAUCES

As well as the popular custards and flavoured white sauces, quick and easy dessert toppings can be made almost instantly from ready-made and store-cupboard (pantry) ingredients, and these are ideal to serve over scoops of ice cream to make them a little more special. They could also be served with pancakes and are particularly popular with children.

HOW TO USE VANILLA PODS

Vanilla pods (beans) are commonly used in sweet dessert sauces, but they are also occasionally used to flavour delicate savoury cream sauces.

To flavour sugar, bury a vanilla pod in a jar of caster (superfine) sugar. It can be used as vanilla-flavoured sugar to add to sweet sauces and desserts.

To infuse (steep) vanilla flavour into milk or cream, heat it gently with the vanilla pod over a low heat until almost boiling. Remove from the heat, cover and leave to stand for 10 minutes. Remove the pod, rinse and dry; it may be re-used several times in this way.

To get maximum flavour from the pod, use a sharp knife to slit the pod lengthways and open out. Use the tip of the knife to scrape out the sticky black seeds inside and add to the hot sauce.

SPEEDY SAUCES FOR TOPPING ICE CREAM

Lots of store-cupboard ingredients can be quickly transformed into irresistible sauces to spoon on top of ice cream.

Marshmallow Melt

Melt 90g/3½oz marshmallows with 30ml/2 tbsp milk or cream in a small pan. Add a little freshly grated nutmeg and spoon over ice cream.

Black Forest Sauce

Drain a can of black cherries, reserving the juice. Blend a little of the juice with a little arrowroot or cornflour (cornstarch). Add the mixture to the remaining juice in a pan. Stir over a medium heat until boiling and lightly thickened, then add the cherries and a dash of Kirsch. Bubble for a few seconds, then spoon over the ice cream and top with grated chocolate.

Chocolate-Toffee Sauce

Chop a toffee-filled chocolate bar and heat very gently in a pan, stirring until just melted. Spoon over scoops of vanilla ice cream and sprinkle with chopped nuts.

Marmalade Whisky Sauce

Heat 60ml/4 tbsp chunky marmalade in a pan with 30ml/2 tbsp whisky, until just melted. Bubble for a few seconds then spoon over ice cream.

Whisky Sauce

Measure 600ml/1 pint/2½ cups milk. Mix together 30ml/2 tbsp cornflour (cornstarch) with 15ml/1 tbsp of the milk. Bring the remaining milk to the boil, remove from the heat and pour a little on the cornflour mixture. Return the mixture to the pan and heat gently, stirring constantly, until thickened. Simmer gently for 2 minutes.

Remove from the heat and stir in 30ml/2 tbsp caster (superfine) sugar and 60–90ml/4–6 tbsp whisky.

QUICK SAUCES FOR CRÊPES
Rich Butterscotch Sauce

Heat 75g/3oz/6 tbsp butter, 175g/6oz/1½ cups brown sugar and 30ml/2 tbsp golden (light corn) syrup in a pan over a low heat until melted. Remove from the heat and add 75ml/5 tbsp double (heavy) cream, stirring constantly, until smooth. If you like, add about 50g/2oz/½ cup chopped walnuts. Serve hot with ice cream and crêpes or waffles.

Orange Sauce

Melt 25g/1oz/2 tbsp unsalted (sweet) butter in a heavy pan. Stir in 50g/2oz/¼ cup caster (superfine) sugar and cook until golden brown. Add the juice of 2 oranges and ½ lemon and stir to dissolve the caramel.

Summer Berries

Melt 25g/1oz/2 tbsp butter in a frying pan. Add 50g/2oz/¼ cup caster (superfine) sugar and cook until golden brown. Add the juice of 2 oranges and the rind of ½ orange and cook until syrupy. Add 350g/12oz/3 cups mixed berries and warm through. Add 45ml/3 tbsp Grand Marnier and set alight. Spoon over the crêpes.

PRESENTATION IDEAS

When you've made a delicious sauce for a special dessert, why not make more of it by using it for decoration on the plate, too?

Marbling

Use this technique when you have two contrasting sauces of similar thickness. Spoon alternate spoonfuls of the sauces into a bowl or on to a serving plate, then stir the two sauces lightly together, swirling to create a marbled effect.

Yin-Yang Sauces

This is ideal for two contrasting colours of purée or coulis. Spoon one sauce on each side of a serving plate and push them together gently with a spoon, swirling one around the other, to make a yin-yang shape.

Drizzling

Pour a smooth sauce or coulis into a jug (pitcher) with a fine pouring lip. Drizzle the sauce in droplets or a fine wavy line on to the plate around the food.

FRUIT SAUCES

From the simplest fresh fruit purée, to a cooked and thickened fruit sauce, there are hundreds of ways to add flavour to desserts, tarts and pies. The addition of a little liqueur or lemon juice can bring out the fruit flavour and prevent discoloration. Some fruit sauces, notably apple and cranberry, partner meat dishes, and fresh fruit salsas can be eaten to cool down spicy hot dishes.

MAKING A FRUIT COULIS
A fruit coulis will add a sophisticated splash of colour and flavour to desserts and ices. It can be made from either fresh or frozen fruit. Soft fruits and berries are ideal, and tropical fruits like mango and kiwi fruit can be quickly transformed into exotically flavoured coulis. A few drops of orange flower water or rose water will give a scented flavour, but use it with caution – too much will overpower delicate ingredients.

1 Remove any hulls, stems, peel or stones (pits) from the fruit.

2 Place all the prepared fruit in a food processor or blender and process until it becomes a smooth purée.

3 Press the purée through a fine sieve to remove the pips or fibrous parts and leave a smooth, syrupy juice. Sweeten to taste with icing (confectioners') sugar and add a dash of lemon juice to sharpen the flavour.

PEACH SAUCE
Purée a 400g/14oz can of peaches, together with their juice and 1.5ml/¼ tsp almond essence (extract) in a blender or food processor. Chill before serving.

PASSION FRUIT COULIS
This would be delicious served with skewers of fresh fruit.

1 Halve 8 passion fruit and scoop out the flesh. Purée in a blender for a few seconds.

2 Press the pulp through a sieve and discard the seeds. Add 30ml/2 tbsp lime juice, 30ml/2 tbsp icing (confectioners') sugar and 30ml/2 tbsp white rum. Stir well until the sugar has dissolved.

3 Spoon some of the coulis on to a serving plate. Place the skewers on top. Drizzle over the remaining coulis and garnish with a little toasted coconut, if you like.

CHOCOLATE SAUCES

Chocolate sauces are enduringly popular, from simple custards to richly indulgent versions combined with liqueur or cream. They can be served with ice cream and other frozen desserts, but are also great with poached pears and a wide range of puddings. Flavoured liqueurs can be chosen to echo the flavour of the dessert, and coffee, brandy and cinnamon all go well with chocolate.

The more cocoa solids chocolate contains, the more chocolatey the flavour will be. Plain (semisweet) chocolate may have between 30–70 per cent of cocoa solids. Plain dark (bittersweet) chocolate has around 75 per cent, so if you're aiming at a really rich, dark sauce, this is the best choice. Milk chocolate is much sweeter, containing 20 per cent cocoa solids. Cocoa is ground from the whole cocoa mass after most of the cocoa butter has been extracted.

White chocolate contains no cocoa solids, so strictly speaking it is not a chocolate at all, but gets its flavour from cocoa butter.

The best method of melting chocolate is in a double boiler or in a bowl over a pan of hot water. Never allow water or steam to come into contact with the chocolate as this may cause it to stiffen. Overheating will also spoil the flavour and texture. Plain chocolate should not be heated above 49°C/120°F, and milk or white chocolate not above 43°C/110°F.

For sauce recipes where the chocolate is melted with a quantity of other liquid such as milk or cream, the chocolate may be melted with the liquid in a pan over direct heat, providing there is plenty of liquid. Heat gently, stirring until melted.

If you run out of chocolate for a sauce recipe, use (unsweetened) cocoa powder as an emergency substitute. Mix 45ml/3 tbsp cocoa powder with 15ml/1 tbsp melted butter to replace each 25g/1oz chocolate.

CREAMY CHOCOLATE SAUCE
Place 120ml/4fl oz/½ cup double (heavy) cream in a pan and add 130g/4½oz chocolate. Stir over a low heat until the chocolate has melted. Serve warm or cold.

CHOCOLATE CUSTARD SAUCE
1 Melt 90g/3½ oz plain dark (bittersweet) chocolate in a heatproof bowl set over a pan of hot water.

2 Heat 200ml/7fl oz/scant 1 cup *crème anglaise* until hot but not boiling and stir in the melted chocolate until evenly mixed. Serve hot or cold.

RICH CHOCOLATE BRANDY SAUCE
Break up 115g/4oz plain chocolate into a bowl over a pan of hot water, then heat gently until melted. Remove from the heat and add 30ml/2 tbsp brandy and 30ml/2 tbsp melted butter, then stir until smooth. Serve hot.

Making Marinades & Dressings

Marinades can be savoury or sweet, spicy, fruity, fragrant or exotic, to add a contrasting or complementary flavour to all kinds of foods. They're useful not only for adding flavour, but also for tenderizing and keeping foods moist during cooking, especially on the barbecue. If that's not enough, they can also be used to form the basis of a sauce to serve with the finished dish.

Oil-based Marinades

Choose an oil-based marinade for low-fat foods, such as lean meat, poultry or white fish, which may dry out during cooking. Oil-based marinades are especially useful for grilling (broiling) and barbecues, and at their simplest consist of oil with crushed garlic and chopped herbs. Avoid adding salt as this draws the juices out of the meat.

1 Place the marinade ingredients in a jug (pitcher) and beat well with a fork. Arrange the food in a single layer in a non-metallic dish and pour the marinade over.

2 Turn the food to coat evenly. Cover and leave in the refrigerator to marinate from 30 minutes to several hours, depending on the recipe. Turn the food occasionally.

3 When ready to cook, remove the food from the marinade. The marinade can be poured into a small pan and simmered for several minutes until thoroughly heated, then served spooned over the cooked food.

Wine- or Vinegar-based Marinades

Choose wine- or vinegar-based mixtures to accompany rich foods, such as game or oily fish. They will add flavour and balance the richness. Use herb-flavoured vinegars for oily fish and add chopped fresh herbs.

The acid in the wine or vinegar starts the tenderizing process well before cooking. For game, which can have a tendency to be tough, leave in the marinade overnight. Add lemon juice, garlic, black pepper and herbs, and even sherry, cider or orange juice according to your preference.

Yogurt is a good marinade and can be flavoured with crushed garlic, lemon juice, and handfuls of chopped mint, thyme or rosemary for lamb or pork. For fish or shellfish, use a marinade based on lemon juice with a little oil and plenty of pepper.

1 Measure the ingredients into a jug (pitcher) and beat with a fork.

2 Arrange the food in a wide, non-metallic dish in a single layer and spoon over the marinade, turning the food to coat evenly. Cover and chill for 30 minutes up to several hours, depending on the recipe.

3 Drain the food of excess marinade before cooking. If the food is to be griddled or grilled (broiled), use the marinade to brush over the food during cooking to add extra flavour and keep it moist.

MAKING AN OIL-BASED DRESSING

A good vinaigrette can do more than dress a salad. It can also be used to baste meat, poultry, seafood or vegetables during cooking. Many classic dressings, such as vinaigrette or French dressing, are based on an oil and acid mixture. The basic proportions are 3 parts oil to 1 part acid beaten together to form an emulsion.

The oil you choose for a dressing adds character to the flavour. A strongly flavoured extra virgin olive oil adds personality to a simple green leaf or potato salad, but can overpower more delicate ingredients. Pure olive oil or sunflower oil adds a lighter flavour. Nut oils, such as walnut or hazelnut, are expensive, but can add an unusual flavour to a salad when used in small quantities.

The acid in a dressing may be vinegar or lemon juice, and this can define the flavour of the finished salad. Choose from wine, sherry or cider vinegars, herb, chilli or fruit vinegars, to balance or contrast with the salad ingredients and the type of oil.

GENERAL VARIATIONS

- *Use red or white wine vinegar. Or use a herb-flavoured vinegar.*
- *Use lemon juice instead of vinegar.*
- *Replace 1 tablespoon of the vinegar with wine.*
- *Other fruit juices such as orange or apple juice can be used instead for a sweeter, less acid flavour.*
- *Use olive oil, or a mixture of vegetable and olive oils.*
- *Use 120ml/4fl oz/½ cup olive oil and 30ml/2 tbsp walnut or hazelnut oil.*
- *Add 1 crushed garlic clove before whisking in the oil.*
- *Add 15–30ml/1–2 tbsp chopped herbs to the vinaigrette.*

CLASSIC VINAIGRETTE

To guarantee the ingredients blend together in a smooth emulsion, make sure all the ingredients are at room temperature. This can be done by simply whisking with a fork, in a jug (pitcher), or the ingredients can be placed in a screw-topped jar and shaken.

Lemon juice adds a sharper flavour, which can be useful to add a lively tang to a bland dish. Other fruit juices, such as orange or apple juice, can be used instead for a sweeter, less acid flavour.

Matured vinegars such as balsamic can be strong in flavour, so the basic proportions should be amended to 5 parts oil and 2 of balsamic vinegar.

Put 30ml/2 tbsp vinegar in a bowl with 10ml/2 tsp Dijon mustard, salt and ground black pepper. Add 1.5ml/¼ tsp caster (superfine) sugar, if you like. Whisk well.

Gradually drizzle in 90ml/6 tbsp oil, whisking constantly, until the vinaigrette is smooth and well blended.

CREAMY ORANGE DRESSING

This tangy orange dressing is versatile enough to complement a mixed green salad with orange segments and tomatoes. It could also partner chicken or smoked duck breasts served on a bed of rice salad.

Serves 4
45ml/3 tbsp half-fat crème fraîche
15ml/1 tbsp white wine vinegar
finely grated rind and juice of
  1 small orange
salt and ground black pepper

1 Measure the crème fraîche and wine vinegar into a screw-topped jar and add the orange rind and juice.

2 Shake well until evenly combined, then adjust the seasoning to taste.

CLASSIC SAUCES

A comprehensive collection of sauce recipes must, by definition, include as its foundation the traditional, classic recipes that have been handed down through many generations of cooks. Every country has its enduring time-honoured sauces, from French favourites, such as elegant Béchamel Sauce and rich, brown Espagnole Sauce, to British favourites, such as Horseradish or Bread Sauce and from all-American Cranberry Sauce to vibrant fresh Italian Pesto. Each has evolved from the imaginative use of local foods and has been created to enhance the flavours of the traditional cuisine of the country. These well-tried classics form the basis of a repertoire essential to every professional cook. They encompass all of the sauce-making techniques, such as flour-thickened roux and rich emulsions, and some of them form an integral part of world-famous dishes. In the past, the art of sauce-making required that stocks and other ingredients were prepared entirely by hand, but cooks today have electric mixers and food processors to assist them. The substitution of commercial stock can also save time and effort, and still provide the busy cook with an impressive result, complementing the flavour of both plain and rich cooking.

Béchamel Sauce

This creamy white sauce with a mellow flavour is ideal for lasagne as well as a suitable base or accompaniment for many fish, egg and vegetable dishes.

SERVES 4

INGREDIENTS
1 small onion
1 small carrot
1 celery stick
bouquet garni
6 black peppercorns
pinch of freshly grated nutmeg or a blade of mace
300ml/½ pint/1¼ cups milk
25g/1oz/2 tbsp butter
25g/1oz/¼ cup plain (all-purpose) flour
30ml/2 tbsp single (light) cream
salt and ground black pepper

1 Peel and finely chop the vegetables. Put the vegetables, bouquet garni, peppercorns, nutmeg or mace and milk in a pan. Bring to the boil. Remove from the heat, cover and leave to infuse (steep) for 30 minutes.

2 Melt the butter in a pan over a low heat, remove from the heat and stir in the flour. Return to the heat and cook for 1–2 minutes, stirring, to make a roux.

3 Reheat the flavoured milk until almost boiling. Strain into a jug (pitcher), pressing the vegetables with the back of a spoon to extract the juices.

4 Off the heat, gradually blend the milk into the roux, stirring vigorously after each addition. Bring to the boil and stir constantly until the sauce thickens. Simmer gently for 3–4 minutes.

5 Remove the pan from the heat. Season with salt and pepper to taste and stir the cream into the sauce.

BASIC WHITE SAUCE

This white sauce is wonderfully adaptable for all kinds of savoury dishes, but it can be bland so always taste and season carefully.

SERVES 6

INGREDIENTS
600ml/1 pint/2½ cups milk
25g/1oz/2 tbsp butter
25g/1oz/¼ cup plain (all-purpose) flour
salt and ground black pepper

1 Pour the milk into a pan and warm over a low heat, but do not allow it to come to the boil.

2 Melt the butter in a separate pan, then stir in the flour and cook gently for 1–2 minutes to make a roux. Do not allow the roux to brown.

3 Remove the pan from the heat, gradually blend in the milk, stirring vigorously after each addition to prevent lumps from forming.

4 Return the pan to the heat and gradually bring to the boil, stirring constantly until the sauce thickens.

5 Simmer gently for a further 3–4 minutes, until thickened and smooth. Season with salt and ground black pepper to taste.

COOK'S TIPS
• *For a thicker, coating sauce, increase the amount of flour to 50g/2oz/½ cup and the butter to 50g/2oz/¼ cup.*
• *If you aren't using a non-stick pan, use a small, balloon whisk to incorporate the flour and milk to make sure the sauce has a smooth consistency.*

VELOUTÉ SAUCE

This savoury pouring sauce is named after its smooth, velvety texture. It's based on a white stock made from fish, vegetables or meat, so it is wonderfully versatile.

SERVES 4

INGREDIENTS
600ml/1 pint/2½ cups stock
25g/1oz/2 tbsp butter
25g/1oz/¼ cup plain (all-purpose) flour
30ml/2 tbsp single (light) cream
salt and ground black pepper

1 Heat the stock until almost boiling, but do not boil. In another pan melt the butter and stir in the flour. Cook, stirring, over a medium heat for 3–4 minutes, or until it becomes a pale, straw colour, stirring constantly.

2 Remove the pan from the heat and gradually blend in the hot stock. Return to the heat and bring to the boil, stirring constantly, until the sauce thickens.

3 Continue to cook at a very slow simmer, stirring occasionally, until reduced by about a quarter.

4 Skim the surface during cooking to remove any scum, or pour through a very fine strainer.

5 Just before serving, remove from the heat and stir in the cream. Season to taste with salt and pepper.

LEMON SAUCE WITH TARRAGON

The tangy sharpness of lemon and the mild aniseed-like flavour of tarragon give added zest to chicken, egg or steamed vegetable dishes.

SERVES 4

INGREDIENTS
1 lemon
small bunch of fresh tarragon
1 shallot, finely chopped
90ml/6 tbsp white wine
1 quantity velouté sauce
45ml/3 tbsp double (heavy) cream
30ml/2 tbsp brandy
salt and ground black pepper

1 Thinly pare the rind from the lemon, taking care not to remove any of the white pith. Set the rind aside. Squeeze the juice from the lemon and pour it into a pan. Discard the lemon.

2 Discard the coarse stalks from the tarragon. Chop the leaves and add all but 15ml/1 tbsp to the pan with the lemon rind and shallot.

3 Add the wine and simmer gently over a low heat until the liquid is reduced by half. Strain into a clean pan.

4 Add the velouté sauce, cream, brandy and reserved tarragon. Heat through, taste and adjust the seasoning, if necessary.

ESPAGNOLE SAUCE

Espagnole is a classic rich brown sauce, ideal for serving with red meat and game.
It also makes a delicious, full-flavoured base for other sauces.

SERVES 4–6

INGREDIENTS
25g/1oz/2 tbsp butter
50g/2oz bacon, chopped
2 shallots, unpeeled and chopped
1 carrot, chopped
1 celery stick, chopped
mushroom trimmings (if available)
25g/1oz/¼ cup plain (all-purpose) flour
600ml/1 pint/2½ cups hot brown stock
bouquet garni
30ml/2 tbsp tomato purée (paste)
15ml/1 tbsp sherry (optional)
salt and ground black pepper

1 Melt the butter in a heavy pan and fry the bacon for 2–3 minutes. Add the shallots, carrot, celery and mushroom trimmings, if using, and cook for a further 5–6 minutes, or until golden.

2 Gradually stir in the flour and cook for 5–10 minutes over a medium heat until the roux has become a rich brown colour. Remove the pan from the heat and gradually blend in the stock.

3 Gradually bring to the boil, stirring constantly until the sauce thickens. Add the bouquet garni, tomato purée, sherry, if using, and seasoning.

4 Reduce the heat and simmer gently for 1 hour, stirring occasionally. Strain the Espagnole sauce, and gently reheat before serving.

CHASSEUR SAUCE

This excellent mushroom and wine sauce will transform simple pan-fried or grilled chicken, grilled or roast pork, rabbit dishes and, of course, game.

SERVES 3–4

INGREDIENTS
25g/1oz/2 tbsp butter
1 shallot, finely chopped
115g/4oz/2 cups mushrooms, sliced
120ml/4fl oz/½ cup white wine
30ml/2 tbsp brandy
1 quantity Espagnole Sauce
15ml/1 tbsp chopped fresh tarragon or chervil

1 Melt the butter in a medium or large pan over a medium heat, and cook the shallot until softened but not brown.

2 Add the mushrooms and sauté gently, stirring occasionally, until they are just beginning to brown.

3 Pour in the white wine and brandy, and simmer over a medium heat until the sauce is reduced by half.

4 Add the Espagnole sauce and tarragon or chervil and heat through, stirring occasionally. Serve hot.

COOK'S TIP
Espagnole sauce is traditionally made with mushrooms known as mousseron, *the French name for a group of white or beige mushrooms, that includes St George's and blewits. Chestnut mushrooms are also a good choice.*

MOUSSELINE SAUCE

This is a truly luscious sauce, that is subtly flavoured, rich and creamy. Try serving it as a dip for prepared artichokes or artichoke hearts, or with shellfish.

SERVES 4

INGREDIENTS
2 egg yolks
15ml/1 tbsp lemon juice
75g/3oz/6 tbsp softened butter
90ml/6 tbsp double (heavy) cream
extra lemon juice (optional)
salt and ground black pepper

1 To make the sauce, whisk the yolks and lemon juice in a heatproof bowl over a pan of barely simmering water, or a double boiler, until very thick and fluffy.

2 Whisk in the butter, but only a very little at a time, until it is thoroughly absorbed and the sauce has the consistency of mayonnaise.

3 In a separate bowl, whisk the cream until it forms stiff peaks. Fold into the warm sauce and adjust the seasoning. You can add a little more lemon juice for extra sharpness if you like.

> VARIATION
> *For a lavish accompaniment to special fish dishes such as lobster or Dover sole, stir in 30–45ml/ 2–3 tbsp caviar before serving.*

HOLLANDAISE SAUCE

A rich butter sauce, like a warm mayonnaise, which is perfect for steamed or grilled fish, such as salmon, or fresh vegetables such as broccoli, asparagus or new potatoes.

SERVES 2–3

INGREDIENTS
30ml/2 tbsp white wine or tarragon vinegar
15ml/1 tbsp water
6 black peppercorns
1 bay leaf
115g/4oz/½ cup butter
2 egg yolks
salt and ground black pepper

1 Place the vinegar, water, peppercorns and bay leaf in a pan. Simmer the liquid gently until it has reduced by half. Strain and leave to cool. Meanwhile, cream the butter in a separate bowl until soft.

2 In a double boiler or a heatproof bowl set over a pan of gently simmering water, whisk the egg yolks and flavoured vinegar liquid together gently until the mixture is light and fluffy.

3 Gradually add the butter a tiny piece at a time. Whisk quickly until all the butter has been absorbed, before adding any more.

4 Season lightly with salt and pepper and, if the sauce is too sharp, add a little more butter. For a thinner version of the sauce, stir in 15–30ml/1–2 tbsp single (light) cream. Serve immediately.

Béarnaise Sauce

For dedicated meat eaters, this herbed butter sauce adds a note of sophistication without swamping your grilled or pan-fried steak. It also enhances plain vegetables.

SERVES 2–3

INGREDIENTS
45ml/3 tbsp white wine vinegar
30ml/2 tbsp water
1 small onion, finely chopped
a few fresh tarragon and chervil sprigs
1 bay leaf
6 crushed black peppercorns
115g/4oz/½ cup butter
2 egg yolks
15ml/1 tbsp chopped fresh herbs, such as tarragon, parsley, chervil
salt and ground black pepper

1 Place the vinegar, water, onion, herb sprigs, bay leaf and peppercorns in a pan. Simmer gently until the liquid is reduced by half. Strain and cool. Meanwhile, cream the butter in a separate bowl until soft.

2 In a heatproof bowl set over a pan of gently simmering water, or a double boiler, whisk the egg yolks and liquid until light and fluffy.

3 Gradually add the butter, half a teaspoonful at a time. Whisk until all the butter has been incorporated before adding any more.

4 Add the chopped fresh herbs and season to taste. Serve warm, not hot, on the side of a grilled (broiled) steak or allow a spoonful to melt over new potatoes.

VARIATION
To make Choron sauce, which is very good with roast or grilled (broiled) lamb, stir in 15ml/1 tbsp tomato purée (paste) at the end of step 1.

TANGY ORANGE SAUCE

Known as sauce bigarade, *this is the perfect accompaniment for roast duckling and rich game. For a full mellow flavour it is best made with the rich roasting-pan juices.*

SERVES 4–6

INGREDIENTS
roasting-pan juices or 25g/1oz/2 tbsp butter
40g/1½oz/⅓ cup plain (all-purpose) flour
300ml/½ pint/1¼ cups hot stock (preferably duck)
150ml/¼ pint/⅔ cup red wine
2 Seville (Temple) oranges or 2 sweet oranges plus 10ml/2 tsp lemon juice (optional)
15ml/1 tbsp orange-flavoured liqueur
30ml/2 tbsp redcurrant jelly
salt and ground black pepper

1 Carefully pour off any excess fat from the roasting pan, leaving the rich meat juices behind, or melt the butter in a small pan.

2 Sprinkle the flour into the meat juices or melted butter and cook gently over a low heat, stirring constantly, for about 4 minutes, or until the mixture is just lightly browned.

3 Remove the pan from the heat and gradually blend in the hot stock and wine. Return to the heat and bring to the boil, stirring constantly. Lower the heat and simmer gently for 5 minutes.

4 Meanwhile, using a citrus zester, peel the rind thinly from one orange. Squeeze the juice from both of the oranges.

5 Place the rind in a small pan, cover with boiling water and bring back to the boil. Simmer for 5 minutes, then strain and add the rind to the sauce.

6 Add the orange juice to the sauce, along with the lemon juice, if using, and the liqueur and redcurrant jelly. Stir until the jelly has dissolved. Season with salt and pepper to taste.

PESTO SAUCE

There is nothing more evocative of the warmth of Italy than a good home-made pesto. Serve in generous spoonfuls with your favourite pasta.

SERVES 3–4

INGREDIENTS
50g/2oz/1 cup basil leaves
2 garlic cloves, crushed
30ml/2 tbsp pine nuts
120ml/4 fl oz/½ cup olive oil
40g/1½oz/½ cup finely grated Parmesan cheese
salt and ground black pepper

1 **By hand:** using a mortar and pestle, grind the basil, garlic, pine nuts and seasoning to a fine paste.

2 Transfer the mixture to a bowl and whisk in the oil a little at a time. Add the cheese and blend well. Adjust the seasoning to taste and heat the sauce gently.

1 **Using a food processor:** place the basil, garlic, pine nuts and seasoning in the food processor and process as finely as possible.

2 With the machine running, gradually add the oil in a thin stream, combining the ingredients until they have formed a smooth paste.

3 Add the cheese and pulse quickly 3–4 times. Adjust the seasoning, if necessary, and heat gently.

VARIATION
Pesto makes an excellent dressing for boiled new potatoes. Serve the dish while hot or allow to cool to room temperature.

NEWBURG SAUCE

The rich flavour of this creamy sauce will not mask delicate foods, and it is therefore ideal for serving with shellfish. It also goes well with pan-fried chicken.

SERVES 4

INGREDIENTS
15g/½oz/1 tbsp butter
1 small shallot, finely chopped
pinch of cayenne pepper
300ml/½ pint/1¼ cups double (heavy) cream
60ml/4 tbsp Madeira
3 egg yolks
salt and ground black pepper

1 Melt the butter in a heatproof bowl placed over a pan of barely simmering water, or in a double boiler. Add the chopped shallot to the butter and cook gently until it is softened and transparent but not coloured.

2 Add the cayenne and all but 60ml/4 tbsp of the cream. Leave over the simmering water for 10 minutes to reduce slightly.

3 Stir in the Madeira. Beat the egg yolks with the remaining cream and stir into the hot sauce. Continue stirring the sauce over barely simmering water until thickened. Season to taste. Serve immediately.

COOK'S TIPS
• *To give the sauce a luxurious festive look, stir in 15–30ml/1–2 tbsp of pink or black lumpfish roe.*
• *Spoon over seafood or chicken, reserving some for pouring, and serve immediately. Garnish the dish with fresh herbs.*

Rich Tomato Sauce

For a full tomato flavour and rich red colour, fresh Italian plum tomatoes are an excellent choice if they are available – make sure that they are completely ripe.

Serves 4–6

Ingredients
30ml/2 tbsp olive oil
1 large onion, chopped
2 garlic cloves, crushed
1 carrot, finely chopped
1 celery stick, finely chopped
675g/1½lb tomatoes, peeled and chopped
150ml/¼ pint/⅔ cup red wine
150ml/¼ pint/⅔ cup Vegetable Stock
bouquet garni
2.5–5ml/½–1 tsp sugar
15ml/1 tbsp tomato purée (paste), or to taste
salt and ground black pepper

1 Heat the oil in a pan, add the onion and garlic and sauté until soft and pale golden brown. Add the carrot and celery and continue to cook, stirring occasionally, until golden.

2 Stir in the tomatoes, wine, stock and bouquet garni. Season with salt and ground black pepper to taste.

3 Bring the tomato mixture to the boil, then cover and simmer gently for 45 minutes, stirring occasionally to avoid the burning. Remove the bouquet garni from the liquid, taste the sauce and adjust the seasoning, adding a pinch of sugar and tomato purée as necessary.

4 Serve the sauce as it is or, for a smoother texture, press through a sieve, or process in a blender or food processor.

BLUE CHEESE & WALNUT SAUCE

This is a very quick but indulgently creamy sauce. The blue cheese melts easily with cream to make a simple sauce to serve with vegetables or pasta.

SERVES 2

INGREDIENTS
50g/2oz/¼ cup butter
50g/2oz/¾ cup button (white) mushrooms, sliced
150g/5oz hard blue cheese, such as Gorgonzola, Stilton or Danish Blue
150ml/¼ pint/⅔ cup sour cream
25g/1oz/⅓ cup grated Pecorino cheese
50g/2oz/½ cup broken walnut pieces
salt and ground black pepper

1 Melt the butter in a pan, add the mushrooms and cook gently, stirring occasionally, for 3–5 minutes, until lightly browned.

2 Place the blue cheese and sour cream in a bowl, add seasoning to taste and mash together well using a fork.

3 Stir the cheese and sour cream mixture into the mushroom mixture and heat gently, stirring, until melted.

4 Finally, stir in the grated Pecorino cheese and the broken walnut pieces. Serve the sauce warm.

COOK'S TIP
It is worth buying the best blue cheese you can find for this sauce to produce the finest flavour. Although blue cheese has a "smelly" reputation, it should never have an unpleasant or sour odour, and the texture should be firm.

GREEN PEPPERCORN SAUCE

This sauce is excellent with pasta, pork steaks or grilled chicken. The green peppercorns in brine have a more rounded flavour than the dry-packed type.

SERVES 3–4

INGREDIENTS
15ml/1 tbsp green peppercorns in brine, drained
1 small onion, finely chopped
25g/1oz/2 tbsp butter
300ml/½ pint/1¼ cups light stock
juice of ½ lemon
15ml/1 tbsp beurre manié
45ml/3 tbsp double (heavy) cream
5ml/1 tsp Dijon mustard
salt and ground black pepper

1 Dry the peppercorns on kitchen paper, then crush lightly under the blade of a heavy-duty knife or use a mortar and pestle.

2 Soften the onion in the butter, add the stock and lemon juice and simmer for 15 minutes.

3 Whisk in the beurre manié a little at a time and continue to cook, stirring, until the sauce thickens. Reduce the heat and stir in the peppercorns, cream and mustard. Heat until boiling, then season to taste. Serve the sauce hot.

QUICK SATAY SAUCE

There are many versions of this tasty peanut sauce. This one is very speedy, and it tastes delicious drizzled over grilled skewers of chicken.

SERVES 4

INGREDIENTS
200ml/7fl oz/scant 1 cup coconut cream
60ml/4 tbsp crunchy peanut butter
1 tsp Worcestershire sauce
Tabasco sauce, to taste
fresh coconut, to garnish (optional)

1 Pour the coconut cream into a small pan and heat it gently over a low heat for about 2 minutes.

2 Add the peanut butter and stir the mixture vigorously until the peanut butter is blended evenly into the coconut cream. Continue to heat until the mixture is warm but not boiling hot.

3 Add the Worcestershire sauce and a dash of Tabasco to taste. Pour into a serving bowl.

4 Use a potato peeler to shave thin curls from a piece of fresh coconut, if using. Sprinkle the coconut over the dish of your choice and serve immediately with the warm sauce.

BARBECUE SAUCE

Brush this sauce over chops, kebabs or chicken drumsticks before cooking on the barbecue, or serve as a hot or cold accompaniment to hot dogs and burgers.

SERVES 4

INGREDIENTS
30ml/2 tbsp vegetable oil
1 large onion, chopped
2 garlic cloves, crushed
400g/14oz can tomatoes
30ml/2 tbsp Worcestershire sauce
15ml/1 tbsp white wine vinegar
45ml/3 tbsp clear honey
5ml/1 tsp mustard powder
2.5ml/½ tsp chilli seasoning or mild chilli powder
salt and ground black pepper

1 Heat the oil in a pan and cook the onion and garlic until soft. Stir in the remaining ingredients and bring to the boil. Simmer gently, uncovered, for 15–20 minutes, stirring occasionally. Cool slightly.

2 Pour the sauce into a food processor or blender and process until smooth. Press the sauce through a sieve if you prefer a smoother result, and adjust the seasoning with salt and pepper to taste before serving.

COOK'S TIP
Chilli seasoning usually contains a mixture of extra spices and/or herbs, while chilli powder tends to be made from pure dried chilli.

APPLE SAUCE

Really more of a condiment than a sauce, this tart purée is usually served cold or warm, rather than hot. It's typically served with rice, roast pork or duck.

SERVES 6

INGREDIENTS
225g/8oz tart cooking apples
30ml/2 tbsp water
thin strip of lemon rind
15ml/1 tbsp butter
15–30ml/1–2 tbsp caster (superfine) sugar

1 Peel the apples, cut into quarters and remove the cores. Cut the quarters into thin, even slices.

2 Place the apples in a pan with the water and lemon rind. Cook, uncovered, over a low heat until very soft, stirring occasionally.

3 Remove the lemon rind from the pan and discard. Beat the apples to a pulp with a spoon, or press through a sieve. Stir the butter into the apple sauce and then add sugar to taste.

VARIATIONS
- *To make a Normandy Apple Sauce, try stirring in 15ml/1 tbsp Calvados or applejack with the butter and sugar in step 3.*
- *To make a deliciously creamy savoury Apple Sauce, stir in 30ml/2 tbsp sour cream or crème fraîche at step 3.*

CRANBERRY SAUCE

This is the traditional sauce for roast turkey, but don't keep it just for festive occasions. The vibrant colour and tart taste make it a perfect partner to any white roast meat, and it is also a great addition to a chicken or Brie sandwich.

SERVES 6

INGREDIENTS
1 orange
225g/8oz/2 cups cranberries
250g/9oz/1¼ cups caster (superfine) sugar
150ml/¼ pint/⅔ cup water

1 Pare the rind thinly from the orange using a swivel-bladed vegetable peeler, taking care not to remove any white pith. Squeeze the juice.

2 Place the orange rind and juice in a heavy pan together with the cranberries, sugar and water.

3 Bring to the boil, stirring until the sugar has dissolved, then simmer gently for 10–15 minutes, or until the berries burst. Remove the orange rind and leave to cool before serving.

Mint Sauce

Tart, yet sweet, this simple sauce is the perfect foil to rich meat. It's best served, of course, with the new season's tender roast lamb, but it is also wonderful with grilled lamb chops or pan-fried duck and makes a refreshing dressing for new potatoes.

SERVES 6

INGREDIENTS
small bunch of fresh mint
15ml/1 tbsp sugar
30ml/2 tbsp boiling water
45ml/3 tbsp white wine vinegar

1 Strip the mint leaves from their stalks and finely chop the leaves. Discard the stalks.

2 Place in a heatproof bowl with the sugar and pour in the boiling water. Stir well to dissolve the sugar and leave the mixture to stand for 5–10 minutes to let the flavours infuse (steep).

3 Add the white wine vinegar, stir well to mix and leave to stand for 1–2 hours before serving.

Horseradish Sauce

This light, creamy sauce is the classic accompaniment to roast beef, but is perfect, too, with herbed sausages and grilled fish, especially oily fish such as mackerel.

Serves 6

Ingredients
7.5cm/3in piece of fresh horseradish
15ml/1 tbsp lemon juice
10ml/2 tsp sugar
2.5ml/½ tsp English (hot) mustard powder
150ml/¼ pint/⅔ cup double (heavy) cream

1 Scrub and peel the piece of fresh horseradish, and then grate it as finely as possible. (If you have sensitive skin, wear rubber gloves.)

2 Combine the grated horseradish, lemon juice, sugar and mustard powder in a bowl and mix well.

3 Whip the cream in another bowl until it stands in soft peaks, then gently fold in the horseradish mixture.

Variation
For a change of flavour, replace the lemon juice with tarragon vinegar.

BREAD SAUCE

Smooth and surprisingly delicate, this old-fashioned sauce dates back to medieval times. It's traditionally served with roast chicken, turkey and game birds.

SERVES 6

INGREDIENTS
1 small onion
4 cloves
bay leaf
300ml/½ pint/1¼ cups milk
90g/3½oz/scant 2 cups fresh white breadcrumbs
15ml/1 tbsp butter
15ml/1 tbsp single (light) cream
salt and ground black pepper

1 Peel the onion and stick the cloves into it. Put it into a pan with the bay leaf and pour in the milk.

2 Bring just to the boil, then remove the pan from the heat and leave to infuse (steep) for about 15–20 minutes. Remove the bay leaf and onion from the milk and discard.

3 Return the pan to the heat and stir in the breadcrumbs. Simmer gently for 4–5 minutes, or until thick and creamy. Stir in the butter and cream, then season to taste. Serve warm.

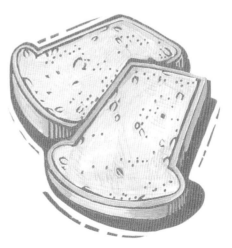

SAUCES FOR PASTA DISHES

There's a wealth of sauce recipes for all types of pasta, and not surprisingly they are often Italian in origin. Endlessly varied in style, they may be delicate, buttery herb mixtures or rich cream sauces, hearty meat ragus or chunky vegetable sauces. Many are based on tomatoes from southern Italy, and make the very best use of those other Mediterranean flavours – olive oil, garlic and basil – all classic partners for pasta. Most pasta sauces are refreshingly simple and foolproof, and do not need hours of preparation. Most are cooked in a matter of minutes, retaining all the natural flavours of fresh ingredients, with the exception of long-simmered rich meat and tomato ragus, which by tradition are simmered at length on a low heat for a more concentrated, mature flavour. Many of these sauces are designed to match particular types or shapes of pasta, but there are no hard-and-fast rules. Many of the sauces work well with other types of pasta, so try experimenting with your favourites. It's rare for a pasta sauce to be flour-thickened, but many are enriched or thickened with eggs, such as Carbonara. Those that are simmered over long periods, such as Bolognese Sauce, reach a thicker consistency as they are reduced and become more concentrated. Many form an integral part of the dish, and may be as simple as olive oil with Parmesan cheese and herbs. The choice is yours.

MAKING PASTA DOUGH

Home-made pasta has a wonderfully light, almost silky texture – quite different from the so-called fresh pasta that you buy in the stores.

PASTA WITH EGGS

INGREDIENTS
300g/11oz/2¾ cups plain (all-purpose) flour
3 eggs
5ml/1 tsp salt

1 Mound the flour on a clean surface and make a large, deep well in the centre with your hands. Keep the sides of the well so that when the eggs are added they will stay in the well.

2 Crack the eggs into the well and add the salt. With a table knife, mix the eggs and salt together, then gradually incorporate the flour from the sides of the well.

3 As soon as the mixture is no longer liquid, dip your fingers in the flour and gradually work the ingredients into a coarse and sticky dough. If the dough is too dry, add just a few drops of cold water; if it is too moist, sprinkle a little extra flour over it.

4 Press the dough into a ball and knead it as you would bread. Push it away from you with the heel of your hand, then fold the dough back on itself so that it faces towards you and push it out again.

5 Continue folding the dough back a little further each time and pushing it out until you have folded it back all the way towards you and all the dough has been kneaded. Give the dough a quarter turn anti-clockwise (counterclockwise), then continue kneading, folding and turning for 10 minutes. The dough should be very smooth and elastic.

6 Wrap the dough in clear film (plastic wrap) and leave to rest for 15–20 minutes at room temperature. It will then be ready to roll. Roll out half the dough at a time on a lightly floured surface until it is 3mm/⅛in thick. Alternatively, you can use a pasta machine at successively thinner settings.

CHILLI SAUCE WITH PASTA

This is a speciality of Lazio in Italy – the Italian name for the sauce, al arrabbiata, *means rabid or angry, and describes the heat that comes from the chilli.*

SERVES 4

INGREDIENTS
300g/11oz dried penne or tortiglioni

FOR THE TOMATO AND CHILLI SAUCE
500g/1¼lb sugocasa
2 garlic cloves, crushed
150ml/¼ pint/⅔ cup dry white wine
15ml/1 tbsp sun-dried tomato paste
1 fresh red chilli
30ml/2 tbsp finely chopped fresh flat leaf parsley, plus extra to garnish
salt and ground black pepper
grated fresh Pecorino cheese, to serve

1 Put the sugocasa, garlic, wine, tomato paste and whole chilli in a pan and bring to the boil. Cover and simmer gently.

2 Drop the pasta into a large pan of rapidly boiling salted water and cook for 10–12 minutes, or until *al dente*.

3 Remove the chilli from the sauce and add the parsley. Taste for seasoning. If you prefer a hotter taste, chop some or all of the chilli and return it to the sauce. Drain the pasta and tip into a warmed large bowl. Pour the sauce over the pasta and toss to mix. Serve immediately, sprinkled with parsley and grated Pecorino.

COOK'S TIPS
• *If you prefer the flavour to be slightly less hot, remove the seeds from the chilli before using. Split the chilli down its length and scrape out the fiery seeds with the tip of a knife.*
• *Sugocasa literally means "house sauce" and consists of coarsely crushed tomatoes.*

Italian Plum Tomato Sauce with Cheese & Ham Ravioli

This tasty sauce uses store-cupboard ingredients, which is time saving if you have an elaborate pasta to make. It can also be served with meat or fish.

Serves 4–6

Ingredients
500g/1¼lb fresh Pasta Dough
60ml/4 tbsp grated fresh Pecorino cheese, plus extra to serve

For the filling
175g/6oz ricotta cheese
30ml/2 tbsp grated fresh Parmesan cheese
115g/4oz prosciutto, finely chopped
150g/5oz fresh mozzarella cheese, drained and finely chopped
1 small (US medium) egg
15ml/1 tbsp chopped fresh flat leaf parsley, plus extra to garnish

For the Italian plum tomato sauce
30ml/2 tbsp olive oil
1 onion, finely chopped
400g/14oz can chopped plum tomatoes
15ml/1 tbsp sun-dried tomato paste
5–10ml/1–2 tsp dried oregano
salt and ground black pepper

1 To make the sauce, heat the oil in a pan, add the onion and cook, stirring frequently, until softened.

2 Add the tomatoes. Fill the empty can with water, pour it into the pan, then stir in the tomato paste, oregano and seasoning to taste. Bring to the boil and stir well, then cover the pan and simmer for 30 minutes, stirring occasionally and adding more water if the sauce becomes too thick.

3 Put the filling ingredients in a bowl and season to taste. Mix with a fork, breaking up the ricotta.

4 Using a pasta machine, roll out one-quarter of the pasta into a 90–100cm/36–40in strip. Cut the strip into two 45–50cm/18–20in lengths.

5 Using two teaspoons, put little mounds of the filling, 10–12 in total, along one side of one of the pasta strips, spacing them evenly. The filling will be quite moist. Brush a little water around each mound, then fold the plain side of the pasta strip over.

6 Starting from the folded edge, press down gently with your fingertips around each mound, pushing the air out at the unfolded edge.

7 Sprinkle lightly with flour. With a fluted pasta wheel, cut along each long side, then in-between each mound, to make small square shapes.

8 Put the ravioli on floured dishtowels; sprinkle lightly with flour. Leave to dry while you are repeating the process with the remaining pasta, to give you 80–96 ravioli altogether.

9 Drop the ravioli into a large pan of lightly salted, boiling water, bring the water back to the boil and boil for 4–5 minutes. Drain well. Spoon about a third of the ravioli into a warmed serving bowl. Sprinkle with 15ml/1 tbsp grated Pecorino and pour over a third of the tomato sauce.

10 Repeat the layers twice, then top with the remaining grated Pecorino. Serve immediately, garnished with chopped parsley.

Sun-dried Tomato & Radicchio Sauce with Paglia e Fieno

This is a light, modern pasta dish of the kind served in fashionable restaurants. It is the presentation that sets it apart. It is very quick and easy to prepare.

SERVES 4

INGREDIENTS
45ml/3 tbsp pine nuts
350g/12oz paglia e fieno pasta
30ml/2 tbsp extra virgin olive oil
4–6 spring onions (scallions), thinly sliced into rings

FOR THE SUN-DRIED TOMATO AND RADICCHIO SAUCE
15ml/1 tbsp extra virgin olive oil
30ml/2 tbsp sun-dried tomato paste
40g/1½oz radicchio leaves, finely shredded (about ½ cup)
salt and ground black pepper

1 Put the pine nuts in a heavy frying pan and toss over a medium heat for 1–2 minutes, until lightly toasted and golden brown. Remove and set aside.

2 Cook the pasta according to the packet instructions, keeping the colours separate by using two pans.

3 To make the sauce, heat the oil in a medium frying pan. Add the sun-dried tomato paste, then stir in two ladlefuls of pasta cooking water. Simmer until the sauce is slightly reduced, stirring constantly.

4 Stir in the radicchio and season to taste. Keep on a low heat. Drain the pasta, keeping the colours separate, and return them to their pans. Add 15ml/1 tbsp of oil to each pan and toss over a medium to high heat until the pasta is glistening.

5 Arrange a portion of green and white pasta in each of four warmed bowls, then spoon the sauce into the centre. Sprinkle the spring onions and toasted pine nuts decoratively over the top and serve immediately. Before eating, each diner should toss the sauce with the pasta to mix well.

Tomato & Courgette Sauce with Tagliatelle

This vegetarian sauce goes well with a variety of pastas and only takes minutes to prepare. Its light, summery flavour is perfect for an al fresco lunch.

SERVES 3–4

INGREDIENTS
225g/8oz wholewheat tagliatelle
50g/2oz/½ cup flaked (sliced) almonds, toasted

FOR THE TOMATO AND COURGETTE (ZUCCHINI) SAUCE
5–6 ripe plum tomatoes
30ml/2 tbsp olive oil
1 onion, chopped
2 celery sticks, chopped
1 garlic clove, crushed
2 courgettes (zucchini), halved lengthways and sliced
30ml/2 tbsp sun-dried tomato paste
salt and ground black pepper

1 To make the sauce, place the tomatoes in a bowl of boiling water for 30 seconds to loosen the skins. Peel, then chop.

2 Bring a large pan of lightly salted water to the boil, add the pasta, bring back to the boil and cook for about 12 minutes, or according to the instructions on the packet, until *al dente*.

3 Meanwhile, heat the oil in another pan and add the chopped onion, celery, garlic and courgettes. Sauté over a gentle heat for 3–4 minutes, until the onions have become lightly browned.

4 Stir in the tomatoes and sun-dried tomato paste. Cook gently for a further 5 minutes, then add salt and pepper to taste.

5 Drain the pasta, return it to the pan and add the sauce. Toss well. Place in a serving dish and sprinkle the toasted almonds over the top to serve.

Cannelloni with Two Sauces

The combination of the full-flavoured tomato sauce and the creamy white sauce makes this cannelloni dish a success. For a special occasion, make it in advance to the baking stage. Add the white sauce and bake on the day.

SERVES 6

INGREDIENTS
15ml/1 tbsp olive oil
1 small onion, finely chopped
450g/1lb minced (ground) beef
1 garlic clove, finely chopped
5ml/1 tsp dried mixed herbs
120ml/4fl oz/½ cup Beef Stock
1 egg
75g/3oz cooked ham or mortadella sausage, finely chopped
45ml/3 tbsp fine fresh white breadcrumbs
115g/4oz/1¼ cups freshly grated Parmesan cheese
18 pre-cooked cannelloni tubes
salt and ground black pepper

FOR THE TOMATO SAUCE
30ml/2 tbsp olive oil
1 small onion, finely chopped
½ carrot, finely chopped
1 celery stalk, finely chopped
1 garlic clove, crushed
400g/14oz can chopped plum tomatoes
a few fresh basil sprigs
2.5ml/½ tsp dried oregano

FOR THE WHITE SAUCE
50g/2oz/¼ cup butter
50g/2oz/½ cup plain (all-purpose) flour
900ml/1½ pints/3¾ cups milk
fresh nutmeg

1 Heat the olive oil in a pan and cook the chopped onion over a low heat, stirring occasionally, for about 5 minutes, until softened.

2 Add the minced beef and garlic and cook for 10 minutes, stirring and breaking up any lumps with a wooden spoon. Add the herbs, and season to taste, then moisten with half the stock. Cover the pan and simmer for 25 minutes, stirring occasionally. Add more stock as it reduces. Spoon into a bowl and leave to cool.

3 To make the tomato sauce, heat the oil in a pan, add the vegetables and garlic and cook over a medium heat, stirring frequently, for 10 minutes. Add the tomatoes. Fill the empty can with water, pour it into the pan, then add the herbs and season. Bring to the boil, lower the heat, cover and simmer for 25–30 minutes, stirring occasionally. Process the tomato sauce in a blender or food processor.

4 Add the egg, ham or mortadella, breadcrumbs and 90ml/6 tbsp of the grated Parmesan to the meat and stir well to mix. Taste for seasoning.

5 Spread a little tomato sauce over the base of a rectangular ovenproof dish. Using a teaspoon, fill the cannelloni with the meat mixture. Place the cannelloni in a single layer on top of the sauce. Pour the remaining sauce over the top.

6 Preheat the oven to 190°C/375°F/Gas 5. For the white sauce, melt the butter in a pan, add the flour and cook for 1–2 minutes. Remove from the heat and blend in the milk. Return to the heat, bring to the boil and stir until smooth and thick. Grate in fresh nutmeg, and season.

7 Pour the sauce over the cannelloni, then sprinkle with Parmesan. Bake for 40–45 minutes. Leave to stand for 10 minutes before serving.

Tomato & Pepper Sauce

A mellow sauce, ideal for serving with pasta. For a more extravagant dish, suitable for non-vegetarians, you could add sliced chorizo sausage.

SERVES 3–4

INGREDIENTS
350g/12oz filled pasta, such as tortelloni

FOR THE TOMATO, (BELL) PEPPER AND CHILLI SAUCE
30ml/2 tbsp olive oil
1 onion, chopped
1 garlic clove, crushed
2 large red or orange (bell) peppers,
  seeded and finely chopped
5ml/1 tsp chilli seasoning
15ml/1 tbsp paprika
2.5ml/½ tsp dried thyme
225g/8oz can chopped tomatoes
300ml/½ pint/1¼ cups vegetable stock
2.5ml/½ tsp sugar
30ml/2 tbsp sun-dried tomatoes in oil,
  drained and chopped
salt and ground black pepper

1 Heat the oil and gently sauté the onion, garlic and red or orange peppers for 4–5 minutes, until softened.

2 Add the chilli, paprika and thyme and cook over a low heat for a further minute, stirring constantly. Stir in the tomatoes, vegetable stock, sugar and seasoning, and bring to the boil. Cover and simmer for 30 minutes, or until soft, adding more stock if necessary.

3 About 10 minutes before the end of cooking, add the sun-dried tomatoes and stir in.

4 Cook the pasta in salted, boiling water according to the packet instructions. Drain and serve with the hot sauce.

AUBERGINE SAUCE WITH PASTA

Full of flavour, this sauce goes well with any short pasta shapes. It can be layered with sheets of pasta and cheese sauce to make lasagne.

SERVES 4–6

INGREDIENTS
350g/12oz dried short pasta shapes

FOR THE AUBERGINE (EGGPLANT) SAUCE
30ml/2 tbsp olive oil
1 small fresh red chilli
2 garlic cloves
2 handfuls fresh flat leaf parsley, coarsely chopped, plus extra to serve
450g/1lb aubergine (eggplant), chopped
200ml/7fl oz/scant 1 cup vegetable stock
1 vegetable stock (bouillon) cube
1 handful fresh basil leaves
8 plum tomatoes, peeled and chopped
60ml/4 tbsp red wine
5ml/1 tsp sugar
1 envelope saffron powder
2.5ml/½ tsp ground paprika
salt and ground black pepper

1 Heat the oil in a large frying pan and add the chilli, garlic and half the parsley. Smash the garlic cloves with a wooden spoon to release their juice, then cover the pan and cook over a low to medium heat for 10 minutes, stirring occasionally.

2 Remove and discard the chilli. Add the aubergine and half the stock, then cover and cook, stirring frequently, for about 10 minutes. Add the remaining ingredients, stir well, replace the lid and cook for 30–40 minutes.

3 About 10 minutes before the sauce is ready, cook the pasta in salted, boiling water according to the instructions on the packet until *al dente*.

4 Check the sauce for seasoning, then toss with the drained pasta in warmed bowls. Garnish with extra chopped parsley.

Carbonara Sauce with Spaghetti

An all-time favourite sauce that is perfect for spaghetti or tagliatelle. This version has plenty of pancetta or bacon and is not too creamy, but you can vary the amounts.

Serves 4

Ingredients
350g/12oz fresh or dried spaghetti

For the carbonara sauce
30ml/2 tbsp olive oil
1 small onion, finely chopped
8 pancetta or lean bacon strips, cut into 1cm/½in strips
4 eggs
60ml/4 tbsp crème fraîche
60ml/4 tbsp freshly grated Parmesan cheese, plus extra to serve
salt and ground black pepper

Cook's Tip
Pancetta, like bacon, is available both smoked and unsmoked. Both taste delicious in this sauce, so use whichever is your favourite.

1 Heat the oil in a frying pan, add the onion and cook over a low heat, stirring occasionally, for 5 minutes, until softened.

2 Add the strips of pancetta or bacon to the onion in the pan and cook for about 10 minutes, stirring almost all the time.

3 Meanwhile, cook the pasta in a pan of salted, boiling water according to the instructions on the packet, until *al dente*.

4 Put the eggs, crème fraîche and grated Parmesan in a bowl. Grind in plenty of pepper, then beat the mixture well.

5 Drain the pasta, turn it into the pan with the pancetta or bacon and toss thoroughly to mix.

6 Turn the heat off under the pan. Immediately add the egg mixture and toss vigorously so that it cooks lightly and coats the pasta.

7 Quickly taste for seasoning, then divide among four warmed bowls and sprinkle with black pepper. Serve immediately, with extra grated Parmesan offered separately.

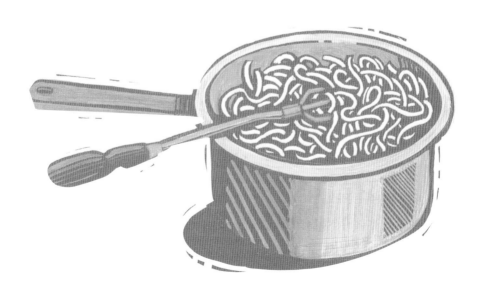

GORGONZOLA SAUCE WITH GNOCCHI

This cheese sauce has a strong flavour and so is ideal with potato dumplings or a plain pasta like macaroni. Either way, it makes a filling dish ideal for a winter supper.

SERVES 4

INGREDIENTS
450g/1lb potatoes, unpeeled
1 large (US extra large) egg
115g/4oz/1 cup plain (all-purpose) flour
salt and ground black pepper
fresh thyme sprigs, to garnish
60ml/4 tbsp freshly grated Parmesan cheese, to serve

FOR THE GORGONZOLA SAUCE
115g/4oz Gorgonzola cheese
60ml/4 tbsp double (heavy) cream
15ml/1 tbsp chopped fresh thyme

> VARIATION
> *The Gorgonzola sauce could also be used in a fondue, with croûtons or vegetable pieces to dip.*

1 Cook the potatoes in boiling salted water for about 20 minutes until they are tender. Drain and, when cool enough to handle, remove the skins.

2 Press the potatoes through a sieve, using the back of a spoon, into a mixing bowl. Season, then beat in the egg. Add the flour a little at a time, stirring well with a wooden spoon after each addition until you have a smooth dough. (You may not need all the flour.)

3 Turn the dough out on to a floured surface and knead it for about 3 minutes, adding more flour if you need to, until it is smooth and soft and not sticky to the touch.

4 Divide the dough into six equal pieces. Flour your hands and gently roll each piece on a board into a log shape measuring 15–20cm/6–8in long and 2.5cm/1in diameter. Cut each log into six to eight pieces, each about 2.5cm/1in long, then gently roll each piece in the flour. Form into gnocchi by gently pressing each piece on to the floured surface with the tines of a fork to form ridges.

5 To cook, drop the gnocchi into a pan of boiling water, about 12 at a time. Once they rise to the surface, after about 2 minutes, cook them for 4–5 minutes more, then drain.

6 To make the sauce, place the Gorgonzola, cream and thyme in a large frying pan and heat gently until the cheese melts to form a thick, creamy consistency, then heat through.

7 Add the drained gnocchi to the sauce and toss well to combine. Serve with Parmesan and garnish with thyme.

CREAM & PARMESAN SAUCE WITH SPINACH & RICOTTA RAVIOLI

This simple, but rich-tasting sauce is the perfect accompaniment to home-made spinach and ricotta ravioli but would be just as delicious on store-bought tortelloni or any other fresh pasta with a stuffing to give flavour.

SERVES 8

INGREDIENTS
500g/1¼lb fresh Pasta Dough
grated fresh Parmesan cheese, to serve
salt and ground black pepper

FOR THE FILLING
40g/1½oz/3 tbsp butter
175g/6oz fresh spinach leaves, trimmed, washed and shredded
200g/7oz/scant 1 cup ricotta cheese
25g/1oz/⅓ cup freshly grated Parmesan cheese
freshly grated nutmeg
1 small (US medium) egg

FOR THE CREAM AND PARMESAN SAUCE
50g/2oz/¼ cup butter
120ml/4fl oz/½ cup double (heavy) cream
50g/2oz/⅔ cup freshly grated Parmesan cheese

VARIATION
This cheese sauce would also work well with a baked pasta dish such as macaroni. Sprinkle the top generously with grated Parmesan before baking.

1 To make the filling, melt the butter in a pan, add the spinach and salt and pepper to taste and cook over a medium heat for 5–8 minutes, stirring frequently, until the spinach is wilted and tender. Increase the heat to high. Stir until the water boils off and the spinach is quite dry.

2 Tip the spinach into a bowl and set aside until cold, then add the ricotta, grated Parmesan and freshly grated nutmeg to taste. Beat well to mix, taste for seasoning, then add the egg and beat well again.

3 Using a pasta machine, roll out one-quarter of the pasta into a 90–100cm/36–40in strip. Cut the strip with a sharp knife into two 45–50cm/18–20in lengths (you can do this during rolling if the strip gets too long to manage).

4 Using a teaspoon, put 10–12 little mounds of the filling along one side of one of the pasta strips, spacing them evenly. Brush a little water around each mound, then fold the plain side of the pasta strip over the filling.

5 Starting from the folded edge, press down gently with your fingertips around each mound of filling, pushing the air out at the unfolded edge. Sprinkle lightly with flour.

6 With a fluted pasta wheel, cut along each long side, then in-between each mound to make small square shapes.

7 Put the ravioli on floured dishtowels, sprinkle lightly with flour and leave to dry while you are repeating the process with the remaining pasta, to give yourself 80–96 ravioli altogether.

8 Drop the ravioli into a large pan of salted, boiling water, bring back to the boil and boil for 4–5 minutes.

9 Meanwhile, make the sauce. Gently heat the butter, cream and Parmesan in a medium pan until the butter and Parmesan have melted.

10 Increase the heat and simmer for 1–2 minutes, until the sauce is slightly reduced, then add salt and pepper to taste.

11 Drain the ravioli and divide them equally among eight warmed large bowls. Drizzle the sauce over them and serve sprinkled with Parmesan and pepper.

BOLOGNESE SAUCE WITH RAVIOLI

Perhaps one of the most famous pasta sauces outside Italy, Bolognese sauce is a rich ragù from the city of Bologna in Emilia-Romagna, an area famous for fine foods.

SERVES 6

INGREDIENTS
225g/8oz/1 cup cottage cheese
30ml/2 tbsp freshly grated Parmesan cheese, plus extra for serving
1 egg white, beaten, including extra for brushing
1.5ml/¼ tsp ground nutmeg
300g/11oz fresh Pasta Dough
plain (all-purpose) flour, for dusting
salt and ground black pepper

FOR THE BOLOGNESE SAUCE
1 medium onion, finely chopped
1 garlic clove, crushed
150ml/¼ pint/⅔ cup Beef Stock
350g/12oz minced (ground) extra-lean beef
120ml/4fl oz/½ cup red wine
30ml/2 tbsp concentrated tomato purée (paste)
400g/14oz can chopped plum tomatoes
2.5ml/½ tsp chopped fresh rosemary
1.5ml/¼ tsp ground allspice

> VARIATION
> Stir in a handful of chopped chicken livers with the minced (ground) beef to add a more meaty richness to the sauce.

1 To make the filling, mix the cottage cheese, grated Parmesan cheese, most of the egg white, seasoning and nutmeg together thoroughly.

2 Roll the pasta into thin sheets, then place small amounts of filling along the pasta in rows, leaving a gap of 5cm/2in between them. Moisten around the filling with beaten egg white.

3 Place a second sheet of pasta lightly over the top. Press between each pocket to remove the air, and seal.

4 Cut into rounds with a fluted ravioli or pastry cutter. Transfer to a floured dishtowel and leave to rest for at least 30 minutes before cooking.

5 To make the Bolognese sauce, cook the onion and garlic in the stock for about 5 minutes or until all the stock has reduced. Add the beef and cook quickly to brown, breaking up the meat with a fork.

6 Add the wine, tomato purée, chopped tomatoes, rosemary and allspice. Bring to the boil and simmer for 1 hour. Season to taste.

7 Cook the ravioli in a large pan of salted, boiling water for 4–5 minutes. (Cook in batches to stop them from sticking together.) Drain thoroughly. Serve topped with the Bolognese sauce. Hand round the grated Parmesan cheese separately.

CREAM & WALNUT SAUCE ON PANSOTTI

This walnut and cream pesto is a simplified version of the one traditionally served with pansotti in Liguria. It would go equally well with any pasta stuffed with ricotta or spinach, or for a less rich alternative serve it with plain pasta shells.

SERVES 6–8

INGREDIENTS
500g/1¼lb herb-flavoured pasta dough with eggs
50g/2oz/¼ cup butter
freshly grated Parmesan cheese, to serve
salt and ground black pepper

FOR THE FILLING
250g/9oz/generous 1 cup ricotta cheese
115g/4oz/1¼ cups freshly grated Parmesan cheese
1 large handful fresh basil leaves, finely chopped
1 large handful fresh flat leaf parsley, finely chopped
a few fresh marjoram or oregano sprigs, leaves removed and finely chopped
1 garlic clove, crushed
1 small (US medium) egg

FOR THE CREAM AND WALNUT SAUCE
90g/3½oz/scant 1 cup shelled walnuts
1 garlic clove
60ml/4 tbsp extra virgin olive oil
120ml/4fl oz/½ cup double (heavy) cream

COOK'S TIP
Take care not to overfill the pansotti, or they will burst open during cooking.

1 To make the filling, put the ricotta cheese, Parmesan cheese, basil, parsley, marjoram or oregano, garlic and egg in a bowl. Season with salt and ground black pepper to taste and beat well to mix.

2 To make the sauce, put the walnuts, garlic clove and oil in a food processor and process to a paste, adding up to 120ml/4fl oz/½ cup warm water, through the feeder tube, to thin down the paste.

3 Spoon the mixture into a bowl and add the cream. Beat well to mix, then season to taste.

4 Using a pasta machine, roll out one-quarter of the pasta into a 90–100cm/36–40in strip. Cut the strip with a sharp knife into two 45–50cm/18–20in lengths (you can do this during rolling if the strip gets too long to manage).

5 Using a 5cm/2in square ravioli cutter, cut eight to ten squares from one of the pasta strips.

6 Using a teaspoon, put a mound of filling in the centre of each square. Brush a little water around the edge of each square, then fold the square diagonally in half over the filling to make a triangle. Press gently to seal.

7 Spread out the pansotti on clean floured dishtowels, sprinkle lightly with flour and set aside to dry, while repeating the process with the remaining dough, to make a total of 64–80 pansotti.

8 Cook the pansotti in a large pan of lightly salted, boiling water for 4–5 minutes. Meanwhile, put the walnut sauce in a large, warmed bowl and add a ladleful of the pasta cooking water to thin it down slightly. Melt the butter in a small pan until sizzling.

9 Drain the pansotti and tip them into the bowl of walnut sauce. Drizzle the butter over them, toss well, then sprinkle with grated Parmesan. Alternatively, toss the pansotti in the melted butter, spoon into warmed individual bowls and drizzle the sauce over them. Serve the dish immediately, with extra Parmesan handed around separately.

SPINACH SAUCE WITH SEAFOOD PASTA SHELLS

The classic combination of soft cheese and spinach complements all kinds of pasta.
This sauce would be perfect with any filled fresh pasta.

SERVES 4

INGREDIENTS
32 large dried pasta shells
salt and ground black pepper

FOR THE FILLING
15g/½oz/1 tbsp butter or margarine
8 spring onions (scallions), thinly sliced
6 tomatoes
225g/8oz cooked peeled prawns (shrimp)
175g/6oz can white crab meat, drained and flaked

FOR THE SPINACH SAUCE
225g/8oz/1 cup soft cheese
90ml/6 tbsp milk
pinch of freshly grated nutmeg
115g/4oz frozen chopped spinach, thawed and drained
salt and ground black pepper

1 Preheat the oven to 150°C/300°F/Gas 2. Melt the butter or margarine in a pan and cook the spring onions for 3–4 minutes, or until soft.

2 Plunge the tomatoes into boiling water for 1 minute, then into cold water. Slip off the skins. Halve the tomatoes, remove the seeds and cores and coarsely chop the flesh.

3 Cook the pasta shells in lightly salted, boiling water for about 10 minutes, or until *al dente*. Drain.

4 To make the sauce, put the soft cheese and milk into a pan and heat gently, stirring constantly until blended. Season with salt, ground black pepper and a pinch of nutmeg.

5 Measure 30ml/2 tbsp of cheese mixture into a bowl. Add the onions, tomatoes, prawns and crab meat. Mix well. Spoon the filling into the shells and place in a single layer in a shallow ovenproof dish. Cover with foil and cook for 10 minutes.

6 Stir the spinach into the remaining sauce. Bring to the boil and simmer gently for 1 minute, stirring constantly. Drizzle the sauce over the pasta and serve hot.

SMOKED HADDOCK & PARSLEY SAUCE

This hearty sauce made with smoked haddock makes any hollow pasta shape into a healthy lunch or supper. Shell-shaped pasta is ideal to hold the sauce, but corkscrew and tube shapes work just as well.

SERVES 4

INGREDIENTS
225g/8oz pasta shells
15g/½oz toasted flaked (sliced) almonds, to serve

FOR THE SMOKED HADDOCK AND PARSLEY SAUCE
450g/1lb smoked haddock fillet
1 small leek or onion, thickly sliced
300ml/½ pint/1¼ cups milk
bouquet garni (bay leaf, thyme and parsley stalks)
25g/1oz/2 tbsp butter or margarine
25g/1oz/¼ cup plain (all-purpose) flour
30ml/2 tbsp chopped fresh parsley
salt and ground black pepper

1 Remove all the skin and any bones from the haddock and discard. Put the fish into a pan with the leek or onion, milk and bouquet garni. Bring to the boil, cover and simmer gently for 8–10 minutes, or until the fish flakes easily.

2 Remove the fish and leek or onion and flake the fish with a fork. Strain and reserve the milk for making the sauce, and discard the bouquet garni.

3 Put the butter or margarine, flour and reserved milk into a pan. Bring to the boil and whisk until smooth. Season and add the fish and leek or onion.

4 Cook the pasta in a large pan of salted, boiling water until *al dente*. Drain thoroughly and stir into the sauce with the chopped parsley. Serve immediately, sprinkled with toasted flaked almonds.

Squid Sauce with Black Pasta

What better partner for a delicious squid sauce than squid ink tagliatelle? The tastes blend perfectly and the dish looks truly spectacular. However, the sauce will enhance any plain pasta, whether flat ribbons or long spirals.

SERVES 4

INGREDIENTS
450g/1lb squid ink tagliatelle

FOR THE SQUID SAUCE
105ml/7 tbsp olive oil
2 shallots, chopped
3 garlic cloves, crushed
45ml/3 tbsp chopped fresh parsley
675g/1½lb cleaned squid, cut into rings and rinsed
150ml/¼ pint/⅔ cup dry white wine
400g/14oz can chopped plum tomatoes
2.5ml/½ tsp dried chilli flakes or powder
salt and ground black pepper

1 Heat the oil in a pan and add the shallots. Cook, stirring occasionally, until pale golden, then add the garlic.

2 When the garlic colours a little, add 30ml/2 tbsp of the parsley, stir, then add the squid and stir again. Cook for 3–4 minutes, then add the wine.

3 Simmer for a few seconds, then add the tomatoes and chilli. Season the mixture with salt and pepper. Cover and simmer gently for about 1 hour, until the squid is tender. Add more water if necessary.

4 Cook the pasta in salted, boiling water, according to the instructions on the packet, until *al dente*. Drain and return the tagliatelle to the pan. Add the squid sauce and mix well. Serve immediately, sprinkled with the remaining parsley.

Clam & Tomato Sauce with Vermicelli

This fabulous seafood sauce is a regular dish in Neapolitan restaurants, and is often served with vermicelli or spaghetti. Fresh mussels could be substituted for the clams.

Serves 4

Ingredients
350g/12oz vermicelli

For the clam and tomato sauce
1kg/2¼lb fresh hard-shell clams
250ml/8fl oz/1 cup dry white wine
2 garlic cloves, bruised
1 large handful fresh flat leaf parsley
30ml/2 tbsp olive oil
1 small onion, finely chopped
8 ripe plum tomatoes, peeled, seeded and finely chopped
½–1 fresh red chilli, seeded and finely chopped
salt and ground black pepper

1 Scrub the clams thoroughly under cold running water and discard any that are open and that do not close immediately when they are sharply tapped against the work surface.

2 Pour the wine into a large pan, add the garlic cloves and half the parsley, then the clams. Cover tightly with the lid and bring to the boil over a high heat. Cook for about 5 minutes, shaking the pan frequently, until the clams have opened.

3 Tip the clams into a large colander set over a bowl and let the liquid drain through. Set aside the clams until they are cool enough to handle, then remove about two-thirds of them from their shells, pouring the clam liquid into the bowl of cooking liquid. Discard any clams that have failed to open. Set both the shelled and unshelled clams aside, keeping the unshelled clams warm in a bowl covered with a lid.

4 Heat the oil in a pan, add the onion and cook gently, stirring frequently, for about 5 minutes, until softened and lightly coloured. Add the tomatoes, then pour in the clam cooking liquid. Add the chilli and salt and pepper to taste. Chop the remaining parsley finely and set aside.

5 Bring to the boil, half-cover the pan, lower the heat and simmer gently for 15–20 minutes.

6 Meanwhile, cook the pasta in salted, boiling water according to the instructions on the packet, until it is *al dente*.

7 Add the shelled clams to the tomato sauce, stir well and heat through very gently for 2–3 minutes.

8 Drain the cooked pasta well and tip it into a warmed bowl. Taste the sauce for seasoning, then pour the sauce over the pasta and toss everything together well. Serve garnished with the reserved clams and sprinkled with parsley.

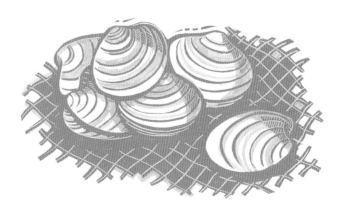

PRAWN & VODKA SAUCE WITH PASTA

The combination of prawns, vodka and pasta may seem unusual, but it has become a modern classic in Italy. Here it is served with two-coloured pasta, but the sauce goes equally well with short shapes such as penne, rigatoni and farfalle.

SERVES 4

INGREDIENTS
350g/12oz fresh or dried paglia e fieno

FOR THE PRAWN (SHRIMP) AND VODKA SAUCE
30ml/2 tbsp olive oil
¼ large onion, finely chopped
1 garlic clove, crushed
15–30ml/1–2 tbsp sun-dried tomato paste
200ml/7fl oz/scant 1 cup double (heavy) cream
12 large raw prawns (shrimp), peeled and chopped
30ml/2 tbsp vodka
salt and ground black pepper

1 Heat the oil in a medium pan, add the onion and garlic and cook gently, stirring frequently, for about 5 minutes, or until softened.

2 Add the tomato paste and stir for 1–2 minutes, then add the cream and bring to the boil, stirring. Season with salt and pepper to taste and let the sauce bubble until it starts to thicken slightly. Remove from the heat.

3 Cook the pasta in a large pan of salted, boiling water according to the instructions on the packet, until *al dente*. When it is almost ready, add the prawns and vodka to the sauce and toss over a medium heat for 2–3 minutes, or until the prawns turn pink.

4 Drain the pasta and turn it into a warmed bowl. Pour the sauce over and toss well. Divide among warmed bowls and serve immediately.

SMOKED SALMON & CREAM SAUCE WITH PENNE

This modern way of serving pasta is popular all over Italy. The three essential ingredients combine beautifully, and the dish is very quick and easy to make. It is the ideal dish for trouble-free, mid-week entertaining.

SERVES 4

INGREDIENTS
350g/12oz penne

FOR THE SMOKED SALMON AND CREAM SAUCE
115g/4oz thinly sliced smoked salmon
2–3 fresh thyme sprigs
30ml/2 tbsp butter
150ml/¼ pint/⅔ cup double (heavy) cream
salt and ground black pepper

1 Cook the pasta in a large pan of salted, boiling salted water according to the packet instructions, until it is *al dente*.

2 Meanwhile, using kitchen scissors, cut the smoked salmon into thin strips, about 5mm/¼in wide. Strip the leaves from the thyme sprigs.

3 Melt the butter in a large pan. Stir in the cream with a quarter of the salmon and thyme leaves, then season with pepper. Heat gently for 3–4 minutes, stirring constantly. Do not allow to boil. Taste for seasoning.

4 Drain the pasta and toss it in the cream and salmon sauce. Divide among four warmed bowls and top with the remaining salmon and thyme leaves.

COOK'S TIP
Although penne is traditional with this sauce, it also goes well with spinach and ricotta ravioli.

Spicy Sausage Sauce with Tortiglioni

Serve this heady pasta dish with a robust Sicilian red wine. It is best made with Italian salami, but you can use whichever variety is your favourite.

SERVES 4

INGREDIENTS
300g/11oz dried tortiglioni
salt and ground black pepper

FOR THE SPICY SAUSAGE SAUCE
30ml/2 tbsp olive oil
1 onion, finely chopped
1 celery stick, finely chopped
2 large garlic cloves, crushed
1 fresh red chilli, seeded and chopped
450g/1lb ripe plum tomatoes, peeled and finely chopped
30ml/2 tbsp tomato purée (paste)
150ml/¼ pint/⅔ cup red wine
5ml/1 tsp sugar
175g/6oz spicy salami, rind removed and chopped into bitesize pieces
30ml/2 tbsp chopped parsley, to garnish
freshly grated Parmesan cheese, to serve

1 Heat the oil in a large pan, then add the onion, celery, garlic and chilli. Cook gently, stirring frequently, for about 10 minutes, until softened.

2 Add the tomatoes, tomato purée, wine, sugar and salt and pepper and bring to the boil, stirring. Lower the heat, cover and simmer gently, stirring occasionally, for about 20 minutes. Add a few spoonfuls of water if the sauce becomes too thick.

3 Meanwhile, cook the pasta in a large pan of rapidly boiling, salted water according to the instructions on the packet, until *al dente*.

4 Add the salami to the sauce and heat. Drain the pasta, tip it into a large bowl, pour the sauce over and toss. Sprinkle with parsley and serve with Parmesan.

WILD MUSHROOM SAUCE WITH FUSILLI

A very rich dish with an earthy flavour and lots of garlic, this makes an ideal main course for vegetarians, especially if it is followed by a crisp green salad.

SERVES 4

INGREDIENTS
150g/5oz wild mushrooms preserved in olive oil
25g/1oz/2 tbsp butter
150g/5oz fresh wild mushrooms, sliced if large
5ml/1 tsp finely chopped fresh thyme
5ml/1 tsp finely chopped fresh marjoram or oregano, plus extra to serve
4 garlic cloves, crushed
350g/12oz fresh or dried fusilli
200ml/7fl oz/scant 1 cup double (heavy) cream
salt and ground black pepper

1 Drain about 15ml/1 tbsp of the oil from the mushrooms into a medium pan. Slice or chop the preserved mushrooms into bitesize pieces, if they are large.

2 Add the butter to the oil in the pan and heat over a low heat until sizzling. Add the preserved and the fresh mushrooms, the chopped herbs and the garlic. Season to taste.

3 Simmer over a medium heat, stirring frequently, for about 10 minutes, or until the fresh mushrooms are soft and tender.

4 Meanwhile, cook the pasta in salted, boiling water according to the packet instructions, until *al dente.*

5 As soon as the mushrooms are cooked, increase the heat to high and toss the mixture with a wooden spoon to boil off any excess liquid. Pour in the cream and bring to the boil. Season if necessary.

6 Drain the pasta and turn it into a warmed bowl. Pour the sauce over and toss well. Serve immediately, sprinkled with chopped fresh herbs.

SAUCES FOR MEAT DISHES

The simplest, most basic sauce for meat is traditional gravy. Based on the juices from the cooked meat, this is one of the most widely used, everyday sauces. It is on this, together with a basic brown sauce, that many meat sauces are based, such as the rich Cumberland sauce flavoured with port. But not only brown sauces are used with meat – you'll also find white, creamy sauces and a delicate butter in this section. Many red meat dishes provide the opportunity for quite robust sauces, featuring warm spices, garlic or pungent herbs, simmered with red wine or tomato mixtures for added richness. The contrasting flavours of tangy fruits or sweet-and-sour mixtures are particularly successful with rich meats, such as beef, lamb, pork, venison and duck, notably the popular combinations of duck with orange, and venison with cranberries. Although it is usually classed as a white meat, pork is also a natural partner for the tangy sweetness of apples, peaches or nectarines and oranges, and pairs exceptionally well with sweet-and-sour type sauces. More delicately flavoured white meats or poultry, such as veal, chicken and turkey, go well with cream sauces or sauces that are based on white wine.

AVOCADO SAUCE WITH LEMON CHICKEN

This great sauce is based on the classic Mexican dip, guacamole. Made without the addition of water, it could be used as a dip with raw vegetables, or even as a sandwich filling. Here it teams perfectly with chicken.

SERVES 4

INGREDIENTS
juice of 2 lemons
45ml/3 tbsp olive oil
2 garlic cloves, crushed
5 chicken breast portions, about 200g/7oz each
2 beefsteak tomatoes, cored and cut in half
salt and ground black pepper

FOR THE AVOCADO SAUCE
1 ripe avocado
50ml/2fl oz/¼ cup sour cream
45ml/3 tbsp fresh lemon juice
2.5ml/½ tsp salt
50ml/2fl oz/¼ cup water

TO SERVE
chopped fresh coriander (cilantro), to garnish

VARIATION
To cook the chicken on the barbecue, prepare the fire, and when the coals are glowing red and covered with grey ash, spread them in a single layer. Set an oiled grill rack about 13cm/5in above the coals and cook the chicken breast portions for 15–20 minutes, until lightly charred and cooked through. Allow extra olive oil for basting.

1 Combine the lemon juice, oil, garlic, 2.5ml/½ tsp salt and a little pepper in a bowl. Stir to mix.

2 Arrange the chicken portions in one layer in a shallow glass or ceramic dish. Pour over the lemon mixture and turn to coat evenly. Cover and leave to stand for at least 1 hour at room temperature, or chill overnight.

3 For the avocado sauce, cut the avocado in half, remove the stone (pit) and scrape the flesh into a food processor or blender.

4 Add the sour cream, lemon juice and salt, and process until smooth. Add the water and process just to blend. If necessary, add more water to thin the sauce. Transfer to a bowl, taste and adjust the seasoning, if necessary. Set aside.

5 Preheat the grill (broiler) to hot. Heat a ridged griddle or heavy frying pan. Remove the chicken from the marinade and pat dry.

6 When the griddle or frying pan is hot, add the chicken portions and cook, turning frequently, for about 10 minutes, until they are cooked through.

7 Meanwhile, arrange the tomato halves, cut sides up, on a baking sheet and season lightly with salt and pepper. Grill for about 5 minutes.

8 To serve, place a chicken portion, tomato half, and a spoonful of avocado sauce on each plate. Sprinkle with coriander and serve.

SALSA PICANTE WITH CHICKEN ENCHILLADAS

This "hot" salsa is actually a low-heat version using seeded green chillies, and is also cooled down by the sour cream. As well as accompanying enchilladas, it would make a good side dish with kebabs of chicken or pork.

SERVES 4

INGREDIENTS
8 wheat tortillas
175g/6oz/1½ cups grated Cheddar cheese
1 onion, finely chopped
350g/12oz cooked chicken, cut into small chunks
300ml/½ pint/1¼ cups sour cream
1 avocado, sliced and tossed in lemon juice, to garnish

FOR THE SALSA PICANTE
1–2 green chillies
15ml/1 tbsp vegetable oil
1 onion, chopped
1 garlic clove, crushed
400g/14oz can chopped tomatoes
30ml/2 tbsp tomato purée (paste)
salt and ground black pepper

1 To make the salsa picante, cut the chillies in half lengthways and carefully remove the cores and seeds. Slice the chillies very finely. Heat the oil in a frying pan and cook the onion and garlic for about 3–4 minutes until softened. Add the tomatoes, tomato purée and chillies. Simmer gently, uncovered, for 12–15 minutes, stirring the mixture frequently.

2 Pour the sauce into a food processor or blender and process until smooth. Return to the heat and cook very gently, uncovered, for a further 15 minutes. Season to taste then set aside.

3 Preheat the oven to 180°C/350°F/Gas 4 and butter a shallow ovenproof dish. Take one tortilla and sprinkle with a good pinch of cheese and chopped onion, about 40g/1½oz of the chicken and 15ml/1 tbsp of salsa picante.

4 Pour over 15ml/1 tbsp of sour cream, roll up and place, seam-side down, in the dish. Make seven more enchilladas.

5 Pour the remaining salsa over the top and sprinkle with cheese and onion. Bake for 25–30 minutes, until golden. Serve with the remaining cream. Garnish with the sliced avocado.

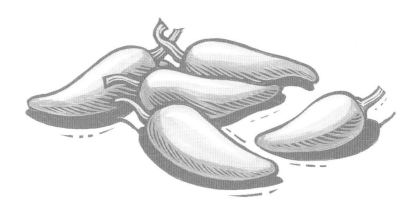

Walnut & Pomegranate Sauce with Duck Breasts

This is an extremely exotic sweet-and-sour sauce which originally comes from Iran, where pomegranates feature in many dishes.

Serves 4

Ingredients
4 duck breasts, about 225g/8oz each

For the walnut and pomegranate sauce
30ml/2 tbsp olive oil
2 onions, very thinly sliced
2.5ml/½ tsp ground turmeric
400g/14oz/3½ cups walnuts, coarsely chopped
1 litre/1¾ pints/4 cups duck or Chicken Stock
6 pomegranates
30ml/2 tbsp caster (superfine) sugar
60ml/4 tbsp lemon juice
salt and ground black pepper

Cook's Tip
Choose pomegranates with shiny, brightly coloured skins. The juice stains, so take care when cutting them. Only the seeds are used in cooking, the bitter pith is discarded.

1 To make the sauce, heat half the oil in a frying pan. Add the onions and turmeric and cook gently until soft.

2 Transfer to a large pan, add the walnuts and stock and season with salt and pepper. Stir, then bring to the boil and simmer, uncovered, for 20 minutes.

3 Halve the pomegranates and scoop out the seeds. Reserve the seeds of one pomegranate. Process the remaining seeds in a blender to break them up. Strain through a sieve to extract the juice, and stir in the sugar and lemon juice.

4 Score the skin of the duck breasts in a diamond pattern with a sharp knife. Heat the remaining oil in a frying pan or griddle and place the duck breasts in it, skin-side down.

5 Cook gently for 10 minutes, pouring off the fat, until the skin is dark golden and crisp. Turn the duck breasts over and cook for a further 3–4 minutes. Transfer to a plate and leave to rest. Deglaze the frying pan with the pomegranate juice, then add the walnut and stock mixture and simmer for about 15 minutes, until thickened.

6 Slice the duck and serve drizzled with a little sauce and garnished with the reserved pomegranate seeds. Serve the remaining sauce separately.

MARSALA CREAM SAUCE WITH TURKEY

Marsala makes a very rich and tasty sauce. The addition of lemon juice gives it a refreshing tang, which helps to offset the richness.

SERVES 6

INGREDIENTS
6 turkey breast steaks
45ml/3 tbsp plain (all-purpose) flour
30ml/2 tbsp olive oil
25g/1oz/2 tbsp butter
salt and ground black pepper

FOR THE MARSALA CREAM SAUCE
175ml/6fl oz/³⁄4 cup dry Marsala
60ml/4 tbsp lemon juice
175ml/6fl oz/³⁄4 cup double (heavy) cream

TO SERVE
lemon wedges and chopped fresh parsley, to garnish
mangetouts (snow peas) and green beans

> COOK'S TIP
> To make this sauce without using the pan drippings, omit the oil and heat the butter in a pan before adding the other ingredients.

1 Put each turkey steak between two sheets of clear film (plastic wrap) and pound with a rolling pin to flatten out evenly. Cut each steak in half or into quarters, cutting away and discarding any sinew.

2 Spread out the flour in a shallow bowl. Season well with salt and pepper and coat the meat, shaking off any excess.

3 Heat the oil and butter in a wide, heavy pan or frying pan until sizzling. Add as many pieces of turkey as you can, and sauté over a medium heat for about 3 minutes on each side until crispy and tender.

4 Transfer to a warmed serving dish with tongs and keep hot. Repeat with the remaining turkey. Lower the heat.

5 To make the sauce, mix the Marsala and lemon juice in a jug (pitcher), add to the oil and butter in the pan and raise the heat. Bring to the boil, stirring in the sediment, then add the cream.

6 Simmer, stirring constantly, until the sauce is reduced and glossy. Taste and adjust the seasoning, if necessary.

7 Spoon the sauce over the turkey, garnish with the lemon wedges and chopped parsley and serve immediately, accompanied by mangetouts and green beans.

Fresh Pesto
with Roast Leg of Lamb

*The intense aromas of fresh basil and garlic combine irresistibly with lamb, and the
pine nuts and Parmesan make a delectable crunchy crust during roasting.*

SERVES 6

INGREDIENTS
2.25–2.75kg/5–6lb leg of lamb

FOR THE PESTO
90g/3½oz/1¾ cups fresh basil leaves
4 garlic cloves, coarsely chopped
45ml/3 tbsp pine nuts
150ml/¼ pint/⅔ cup olive oil
50g/2oz/⅔ cup freshly grated Parmesan cheese
5ml/1 tsp salt, or to taste

1 To make the pesto, combine the basil, garlic and pine nuts in a food processor
and process until finely chopped. With the motor running, slowly add the oil in
a steady stream. Scrape the mixture into a bowl. Stir in the Parmesan and salt.

2 Set the lamb in a roasting pan. Make several slits in the meat with a knife and
spoon pesto into each slit. Coat the surface of the lamb in a thick, even layer of
the remaining pesto. Cover the meat and leave to stand for 2 hours at room
temperature, or chill overnight. Preheat the oven to 180°C/350°F/Gas 4.

3 Roast the lamb, allowing 20 minutes per 450g/1lb for rare meat, or 25 minutes
per 450g/1lb for medium-rare. Turn the lamb occasionally.

4 Remove the leg of lamb from the oven, cover it loosely with foil and let it rest
for about 15 minutes before carving and serving.

VARIATION
*Lamb steaks or lamb chops could also be coated
with this delicious pesto.*

REDCURRANT SAUCE WITH LAMB BURGERS

The sweet-sour redcurrant sauce is the perfect complement to the taste of lamb and would go equally well with grilled or roast lamb steaks.

SERVES 4

INGREDIENTS
500g/1¼lb minced (ground) lean lamb
1 small onion, finely chopped
30ml/2 tbsp finely chopped fresh mint
30ml/2 tbsp finely chopped fresh parsley
115g/4oz mozzarella cheese
30ml/2 tbsp oil, for basting
salt and ground black pepper

FOR THE REDCURRANT SAUCE
115g/4oz/1 cup fresh or frozen redcurrants
10ml/2 tsp clear honey
5ml/1 tsp balsamic vinegar
30ml/2 tbsp finely chopped mint

1 Mix together the lamb, onion, mint and parsley in a large bowl until evenly combined. Season well with salt and pepper. Divide the mixture into eight equal pieces and use your hands to press each of the pieces into flat rounds.

2 Cut the mozzarella into four chunks. Place a chunk of cheese on half the lamb rounds. Top each with another round of meat mixture. Press each of the two rounds of meat together firmly, making four flattish burger shapes. Use your fingers to blend the edges and seal in the cheese completely.

3 To make the sauce, place all the ingredients in a bowl and mash them together with a fork. Season well with salt and ground black pepper.

4 Brush the lamb burgers with olive oil and cook over a moderately hot barbecue for about 15 minutes, or grill (broil) for 10 minutes, turning once, until golden brown. Serve with the sauce.

TOMATO SAUCE WITH GREEK LAMB SAUSAGES

For a quick and easy tomato sauce, passata can be enlivened with sugar, bay leaves and onions. The sausages also add flavour as they simmer in the smooth sauce.

SERVES 4

INGREDIENTS
50g/2oz/1 cup fresh breadcrumbs
150ml/¼ pint/⅔ cup milk
675g/1½lb minced (ground) lamb or minced (ground) turkey
30ml/2 tbsp grated onion
3 garlic cloves, crushed
10ml/2 tsp ground cumin
30ml/2 tbsp chopped fresh parsley
plain (all-purpose) flour, for dusting
olive oil, for frying
salt and ground black pepper
fresh flat leaf parsley, to garnish

FOR THE TOMATO SAUCE
600ml/1 pint/2½ cups passata (bottled strained tomatoes)
5ml/1 tsp sugar
2 bay leaves
1 small onion, peeled

1 Mix together the breadcrumbs and milk. Add the lamb or turkey, onion, garlic, cumin and parsley and season with salt and pepper. Shape the mixture into little fat sausages, about 5cm/2in long and roll them in flour.

2 Heat about 60ml/4 tbsp olive oil in a pan. Add the sausages and cook for about 8 minutes, turning them until evenly browned. Remove and place on kitchen paper to drain.

3 Put the passata, sugar, bay leaves and whole onion in a pan and simmer for 20 minutes. Add the sausages and cook for 10 minutes more. Serve immediately, garnished with parsley.

Smoked Cheese Sauce with Veal Escalopes

Sheep's milk cheese melted with cream makes a simple sauce for serving with pan-fried veal escalopes. The escalopes are used as purchased, not beaten thin.

SERVES 4

INGREDIENTS
25g/1oz/2 tbsp butter
15ml/1 tbsp extra virgin olive oil
8 small veal escalopes (US scallops)
2 garlic cloves, crushed
250g/9oz/3½ cups button (white) mushrooms or closed-cup mushrooms, sliced
150g/5oz/1¼ cups frozen peas, thawed
60ml/4 tbsp brandy
250ml/8fl oz/1 cup whipping cream
150g/5oz smoked sheep's milk cheese, diced
ground black pepper
fresh flat leaf parsley sprigs, to garnish

1 Melt half the butter with the oil in a large, heavy frying pan. Season the escalopes with plenty of pepper and brown them, in batches, on each side over a high heat. Reduce the heat and cook for about 5 minutes on each side until just done. The escalopes should feel firm to the touch, with a very light springiness. Lift the escalopes on to a serving dish and keep hot.

2 Add the remaining butter to the pan. When it melts, stir-fry the garlic and mushrooms for about 3 minutes.

3 Add the peas, pour in the brandy and cook until all the pan juices have been absorbed. Season lightly. Using a slotted spoon, remove the mushrooms and peas and place on top of the escalopes. Pour the cream into the pan.

4 Stir in the diced cheese. Heat gently until the cheese has melted. Season with pepper only and pour over the escalopes and vegetables. Serve immediately, garnished with sprigs of flat leaf parsley.

CHILLI-NECTARINE RELISH WITH PORK CHOPS

Pork and fruit are a classic combination, and this spicy nectarine relish is the perfect partner for griddled pork chops. It also goes well with cold meats.

SERVES 4

INGREDIENTS
250ml/8fl oz/1 cup fresh orange juice
45ml/3 tbsp olive oil
2 garlic cloves, finely chopped
5ml/1 tsp ground cumin
15ml/1 tbsp coarsely ground black pepper
8 pork loin chops, about 2cm/³⁄4in thick, well trimmed
salt

FOR THE CHILLI-NECTARINE RELISH
1 small fresh green chilli
30ml/2 tbsp clear honey
juice of ½ lemon
250ml/8fl oz/1 cup Chicken Stock
2 nectarines, stoned (pitted) and chopped
1 garlic clove, crushed
½ onion, finely chopped
5ml/1 tsp grated fresh ginger root
1.5ml/¼ tsp salt
15ml/1 tbsp chopped fresh coriander (cilantro)

COOK'S TIP
The relish can be made in advance, then covered and stored in the refrigerator overnight for the flavours to mature.

1 Roast the chilli over a gas flame, holding it with tongs, until charred on all sides. Alternatively, char the skin under the grill (broiler). Cool for 5 minutes.

2 Wearing rubber gloves, remove the charred skin of the chilli. Discard the seeds if a less hot flavour is desired. Finely chop the chilli and place in a pan.

3 Add the honey, lemon juice, chicken stock, nectarines, garlic, onion, ginger and salt. Bring to the boil, then simmer, stirring occasionally, for about 30 minutes. Stir in the coriander and set aside.

4 Combine the orange juice, oil, garlic, cumin and pepper in a small bowl. Stir well to mix.

5 Arrange the pork chops, in one layer, in a shallow dish. Pour over the orange juice mixture and turn to coat. Cover with clear film (plastic wrap) and leave to stand for at least 1 hour, or chill overnight.

6 Remove the pork from the marinade and pat dry with kitchen paper. Season lightly with salt.

7 Heat a frying pan or ridged griddle. Add the meat and cook for about 5 minutes, or until browned. Turn and cook on the other side for about 10 minutes more. (Work in batches if necessary.) Serve immediately, with the relish.

Noisettes of Pork with Calvados & Apple Sauce

This dish is ideal as part of a formal menu to impress guests. Buttered gnocchi or griddled polenta and red cabbage are suitable accompaniments.

Serves 4

Ingredients
30ml/2 tbsp plain (all-purpose) flour
4 noisettes of pork, about 175g/6oz each, firmly tied
25g/1oz/2 tbsp butter
4 baby leeks, thinly sliced
5ml/1 tsp mustard seeds, coarsely crushed
30ml/2 tbsp Calvados
150ml/¼ pint/⅔ cup dry white wine
2 Golden Delicious apples, peeled, cored and sliced
150ml/¼ pint/⅔ cup double (heavy) cream
30ml/2 tbsp chopped fresh parsley
salt and ground black pepper

1 Place the flour in a bowl and add plenty of seasoning. Turn the noisettes in the flour mixture to coat them lightly.

2 Melt the butter in a heavy frying pan and cook the noisettes until golden on both sides. Remove from the pan and set aside.

3 Add the leeks to the fat remaining in the pan and cook for 5 minutes. Stir in the mustard seeds and pour in the Calvados, then carefully ignite it to burn off the alcohol.

4 When the flames have died down, pour in the wine and replace the pork. Cook gently for 10 minutes, turning the pork frequently.

5 Add the apples and cream, and simmer gently for 5 minutes, or until the apples are tender, but have not disintegrated. Taste for seasoning, then stir in the chopped parsley and serve immediately.

Sweet-&-sour Sauce with Pork

The combination of sweet-and-sour flavours is popular in Venetian cooking. This recipe is given extra bite with the addition of crushed mixed peppercorns.

SERVES 2

INGREDIENTS
1 whole pork fillet (tenderloin), about 350g/12oz
25ml/1½ tbsp plain (all-purpose) flour
30–45ml/2–3 tbsp olive oil
salt and ground black pepper
broad (fava) beans tossed with grilled (broiled) bacon, to serve

FOR THE SWEET-AND-SOUR SAUCE
250ml/8fl oz/1 cup dry white wine
30ml/2 tbsp white wine vinegar
10ml/2 tsp sugar
15ml/1 tbsp mixed peppercorns, coarsely ground

1 Cut the pork diagonally into thin slices. Place between two sheets of clear film (plastic wrap) and pound lightly with a rolling pin to flatten them evenly.

2 Spread out the flour in a shallow bowl. Season well with salt and pepper and coat the meat, shaking off any excess.

3 Heat 15ml/1 tbsp of the oil in a wide, heavy pan or frying pan and add as many slices of pork as the pan will hold. Cook over a medium heat for 2–3 minutes on each side, or until crispy and tender. Remove with a fish slice (metal spatula) and set aside. Repeat with the remaining pork, adding more oil as necessary.

4 Mix the wine, wine vinegar and sugar in a jug (pitcher). Pour into the pan and stir vigorously over a high heat until reduced, scraping the pan to incorporate the sediment. Stir in the peppercorns and return the pork to the pan. Spoon the sauce over the pork until it is evenly coated and heated through. Serve with the broad beans tossed with grilled bacon.

Sage & Orange Sauce with Pork Fillet

Sage is often partnered with pork – there seems to be a natural affinity – and the addition of orange to the sauce balances the flavour.

SERVES 4

INGREDIENTS
2 pork fillets (tenderloin), about 350g/12oz each
10ml/2 tsp unsalted (sweet) butter
salt and ground black pepper
orange wedges and sage leaves, to garnish

FOR THE SAGE AND ORANGE SAUCE
120ml/4fl oz/½ cup dry sherry
175ml/6fl oz/¾ cup Chicken Stock
2 garlic cloves, very finely chopped
grated rind and juice of 1 unwaxed orange
3 or 4 sage leaves, finely chopped
10ml/2 tsp cornflour (cornstarch)

COOK'S TIPS
• *The meat is cooked if the juices are clear when the meat is pierced or a meat thermometer inserted into the thickest part registers 66°C/150°F.*
• *If fresh sage is not available, try using rosemary as a substitute, as this also goes very well with pork.*

1 Season the pork fillets lightly with salt and pepper. Melt the butter in a heavy, flameproof casserole over a medium-high heat, then add the meat and cook the fillets for 5–6 minutes, turning to brown all sides evenly, making sure that the butter does not burn.

2 Add the sherry, boil for about 1 minute, then add the stock, garlic, orange rind and chopped sage. Bring to the boil and reduce the heat to low, then cover and simmer for 20 minutes, turning once.

3 Using tongs or a slotted spoon, transfer the pork to a warmed platter and cover to keep warm.

4 Bring the sauce to the boil. Blend the cornflour and orange juice together and stir into the sauce, then boil gently over a medium heat for a few minutes, stirring frequently, until the sauce is slightly thickened.

5 Transfer the pork to a board, cut into diagonal slices and arrange on a serving dish. Pour the meat juices into the sauce.

6 Spoon a little sauce over the pork and garnish with orange wedges and sage leaves. Serve the remaining sauce separately.

GAMMON WITH CUMBERLAND SAUCE

Cumberland sauce was invented to honour the Duke of Cumberland, who commanded the troops at the last battle on English soil, against the Scots. It can be served hot or cold, with gammon or venison.

SERVES 8–10

INGREDIENTS
2.25kg/5lb smoked or unsmoked gammon (cured ham)
1 onion
1 carrot
1 celery stick
bouquet garni
6 peppercorns

FOR THE GLAZE
whole cloves
50g/2oz/¼ cup soft light brown or demerara (raw) sugar
30ml/2 tbsp golden (light corn) syrup
5ml/1 tsp English (hot) mustard powder

FOR THE CUMBERLAND SAUCE
juice and shredded rind of 1 orange
30ml/2 tbsp lemon juice
120ml/4fl oz/½ cup port or red wine
60ml/4 tbsp redcurrant jelly

COOK'S TIP
Nowadays, gammon (cured ham) is often not so strongly salted as it once was, so it may not be necessary to soak overnight before cooking to remove the salty flavour.

1 Soak the gammon overnight in a cool place in plenty of cold water to cover. Discard this water. Put the meat into a large pan and cover with cold water. Bring to the boil slowly and skim any scum from the surface with a slotted spoon.

2 Add the vegetables and seasonings, cover and simmer very gently for 2 hours. (The meat can also be cooked in the oven at 180°C/350°F/Gas 4. Allow 30 minutes per 450g/1lb.)

3 Leave the meat to cool in the liquid for 30 minutes. Then remove it from the liquid and strip off the skin neatly with the help of a knife (use rubber gloves if the gammon is too hot to handle).

4 Score the fat in diamonds with a sharp knife and stick a clove in the centre of each diamond. Preheat the oven to 180°C/350°F/Gas 4.

5 Put the sugar, syrup and mustard powder in a small pan and heat gently to melt them. Place the gammon in a roasting pan and spoon the hot glaze evenly over it. Bake it for about 20 minutes, or until golden brown, then put it under a hot grill (broiler) to colour.

6 Leave the meat to stand in a warm place for 15 minutes before carving (this makes carving much easier and tenderizes the meat).

7 For the Cumberland sauce, put the orange and lemon juice into a pan with the port or wine and redcurrant jelly and heat gently to melt the jelly. Pour boiling water on to the orange rind, strain, and add the rind to the sauce. Cook gently for 2 minutes. Serve the sauce hot.

CRANBERRY SAUCE WITH VENISON

Venison steaks are now readily available. Lean and low in fat, they are a healthy choice for a special occasion. Served with a sauce of fresh seasonal cranberries, port and ginger, they make a dish with a wonderful combination of flavours.

SERVES 4

INGREDIENTS
30ml/2 tbsp sunflower oil
4 venison steaks
2 shallots, finely chopped
salt and ground black pepper
fresh thyme sprigs, to garnish
creamy mashed potatoes and broccoli, to serve

FOR THE CRANBERRY SAUCE
1 orange
1 lemon
75g/3oz/³⁄₄ cup fresh or frozen cranberries
5ml/1 tsp grated fresh root ginger
1 fresh thyme sprig
5ml/1 tsp Dijon mustard
60ml/4 tbsp redcurrant jelly
150ml/¹⁄₄ pint/²⁄₃ cup ruby port

> COOK'S TIP
> *When frying venison, always remember the briefer the better; venison will turn to leather if subjected to fierce heat after it has reached the medium-rare stage. If you dislike any hint of pink, cook it to this stage, then let it rest in a low oven for a few minutes.*

1 For the sauce, pare the rind thinly from half the orange and half the lemon using a vegetable peeler, then cut into very fine strips.

2 Blanch the strips in a small pan of boiling water for about 5 minutes, until tender. Strain the strips and refresh under cold water.

3 Squeeze the juice from the orange and lemon and then pour into a small pan. Add the fresh or frozen cranberries, ginger, thyme sprig, mustard, redcurrant jelly and port. Cook the sauce mixture over a low heat until the jelly melts.

4 Bring the sauce to the boil, stirring occasionally, then cover the pan and reduce the heat. Cook very gently, for about 15 minutes, or until the cranberries are just tender.

5 Heat the oil in a heavy frying pan, add the venison steaks and cook over a high heat for 2–3 minutes.

6 Turn the steaks over and add the shallots to the pan. Cook the steaks on the other side for 2–3 minutes, depending on whether you like rare or medium cooked meat.

7 Just before the end of cooking, pour in the sauce and add the strips of orange and lemon rind. Leave the sauce to bubble for a few seconds to thicken slightly, then remove the thyme sprig and adjust the seasoning to taste.

8 Transfer the venison steaks to warmed serving plates and spoon the sauce over them. Garnish with thyme sprigs and serve accompanied by creamy mashed potatoes and broccoli.

GRAVY WITH BEEF POT ROAST

A traditional British dish that will feed a crowd at a low cost. The rich gravy gathers all the flavour from the meat and vegetables, so nothing is wasted.

SERVES 8

INGREDIENTS

1.8kg/4lb brisket or other beef pot-roast
3 garlic cloves, cut in half or in thirds
225g/8oz piece salt pork or bacon
275g/10oz onions, chopped
3 celery sticks, chopped
2 carrots, chopped
115g/4oz turnip, diced
450ml/³/4 pint/scant 2 cups Beef or Chicken Stock
450ml/³/4 pint/scant 2 cups dry red or white wine
1 bay leaf
5ml/1 tsp fresh thyme, or 2.5ml/¹/2 tsp dried
4–6 small whole potatoes, or 3 large potatoes, quartered
75g/3oz beurre manié
salt and ground black pepper
watercress, to garnish

COOK'S TIP
Suitable cuts of beef for pot roasting include brisket, thin and thick rump (round), thick flank and topside (pot roast).

1 Preheat the oven to 160°C/325°F/Gas 3. Make deep incisions in the beef on all sides with the tip of a sharp knife and insert the garlic pieces.

2 In a large, flameproof casserole, cook the salt pork or bacon over a low heat until the fat runs and the pork or bacon begins to brown.

3 Remove the pork or bacon with a slotted spoon and discard. Increase the heat to medium-high and add the beef to the casserole. Brown it evenly on all sides. Remove and set aside on a plate or dish while you prepare the remaining vegetables.

4 Add the chopped onions, celery and carrots to the casserole and cook them for 8–10 minutes, stirring occasionally, until all the vegetables are softened.

5 Stir in the diced turnips, add the beef or chicken stock, red or white wine, bay leaf and thyme and mix well. Return the beef and any juices to the casserole, cover and cook in the preheated oven for 2 hours.

6 Add the whole or quartered potatoes to the casserole, pushing them down under the other vegetables. Season with salt and pepper to taste. Cover the casserole again and cook for a further 45 minutes, or until the potatoes are tender.

7 Transfer the meat to a warmed serving dish. Remove the potatoes and other vegetables from the casserole with a slotted spoon and arrange them around the beef.

8 Discard the bay leaf and skim off excess fat from the cooking liquid. Bring to the boil on the hob (stovetop), then stir teaspoonfuls of the beurre manié into the liquid, whisking thoroughly to blend and adding just enough to thicken to taste. Strain into a gravy boat.

9 Serve the meat with some of the gravy poured over it and the vegetables alongside. Garnish with watercress. Offer the remaining gravy for pouring.

BLACK BEAN SAUCE WITH BEEF & BROCCOLI STIR-FRY

This Chinese dish is a quick stir-fry with a richly flavoured marinade that bubbles down into a luscious, dark sauce. It's a great choice for midweek meals, as you can leave the meat to marinate throughout the day, so it's ready to cook in the evening.

SERVES 4

INGREDIENTS
225g/8oz lean fillet or rump (round) steak
15ml/1 tbsp sunflower oil
225g/8oz broccoli
115g/4oz baby corn, diagonally halved
45–60ml/3–4 tbsp water
2 leeks, diagonally sliced
225g/8oz can water chestnuts, sliced

FOR THE MARINADE
15ml/1 tbsp fermented black beans
30ml/2 tbsp dark soy sauce
30ml/2 tbsp Chinese rice vinegar or cider vinegar
15ml/1 tbsp sunflower oil
5ml/1 tsp sugar
2 garlic cloves, crushed
2.5cm/1in piece of fresh root ginger, peeled and finely chopped

COOK'S TIP
Fermented black beans are cooked, salted and fermented whole soya beans; they are available from Asian stores and many supermarkets.

1 To make the marinade, mash the fermented black beans in a non-metallic bowl. Add the remaining ingredients and stir well.

2 Cut the steak into thin slices across the grain, then add them to the marinade. Stir the steak well to coat it in the marinade. Cover the bowl with clear film (plastic wrap) and leave for several hours.

3 Heat the oil in a large frying pan. Drain the steak (reserving the marinade). When the oil is hot, add the meat and stir-fry for 3–4 minutes. Transfer it to a plate and set aside.

4 Cut the broccoli into small florets. Reheat the oil in the pan, add the broccoli, corn and water. Cover and steam gently for 5 minutes.

5 Add the leeks and water chestnuts to the broccoli mixture and toss over the heat for 1–2 minutes. Return the meat to the pan, pour over the reserved marinade and toss briefly over a high heat before serving.

ROQUEFORT & WALNUT BUTTER WITH RUMP STEAK

Make a roll of this unusual savoury cheese butter to keep in the refrigerator, ready to top plain steaks or pork chops for something a little more special.

SERVES 4

INGREDIENTS

15ml/1 tbsp olive oil or sunflower oil
4 lean rump (round) steaks, about 130g/4½oz each
120ml/4fl oz/½ cup dry white wine
30ml/2 tbsp crème fraîche or double (heavy) cream
salt and ground black pepper
fresh chives, to garnish

FOR THE ROQUEFORT AND WALNUT BUTTER

2 shallots, chopped
75g/3oz/6 tbsp butter, slightly softened
150g/5oz Roquefort cheese
30ml/2 tbsp finely chopped walnuts
15ml/1 tbsp finely chopped fresh chives

COOK'S TIP
The butter can also be stored in the freezer, but it is easier to cut it into rounds before freezing, so you can remove just as many as you need, without thawing the rest.

---

1 To make the Roquefort and walnut butter, sauté the shallots in a third of the butter. Tip into a bowl and add half the remaining butter, the cheese, walnuts, chopped chives and pepper to taste. Chill lightly, roll in foil to a sausage shape and chill again until firm.

2 Heat the remaining butter with the oil and cook the steaks to your liking. Season and remove from the pan.

3 Pour the wine into the pan and stir to incorporate any sediment. Bubble up the liquid for a minute or two, then stir in the crème fraîche or cream. Season with salt and pepper and pour over the steaks.

4 Cut pats of the Roquefort butter from the roll and put one pat on top of each steak. Garnish with chives and serve immediately. Green beans make an ideal accompaniment to this dish.

SAUCES FOR FISH DISHES

You might expect all sauces for fish to be very delicate and light in flavour, but that's not always the case. Certainly in this chapter you'll find a classic white Parsley Sauce and a deliciously subtle Lemon & Chive Sauce, which are the perfect partners for white fish or fishcakes. But you'll also discover some more surprising combinations – a tangy Orange Caper Sauce to pep up plain white fish, and a Chilli Barbecue Sauce to serve with salmon fillets. There are some flavours that are natural partners for fish, such as lemon or dill, which can be used in classic white or white wine sauces, or in butters to serve with whole fish, fillets or steaks. Some of the classic pairings that have become enduring favourites cannot be ignored. The rich, oily flesh of mackerel balances perfectly with the tangy acidity of Gooseberry Sauce, and the slightly sharp flavour of sorrel offsets the richness of salmon and transforms it into a sophisticated dinner-party dish. As with any sauce, there are no hard-and-fast rules, but the general guideline is that white fish pairs best with subtle cream sauces and herb butters, whereas oily fish can take more robust flavours, such as spices or tangy fruits.

Orange Caper Sauce with Skate

A wonderfully sweet-sour, creamy sauce to add zest to otherwise plain white fish. It would also go well with flat fish fillets, such as lemon sole.

SERVES 4

INGREDIENTS
4 skate wings, about 200g/7oz each
25g/1oz/2 tbsp butter
350ml/12fl oz/1½ cups Fish Stock

FOR THE ORANGE AND CAPER SAUCE
25g/1oz/2 tbsp butter
1 onion, chopped
fish bones and trimmings
5ml/1 tsp black peppercorns
300ml/½ pint/1¼ cups dry white wine
2 small oranges
15ml/1 tbsp capers, drained
60ml/4 tbsp crème fraîche
salt and ground white pepper

> VARIATION
> *For an unusual change, try using ruby grapefruit instead of the orange – this goes particularly well with oily fish such as trout or tuna.*

1 To make the sauce, melt the butter and add the onion. Sauté over a medium heat until the onion is lightly browned.

2 Add the fish bones and trimmings and peppercorns to the pan, then pour in the wine. Cover and simmer gently for 30 minutes.

3 Using a serrated knife, peel the oranges, making sure that all the white pith is removed. Ease the segments away from the membranes.

4 Place the skate in a frying pan, add the butter and the fish stock and poach for 10–15 minutes, depending on thickness.

5 Strain the wine mixture into a clean pan. Add the capers and orange segments, together with any juice, and heat through. Lower the heat and gently stir in the crème fraîche and seasoning to taste. Serve the skate wings with the sauce.

PARSLEY SAUCE WITH HADDOCK

One of the most classic sauces to serve with fish, and still a tremendous favourite, is parsley sauce – a perfect partner for almost any white fish.

SERVES 4

INGREDIENTS
4 haddock fillets, about 175g/6oz each
25g/1oz/2 tbsp butter
150ml/¼ pint/⅔ cup milk
150ml/¼ pint/⅔ cup Fish Stock
1 bay leaf
salt and ground black pepper

FOR THE PARSLEY SAUCE
25g/1oz/2 tbsp butter
20ml/4 tsp plain (all-purpose) flour
60ml/4 tbsp single (light) cream
1 egg yolk
45ml/3 tbsp chopped fresh parsley
grated rind and juice of ½ lemon

1 Place the fish in a frying pan, add the butter, milk, fish stock, bay leaf and seasoning and heat to simmering point.

2 Lower the heat, cover the pan and poach the fish for 10–15 minutes, depending on the thickness of the fillets, until the fish is tender and the flesh begins to flake. Using a fish slice (metal spatula), transfer to a warm serving plate, cover and keep warm. Reserve the cooking liquid.

3 Make the sauce. Return the cooking liquid to the heat and bring to the boil, stirring constantly. Lower the heat and simmer for about 4 minutes, then remove and discard the bay leaf.

4 Melt the butter in a pan, stir in the flour and cook, stirring constantly, for 1 minute, but do not let it brown. Remove the pan from the heat and gradually stir in the fish cooking liquid.

5 Return the pan to the heat and bring to the boil, stirring constantly. Simmer for about 4 minutes, stirring frequently.

6 Remove the pan from the heat. In a bowl, blend the cream into the egg yolk, then stir this and the parsley into the sauce.

7 Reheat gently, stirring, for a few minutes; do not allow to boil. Remove from the heat, add the lemon juice and rind and season to taste. Pour into a warmed sauceboat and serve with the fish.

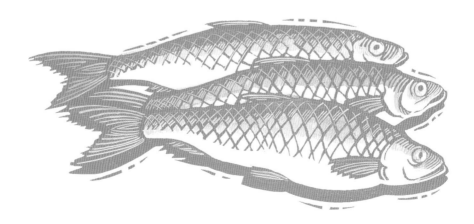

VERMOUTH & CHÈVRE SAUCE WITH PAN-FRIED COD

A smooth sauce of vermouth and light, creamy goat's cheese teams deliciously with chunky, white cod and would also go well with other firm-fleshed fish.

SERVES 4

INGREDIENTS
4 cod fillets, about 150g/5oz each, skinned
15ml/1 tbsp olive oil
salt and ground black pepper
fresh flat leaf parsley, to garnish

FOR THE VERMOUTH AND CHÈVRE SAUCE
15ml/1 tbsp olive oil
4 spring onions (scallions), chopped
150ml/¼ pint/⅔ cup dry vermouth, preferably Noilly Prat
300ml/½ pint/1¼ cups Fish Stock
45ml/3 tbsp crème fraîche or double (heavy) cream
65g/2½oz chèvre or other goat's cheese, rind removed and chopped
30ml/2 tbsp chopped fresh parsley
15ml/1 tbsp chopped fresh chervil

1 Remove any stray bones from the cod fillets. Rinse the fish under cold running water and pat dry with kitchen paper. Place the pieces on a plate and season.

2 Heat a non-stick frying pan, add the oil, swirling it around to coat the base. Add the fillets and cook, without turning or moving them, for 4 minutes, or until caramelized. Turn each piece over and cook the other side for 3 minutes, or until just firm. Remove them to a serving plate and keep hot.

3 To make the sauce, heat the oil and stir-fry the spring onions for 1 minute. Add the vermouth and cook until reduced by half. Add the stock and reduce by half. Stir in the crème fraîche or cream and the cheese and simmer for 3 minutes.

4 Season with salt and pepper to taste, stir in the herbs and spoon the sauce over the fish. Garnish with parsley and serve immediately.

DILL & MUSTARD SAUCE WITH SOLE

This sauce will give a tangy, Scandinavian flavour that is perfect with grilled fish. Sole is used here, but the dill and mustard would combine with virtually any fish.

SERVES 3–4

INGREDIENTS
3–4 lemon sole fillets
melted butter, for brushing
salt and ground black pepper
lemon slices and fresh dill sprigs, to garnish

FOR THE DILL AND MUSTARD SAUCE
25g/1oz/2 tbsp butter
20g/³⁄₄oz/3 tbsp plain (all-purpose) flour
300ml/¹⁄₂ pint/1¹⁄₄ cups hot Fish Stock
15ml/1 tbsp white wine vinegar
45ml/3 tbsp chopped fresh dill
15ml/1 tbsp wholegrain mustard
10ml/2 tsp sugar
2 egg yolks

1 Preheat the grill (broiler) to medium-high. Brush the fish with melted butter, season on both sides and cut two or three slashes in the flesh. Grill (broil) for 4 minutes, then transfer to a warmed place and keep warm.

2 To make the sauce, melt the butter over a medium heat and stir in the flour. Cook for 1–2 minutes over a low heat, stirring constantly. Remove from the heat and gradually blend in the hot stock. Return to the heat, bring to the boil, stirring continuously, then simmer for 2–3 minutes. Remove the saucepan from the heat and beat in the vinegar, dill, mustard and sugar.

3 Using a fork, beat the egg yolks in a small bowl and gradually add a small quantity of the hot sauce. Return to the pan, whisking vigorously. Continue whisking over a very low heat for a further minute. Serve immediately with the grilled sole, garnished with lemon slices and dill sprigs.

HERB SAUCE WITH SARDINES

The only essential accompaniment to this luscious herb sauce is crusty bread to mop up the tasty juices. The sauce is also delicious served with plain, grilled chicken.

SERVES 4

INGREDIENTS
12–16 fresh sardines
oil, for brushing
juice of 1 lemon
crusty bread, to serve

FOR THE HERB SAUCE
15g/¹⁄₂oz/1 tbsp butter
4 spring onions (scallions), chopped
1 garlic clove, finely chopped
grated rind of 1 lemon
30ml/2 tbsp finely chopped fresh parsley
30ml/2 tbsp finely chopped fresh chives
30ml/2 tbsp finely chopped fresh basil
30ml/2 tbsp green olive paste
10ml/2 tsp balsamic vinegar
salt and ground black pepper

1 Use a pair of small kitchen scissors to slit the fish along the belly, then pull out the innards. Wipe the fish with kitchen paper and arrange on a wire rack.

2 To make the sauce, melt the butter in a small pan and gently sauté the spring onions and garlic for about 2 minutes, shaking the pan occasionally, until softened but not browned.

3 Add the lemon rind and remaining sauce ingredients to the spring onions and garlic in the pan and keep warm on the edge of the hob (stovetop) or barbecue, stirring occasionally. Do not allow the mixture to boil.

4 Brush the sardines lightly with oil and sprinkle with lemon juice, salt and pepper. Cook for about 2 minutes on each side, over a medium heat. Serve with the warm sauce and fresh crusty bread.

GOOSEBERRY SAUCE & MACKEREL

Gooseberries and mackerel are a classic combination; the tart sauce offsets the rich, oily fish. In France, gooseberries are actually called "mackerel currants".

SERVES 4

INGREDIENTS
4 fresh mackerel, about 350g/12oz each, cleaned
salt and ground black pepper

FOR THE GOOSEBERRY SAUCE
15g/½oz/1 tbsp butter
225g/8oz gooseberries, trimmed
1 egg, beaten
pinch of ground mace or ginger, or a few drops of orange flower water (optional)
fresh flat leaf parsley, to garnish

1 Melt the butter in a pan, add the gooseberries, then cover and cook over a low heat, shaking the pan occasionally, until the gooseberries are just tender.

2 Meanwhile, preheat the grill (broiler). Season the fish inside and out with salt and black pepper. Cut two or three slashes in the skin on both sides of each mackerel, then grill (broil) for 15–20 minutes, or until cooked, turning once.

3 Purée the gooseberries with the egg in a food processor or blender, or mash the gooseberries thoroughly in a bowl with the egg. Press the gooseberry mixture through a sieve.

4 Return the gooseberry mixture to the pan and reheat gently, stirring, but do not allow to boil. Add the mace, ginger or orange flower water, if using, and season to taste. Serve the sauce hot with the mackerel, garnished with fresh parsley.

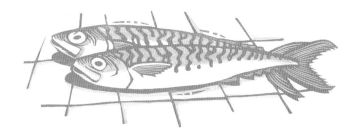

ORANGE SAUCE WITH SEA BREAM

This rich buttery sauce, sharpened with tangy orange juice, goes well with the firm white flesh of sea bream to create a dish of elegant simplicity.

SERVES 2

INGREDIENTS
2 sea bream, about 350g/12oz each,
  scaled and gutted
10ml/2 tsp Dijon mustard
5ml/1 tsp fennel seeds
30ml/2 tbsp olive oil
50g/2oz watercress
175g/6oz mixed lettuce leaves

FOR THE ORANGE BUTTER SAUCE
30ml/2 tbsp frozen orange
  juice concentrate
175g/6oz/¾ cup unsalted (sweet)
  butter, diced
salt and cayenne pepper

1 Wash and dry the sea bream using kitchen paper. Slash the fish four times on each side with a sharp knife. Combine the mustard and fennel seeds together in a small bowl, then spread the mixture over both sides of the fish, pressing the seeds firmly into the flesh.

2 Brush each side of the fish with olive oil and grill (broil) under a preheated grill (broiler) for 10–12 minutes without burning, turning the fish once halfway through the cooking time.

3 Place the orange juice concentrate in a bowl and heat over a pan of simmering water. Remove the pan from the heat and gradually whisk in the butter until creamy. Season well.

4 To make the salad, dress the watercress and the lettuce leaves with the remaining olive oil and arrange the salad with the fish on two plates. Spoon the sauce over the fish and serve.

Tahini Sauce
with Baked Fish

This North African recipe evokes all the colour and rich flavours of Mediterranean cuisine, and the tahini sauce makes an unusual combination of tastes.

SERVES 4

INGREDIENTS
1 whole cod or haddock, about 1.2kg/2½lb, scaled and cleaned
10ml/2 tsp coriander seeds, finely crushed
4 garlic cloves, sliced and crushed
10ml/2 tsp harissa sauce
90ml/6 tbsp olive oil
6 plum tomatoes, sliced
1 mild onion, sliced
3 preserved lemons or 1 fresh lemon, quartered
plenty of fresh herbs, such as bay leaves, thyme and rosemary, plus extra to garnish
salt and ground black pepper

FOR THE TAHINI SAUCE
75ml/5 tbsp light tahini
juice of 1 lemon
1 garlic clove, crushed
45ml/3 tbsp finely chopped fresh parsley or coriander (cilantro)

1 Preheat the oven to 200°C/400°F/Gas 6. Grease a large, shallow ovenproof dish. Slash the fish diagonally on both sides. Mix the coriander seeds and garlic with the harissa sauce and about 60ml/4 tbsp of the olive oil. Spread a little paste inside the fish. Spread the remainder over each side of the fish and set aside.

2 Place the tomatoes, onion and lemon in the dish. Sprinkle with remaining oil and season. Put the fish on top. Tuck plenty of herbs around it. Bake the fish, uncovered, for about 25 minutes, or until it has turned opaque.

3 Meanwhile, to make the sauce, put the ingredients in a small pan with 120ml/4fl oz/½ cup cold water and season. Cook gently until smooth and heated through. Garnish the fish with the herbs and serve the sauce separately.

TOMATO COULIS WITH MARINATED MONKFISH

A light but well-flavoured sauce, this should be made when Italian plum tomatoes are at their ripest. The lime and herb marinade is offset by the sweet tomatoes in the coulis. Serve this delicious dish with a glass of chilled white wine.

SERVES 4

INGREDIENTS
30ml/2 tbsp olive oil
finely grated rind and juice of 1 lime
30ml/2 tbsp chopped fresh mixed herbs
5ml/1 tsp Dijon mustard
4 skinless monkfish fillets
salt and ground black pepper
fresh herb sprigs, to garnish

FOR THE TOMATO COULIS
4 plum tomatoes, peeled and chopped
1 garlic clove, chopped
15ml/1 tbsp olive oil
15ml/1 tbsp tomato purée (paste)
30ml/2 tbsp chopped fresh oregano
5ml/1 tsp soft light brown sugar

COOK'S TIP
The coulis can be served hot, if you prefer. Simply make as directed in the recipe and heat gently in a pan until almost boiling, just before serving.

1 Place the oil, lime rind and juice, herbs, mustard, and salt and pepper in a small bowl or jug (pitcher) and whisk together until thoroughly mixed.

2 Place the monkfish fillets in a shallow, non-metallic container and pour the lime mixture over. Turn the fish several times in the marinade to coat it. Cover and chill in the refrigerator for 1–2 hours.

3 Meanwhile, make the tomato coulis. Place all the coulis ingredients in a food processor or blender and process until smooth. Season to taste, then cover and chill until required.

4 Preheat the oven to 180°C/350°F/Gas 4. Using a fish slice (metal spatula), place each fish fillet on a sheet of greaseproof (waxed) paper large enough to hold it in a parcel.

5 Spoon a little marinade over each piece of fish. Gather the paper loosely over the fish and fold over the edges to secure the parcel tightly. Place the parcels on a baking sheet.

6 Bake for 20–30 minutes, or until the fish fillets are cooked, tender and just beginning to flake.

7 Carefully unwrap the parcels, transfer the fish fillets to warmed plates and serve immediately with a little of the chilled coulis spooned alongside, and garnished with a few fresh herb sprigs.

WATERCRESS CREAM WITH POACHED SALMON

The delicate green colour of this cream sauce looks wonderful against pink-fleshed fish such as salmon or salmon trout – a great choice for a dinner party.

SERVES 4

INGREDIENTS
4 salmon fillets or steaks, about 175g/6oz each
25g/1oz/2 tbsp butter
150ml/¼ pint/²⁄₃ cup hot Fish Stock
150ml/¼ pint/²⁄₃ cup dry white wine
1 bay leaf
salt
pinch of cayenne pepper

FOR THE WATERCRESS CREAM
2 bunches watercress
25g/1oz/2 tbsp butter
2 shallots, chopped
25g/1oz/¼ cup plain (all-purpose) flour
5ml/1 tsp anchovy essence (extract)
150ml/¼ pint/²⁄₃ cup single (light) cream
lemon juice

> VARIATION
> To make rocket (arugula) cream, replace the watercress with 25g/1oz rocket leaves.

1 Trim the watercress of any bruised leaves and coarse stalks. Blanch in boiling water for 5 minutes. Drain and refresh under cold running water. In a sieve, press with a spoon to remove excess moisture. Chop finely.

2 Place the fish in a pan, add the butter, the fish stock, wine, bay leaf and seasoning, and heat over a low-medium heat to simmering point.

3 Lower the heat, cover the pan and poach the fish for 10–15 minutes, depending on thickness, until tender.

4 Transfer the fish to a warmed plate, cover and keep warm. Discard the bay leaf and reserve the cooking liquid for the sauce.

5 To make the sauce, melt the butter and cook the shallots until soft. Stir in the flour and cook for 1–2 minutes.

6 Remove the pan from the heat and gradually blend in the reserved fish cooking liquid. Return to the heat, bring to the boil, stirring constantly, and simmer gently for 2–3 minutes.

7 Strain the sauce into a clean pan, then add the watercress, anchovy essence and cream. Warm over a low heat. Season with salt and cayenne pepper and sharpen with lemon juice to taste. Serve immediately with the poached salmon.

LEMON & CHIVE SAUCE WITH HERBED FISHCAKES

This piquant and aromatic sauce makes a delicious accompaniment to fishcakes but would also team with most grilled or baked fish dishes.

SERVES 4

INGREDIENTS
350g/12oz potatoes, peeled
75ml/5 tbsp skimmed milk
350g/12oz haddock or hoki fillets, skinned
15ml/1 tbsp lemon juice
15ml/1 tbsp creamed horseradish sauce
30ml/2 tbsp chopped fresh parsley
plain (all-purpose) flour, for dusting
115g/4oz/2 cups fresh wholemeal (whole-wheat) breadcrumbs
salt and ground black pepper
fresh flat leaf parsley sprigs, to garnish
vegetables in season, to serve

FOR THE LEMON AND CHIVE SAUCE
thinly pared rind and juice of ½ small lemon
120ml/4fl oz/½ cup dry white wine
2 thin slices fresh root ginger
10ml/2 tsp cornflour (cornstarch)
30ml/2 tbsp chopped fresh chives

1 Place the potatoes in a large pan of boiling water and cook for 15–20 minutes. Drain and mash with the milk, then season to taste.

2 Process the fish together with the lemon juice and horseradish sauce in a food processor or blender. Mix together with the potatoes and parsley.

3 With floured hands, shape the mixture into eight fishcakes and coat with the breadcrumbs. Chill in the refrigerator for 30 minutes.

4 Cook the fishcakes under a preheated medium-hot grill (broiler) for about 5 minutes on each side, until browned.

5 To make the sauce, cut the lemon rind into julienne strips and put into a large pan together with the lemon juice, wine and ginger, and season to taste. Simmer the sauce uncovered for 6 minutes.

6 Blend the cornflour with 15ml/1 tbsp of cold water. Add to the ingredients in the pan and simmer, stirring, until the sauce has thickened and is clear.

7 Stir in the chives immediately before serving. Serve the sauce hot with the fishcakes. Garnish the dish with sprigs of flat leaf parsley and serve with a selection of vegetables.

SORREL SAUCE WITH SALMON STEAKS

The sharp flavour of the sorrel sauce balances the richness of the fish. The young plant has the mildest flavour, so try to buy the herb in its spring season.

SERVES 2

INGREDIENTS
2 salmon steaks, about 250g/9oz each
5ml/1 tsp olive oil
salt and ground black pepper
fresh sage, to garnish

FOR THE SORREL SAUCE
15g/½oz/1 tbsp butter
2 shallots, finely chopped
45ml/3 tbsp crème fraîche
90g/3½oz fresh sorrel leaves, washed and patted dry

1 Season the salmon steaks with salt and pepper. Brush a non-stick frying pan with the olive oil.

2 Make the sauce. Melt the butter in a small pan over a medium heat. Add the shallots and cook for 2–3 minutes, stirring frequently, until just softened.

3 Add the crème fraîche and the sorrel leaves to the shallots and cook until the sorrel is completely wilted, stirring constantly.

4 Meanwhile, place the frying pan over a medium heat until hot. Add the salmon steaks and cook for about 5 minutes, turning once, until the flesh is opaque next to the bone. If you're not sure, pierce the flesh with the tip of a sharp knife; the fish should flake easily.

5 Arrange the salmon steaks on two warmed plates, garnish with sage and serve with the sorrel sauce.

BUTTER SAUCE
WITH SALMON CAKES

The lemony butter sauce keeps the salmon fishcakes deliciously moist; they make a real treat for supper or a leisurely breakfast at the weekend.

MAKES 6

INGREDIENTS
225g/8oz tail piece of salmon, cooked
30ml/2 tbsp chopped fresh parsley
2 spring onions (scallions), trimmed and chopped
225g/8oz/2⅔ cups firm mashed potato
1 egg, beaten
50g/2oz/1 cup fresh white breadcrumbs
butter and oil, for frying (optional)
salt and ground black pepper

FOR THE BUTTER SAUCE
75g/3oz/6 tbsp butter
grated rind and juice of ½ lemon

1 Remove all the skin and bones from the fish and mash or flake it well. Add the chopped parsley, spring onions and 5ml/1 tsp of the lemon rind (from the sauce ingredients) and season with salt and black pepper. Gently work in the potato and then shape into six rounds.

2 Chill the fishcakes for 20 minutes to allow them to firm up. Coat each fishcake well in beaten egg and then in the breadcrumbs. Grill (broil) gently for about 5 minutes each side, or until evenly golden. Alternatively, cook the fishcakes in butter and oil over a medium-hot heat.

3 To make the butter sauce, melt the butter in a pan over a low heat, then whisk in the remaining lemon rind and the lemon juice, together with 15–30ml/ 1–2 tbsp cold water. Season with salt and ground black pepper to taste. Simmer the sauce for a few minutes and then serve immediately with the fish cakes.

CHILLI BARBECUE SAUCE WITH SALMON

This spicy tomato and mustard sauce is delicious served with chargrilled salmon fillets – cook them either on a barbecue or under a hot grill.

SERVES 4

INGREDIENTS
4 salmon fillets, about 175g/6oz

FOR THE CHILLI BARBECUE SAUCE
10ml/2 tsp butter
1 small red onion, finely chopped
1 garlic clove, finely chopped
6 plum tomatoes, diced
45ml/3 tbsp tomato ketchup
30ml/2 tbsp Dijon mustard
30ml/2 tbsp dark brown sugar
15ml/1 tbsp clear honey
5ml/1 tsp cayenne pepper
15ml/1 tbsp ancho chilli powder
15ml/1 tbsp paprika
15ml/1 tbsp Worcestershire sauce

1 To make the barbecue sauce, melt the butter in a large, heavy pan and gently cook the chopped onion and garlic until they are tender and translucent.

2 Stir in the tomatoes and simmer for 15 minutes, stirring occasionally to break up the tomato pieces. Add the remaining sauce ingredients and simmer for a further 20 minutes.

3 Process the mixture until smooth in a food processor fitted with a metal blade. Leave to cool.

4 Brush the salmon with the sauce and chill for at least 2 hours. Cook on the barbecue or grill (broil) for about 2–3 minutes on each side, brushing with the sauce when necessary. Serve drizzled with the remaining sauce.

Five-spice & Black Bean Sauce with Stir-fried Squid

The spicy Asian sauce is the ideal accompaniment for stir-fried squid and is very easy to make. It is important to have all the ingredients ready before you start to cook.

SERVES 6

INGREDIENTS
450g/1lb small squid cleaned
45ml/3 tbsp oil

FOR THE FIVE-SPICE AND BLACK BEAN SAUCE
2.5cm/1in piece of fresh root ginger, grated
1 garlic clove, crushed
8 spring onions (scallions), cut diagonally into 2.5cm/1in lengths
1 red (bell) pepper, seeded and cut into strips
1 fresh green chilli, seeded and thinly sliced
6 chestnut mushrooms, sliced
5ml/1 tsp Chinese five-spice powder
30ml/2 tbsp black bean sauce
30ml/2 tbsp soy sauce
5ml/1 tsp sugar
15ml/1 tbsp rice wine or dry sherry

1 Rinse the squid and pull away the outer skin. Dry on kitchen paper. Slit the squid open and score the outside into diamonds with a sharp knife. Cut the squid into strips.

2 Heat a wok and add the oil. When it is hot, stir-fry the squid quickly. Remove the squid strips from the wok with a slotted spoon and set aside.

3 For the sauce, add the ginger, garlic, spring onions, red pepper, chilli and mushrooms to the oil remaining in the wok and stir-fry for 2 minutes.

4 Return the squid to the wok and stir in the five-spice powder. Stir in the black bean sauce, soy sauce, sugar and rice wine or sherry. Bring to the boil and cook, stirring, for 1 minute. Serve immediately.

SEAFOOD WITH WARM GREEN TARTARE SAUCE

A colourful sauce that's good with all kinds of seafood, particularly fresh scallops, and it looks stunning over black pasta.

SERVES 4

INGREDIENTS
350g/12oz black tagliatelle
12 large scallops
60ml/4 tbsp white wine
150ml/¼ pint/⅔ cup Fish Stock
lime wedges and fresh parsley sprigs, to garnish

FOR THE WARM GREEN TARTARE SAUCE
120ml/4fl oz/½ cup crème fraîche
10ml/2 tsp wholegrain mustard
2 garlic cloves, crushed
30–45ml/2–3 tbsp fresh lime juice
60ml/4 tbsp chopped fresh parsley
30ml/2 tbsp chopped fresh chives
salt and ground black pepper

> COOK'S TIPS
> • If you are removing the scallops from the shells yourself, wash them first in plenty of cold water.
> • If the scallops are frozen, thaw them before cooking, as they will probably have been glazed with water and will need to be drained well.

1 To make the tartare sauce, blend the crème fraîche, mustard, garlic, lime juice, parsley, chives and seasoning together in a food processor or blender.

2 Cook the pasta in a large pan of salted, boiling water according to the instructions on the packet until *al dente*. Drain thoroughly.

3 Meanwhile, slice the scallops in half horizontally. Keep any corals whole. Put the white wine and fish stock into a pan and heat to simmering point. Add the scallops and cook very gently for 3–4 minutes (do not cook them for any longer or they will become tough).

4 Remove the scallops from the pan. Boil the wine and stock to reduce by half and add the tartare sauce to the pan. Heat gently to warm the sauce.

5 Replace the scallops and cook for 1 minute. Spoon over the pasta and garnish with lime wedges and parsley.

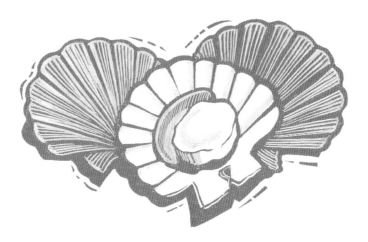

ROMESCO SAUCE WITH GRILLED KING PRAWNS

This sauce, from the Catalan region of Spain, is served with fish and shellfish. Its main ingredients are pimiento, tomatoes, garlic and toasted almonds.

SERVES 4

INGREDIENTS
24 raw king prawns (jumbo shrimp)
30–45ml/2–3 tbsp olive oil
fresh flat leaf parsley, to garnish
lemon wedges, to serve

FOR THE ROMESCO SAUCE
2 well-flavoured tomatoes
60ml/4 tbsp olive oil
1 onion, chopped
4 garlic cloves, chopped
1 canned pimiento, chopped
2.5ml/½ tsp dried chilli flakes or powder
75ml/5 tbsp Fish Stock
30ml/2 tbsp sherry or white wine
10 blanched almonds
15ml/1 tbsp red wine vinegar
salt

> ## VARIATION
> *In Catalonia, romesco sauce is also served with local spicy sausages, grilled (broiled) fish and poultry dishes. Spoonfuls can also be added to enrich a fish or chicken stew, rather like a rouille is used in French cooking.*

1 To make the sauce, immerse the tomatoes in boiling water for about 30 seconds, remove from the pan with a slotted spoon, then refresh them under cold water. Peel off the skins and coarsely chop the flesh.

2 Heat 30ml/2 tbsp of the oil in a pan, add the onion and 3 of the garlic cloves, and cook until soft.

3 Add the pimiento, tomatoes, chilli, fish stock and sherry or wine, then cover and simmer for 30 minutes. Leave to cool slightly.

4 Meanwhile, toast the almonds under the grill (broiler) until golden. Transfer the almonds to a blender or food processor and grind coarsely.

5 Add the remaining 30ml/2 tbsp of oil, the vinegar and the last garlic clove and process the mixture until it is evenly combined.

6 Carefully add the tomato and pimiento sauce (in batches if necessary) and process until smooth. Season with salt to taste and return to the rinsed pan to keep warm.

7 Remove the heads from the prawns, leaving them otherwise unshelled. With a sharp knife, slit each one down the back and remove the dark vein. Rinse and pat dry on kitchen paper. Preheat the grill.

8 Toss the prawns in olive oil, then spread out in the grill pan. Grill for 2–3 minutes on each side, until pink. Arrange them on a serving platter and garnish with parsley. Serve with the lemon wedges and the sauce in a small bowl.

Tartare Sauce with Crab Cakes

Tartare sauce is the traditional accompaniment to any kind of fried fish, but it is also surprisingly delicious with vegetables. Maryland is renowned for its seafood, and these little crab cakes hail from there.

Serves 4

Ingredients
675g/1½lb fresh white crab meat
1 egg, beaten
30ml/2 tbsp mayonnaise
15ml/1 tbsp Worcestershire sauce
15ml/1 tbsp sherry
30ml/2 tbsp finely chopped fresh parsley
15ml/1 tbsp finely chopped fresh chives
45ml/3 tbsp olive oil
salt and ground black pepper

For the tartare sauce
1 egg yolk
15ml/1 tbsp white wine vinegar
30ml/2 tbsp Dijon-style mustard
250ml/8fl oz/1 cup vegetable or groundnut (peanut) oil
30ml/2 tbsp fresh lemon juice
45ml/3 tbsp finely chopped spring onions (scallions)
30ml/2 tbsp chopped drained capers
45ml/3 tbsp finely chopped sour dill pickles
45ml/3 tbsp finely chopped fresh parsley

Cook's Tip
For easier handling and to make the crab meat go further, add 50g/2oz/1 cup fresh breadcrumbs and 1 more egg to the crab mixture. Divide the mixture into 12 cakes to serve 6. Use dill instead of chives if you prefer.

1 Pick over the crab meat, removing any shell or cartilage. Keep the pieces of crab as large as possible.

2 Combine the beaten egg with the mayonnaise, Worcestershire sauce, sherry and herbs in a bowl. Season to taste. Gently fold in the crab meat.

3 Divide the mixture into eight portions and gently form each into an oval cake. Place on a baking sheet between layers of greasepoof (waxed) paper and chill for at least 1 hour.

4 To make the sauce, beat the egg yolk in a bowl with a wire whisk. Add the vinegar, mustard, and seasoning, and whisk for about 10 seconds. Whisk in the oil in a slow, steady stream.

5 Add the lemon juice, spring onions, capers, sour dill pickles and parsley and mix well. Check the seasoning. Cover and chill.

6 Preheat the grill (broiler). Brush the crab cakes with the olive oil. Place on an oiled baking sheet in a single layer. Grill (broil) 15cm/6in from the heat for about 5 minutes on each side, until golden brown. Alternatively, fry the crab cakes over a medium heat for a few minutes on each side. Serve the crab cakes hot with the tartare sauce.

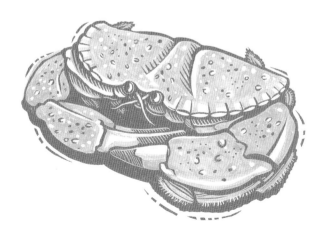

SAUCES FOR VEGETARIAN DISHES

Vegetable dishes have, until recently, been considered the poor-relation among other areas of cookery, but it is not only vegetarians who are becoming increasingly interested in making vegetable dishes more appetizing and exciting. Everyone who is interested in healthy eating is including more vegetable-based meals in their diet. Vegetables are among the most versatile of all ingredients – they can provide hearty, cold-weather meals, such as Baked Marrow and Parsley Sauce and the family favourite, Cheddar Cheese Sauce with Cauliflower, or light summer dishes consisting of steamed and fresh vegetables, such as Warm Vegetable Salad served with Peanut Sauce. The sauces in this chapter, however, are not intended to be served exclusively with vegetable meals. They provide flavour and texture that can be teamed with freshly cooked pasta, such as Green Vegetable Sauce, or polenta, as in Wild Mushroom Sauce. Others provide a piquant taste to add flavour to a plainer dish, like Citrus Sauce or Mustard Sauce, which add spice to liven up courgettes (zucchini) or potatoes but would be equally at home with fish or meat dishes. Any of these sauces will enhance and complement a variety of dishes – whether the flavours are similar or contrasting – if you choose carefully.

CITRUS SAUCE WITH COURGETTES

This piquant sauce is a refreshing change served with steamed green vegetables, or it would also make a tasty dip with roast potato wedges.

SERVES 4

INGREDIENTS
350g/12oz baby courgettes (zucchini)

FOR THE CITRUS SAUCE
4 spring onions (scallions), finely sliced
2.5cm/1in piece fresh root ginger, grated
30ml/2 tbsp cider vinegar
15ml/1 tbsp light soy sauce
5ml/1 tsp soft light brown sugar
45ml/3 tbsp vegetable stock
finely grated rind and juice of ½ lemon and ½ orange
5ml/1 tsp cornflour (cornstarch)

1 Cook the courgettes in lightly salted, boiling water for 3–4 minutes, or until just tender. Drain well.

2 Meanwhile, make the sauce. Put all the sauce ingredients, except the cornflour, into a small pan and bring to the boil. Simmer for 3 minutes.

3 Blend the cornflour with 10ml/2 tsp cold water and add to the sauce. Bring the sauce to the boil, stirring constantly, until thickened.

4 Pour the sauce over the courgettes and heat gently, shaking the pan to coat evenly. Transfer to a warmed dish and serve.

VARIATION
Try this sauce with a mixture of baby vegetables, such as courgettes (zucchini), carrots, turnips, baby corn, patty pan squash, etc.

GREEN VEGETABLE SAUCE

This sauce is a wonderful medley of cooked fresh vegetables. Tossed with pasta, it's ideal for a fresh, light lunch or supper dish in the middle of summer.

SERVES 4

INGREDIENTS
450g/1lb/4 cups dried pasta shapes

FOR THE GREEN VEGETABLE SAUCE
25g/1oz/2 tbsp butter
45ml/3 tbsp extra virgin olive oil
1 small leek, thinly sliced
2 carrots, diced
2.5ml/½ tsp sugar
1 courgette (zucchini), diced
75g/3oz/generous ½ cup green beans
115g/4oz/1 cup frozen peas
1 handful fresh flat leaf parsley, chopped
2 ripe plum tomatoes, peeled and diced
salt and ground black pepper
fried parsley sprigs, to garnish

1 Melt the butter and oil in a medium frying pan. When the mixture sizzles, add the leek and carrots. Sprinkle the sugar over the vegetables and cook over a medium heat, stirring frequently, for about 5 minutes.

2 Stir the courgette, green beans and peas into the sauce and season with plenty of salt and pepper. Cover and cook over a low to medium heat, stirring occasionally, for 5–8 minutes, or until the vegetables are tender. Meanwhile, cook the pasta in a large pan of salted, boiling water according to the instructions on the packet until *al dente*.

3 Stir the chopped parsley and diced tomatoes into the sauce. Drain the pasta and serve immediately, tossed with the sauce and garnished with fried parsley sprigs.

MUSTARD SAUCE WITH POTATO SKEWERS

This thick, garlic-rich dipping sauce is versatile enough to serve with any vegetable kebab or even with crudités, but it is especially delicious with tiny new potatoes.

SERVES 4

INGREDIENTS
1kg/2¼lb small new potatoes
200g/7oz shallots, halved
30ml/2 tbsp olive oil
15ml/1 tbsp sea salt

FOR THE MUSTARD SAUCE
4 garlic cloves, crushed
2 egg yolks
30ml/2 tbsp lemon juice
300ml/½ pint/1¼ cups extra virgin olive oil
10ml/2 tsp wholegrain mustard
salt and ground black pepper

1 To make the mustard sauce, place the garlic, egg yolks and lemon juice in a food processor or blender and process briefly until smooth.

2 With the motor running, gradually add the oil until the mixture forms a thick cream. Add the mustard and season.

3 Par-boil the potatoes in salted, boiling water for about 5 minutes. Drain well and then thread them on to metal skewers with the shallots. Brush the vegetable skewers lightly with olive oil and sprinkle with sea salt.

4 Cook the vegetables for 10–12 minutes over a hot barbecue or under a preheated grill (broiler), turning frequently, until tender. Serve immediately with the mustard dipping sauce.

Baked Marrow & Parsley Sauce

This is a glorious way to treat a modest vegetable. Try to find a small, firm and unblemished marrow for this recipe, as the flavour will be sweet, fresh and delicate.

SERVES 4

INGREDIENTS
1 small young marrow (large zucchini), about 900g/2lb
30ml/2 tbsp olive oil
15g/½oz/1 tbsp butter
1 onion, chopped
15ml/1 tbsp plain (all-purpose) flour
300ml/½ pint/1¼ cups milk and single (light) cream, mixed
30ml/2 tbsp chopped fresh parsley
salt and ground black pepper

1 Preheat the oven to 180°C/350°F/Gas 4 and cut the marrow into pieces measuring about 5 × 2.5cm/2 × 1in.

2 Heat the oil and butter in a flameproof casserole and cook the onion over a low heat until very soft.

3 Add the marrow and sauté for 1–2 minutes and then stir in the flour. Cook for a few minutes. Stir the milk and cream into the vegetable mixture. Add the parsley and seasoning and stir well.

4 Cover and cook in the oven for 30–35 minutes. If you like, uncover for the final 5 minutes of cooking to brown the top.

VARIATION
*Chopped fresh basil or a mixture of basil and chervil
also tastes good in this dish.*

CHILLI SAUCE WITH SPICY POTATO WEDGES

For a healthy snack with superb flavour, try these dry-roasted potato wedges. The crisp spice crust makes them irresistible, especially when served with this chilli sauce.

SERVES 2

INGREDIENTS
2 baking potatoes, about 225g/8oz each, unpeeled
30ml/2 tbsp olive oil
2 garlic cloves, crushed
5ml/1 tsp ground allspice
5ml/1 tsp ground coriander
15ml/1 tbsp paprika
sea salt and ground black pepper

FOR THE CHILLI SAUCE
15ml/1 tbsp olive oil
1 small onion, finely chopped
1 garlic clove, crushed
200g/7oz can chopped tomatoes
1 fresh red chilli, seeded and finely chopped
15ml/1 tbsp balsamic vinegar
15ml/1 tbsp chopped fresh coriander (cilantro), plus extra to garnish

COOK'S TIPS
- To save time, the potatoes can be par-boiled and tossed with the spices in advance.
- Make sure that the potato wedges are perfectly dry and completely covered in the spice mixture before roasting them.

1 Preheat the oven to 200°C/400°F/Gas 6. Cut the potatoes in half, then into eight wedges.

2 Place the wedges in a pan of cold water. Bring to the boil, then lower the heat and simmer gently for 10 minutes, or until the potatoes have softened slightly. Drain well and pat dry on kitchen paper.

3 Mix the oil, garlic, allspice, ground coriander and paprika in a roasting pan. Add salt and pepper to taste. Add the potatoes to the pan and shake to coat them thoroughly. Roast for 20 minutes, turning the potato wedges occasionally, or until they are browned, crisp and fully cooked.

4 Meanwhile, make the chilli sauce. Heat the oil in a pan, add the onion and garlic and cook for 5–10 minutes, or until soft. Add the chopped tomatoes, with their juice. Stir in the chilli and vinegar.

5 Cook gently for 10 minutes, or until the mixture has reduced and thickened, then check the seasoning. Stir in the fresh coriander and serve hot with the potato wedges. Garnish with salt and fresh coriander.

Peanut Sauce with Warm Vegetable Salad

This spicy sauce is based on the classic Indonesian sauce served with satay, but is equally delicious served with this main-course salad which mixes steamed and raw vegetables. It would also partner vegetable kebabs.

Serves 2–4

Ingredients
8 new potatoes
225g/8oz broccoli, cut into small florets
200g/7oz/1⅓ cups fine green beans
2 carrots, cut into thin ribbons with a vegetable peeler
1 red (bell) pepper, seeded and cut into strips
50g/2oz sprouted beans
watercress sprigs, to garnish

For the peanut sauce
15ml/1 tbsp sunflower oil
1 bird's-eye chilli, seeded and sliced
1 garlic clove, crushed
5ml/1 tsp ground coriander
5ml/1 tsp ground cumin
60ml/4 tbsp crunchy peanut butter
75ml/5 tbsp water
15ml/1 tbsp dark soy sauce
1cm/½in piece of fresh root ginger, finely grated
5ml/1 tsp soft dark brown sugar
15ml/1 tbsp lime juice
60ml/4 tbsp coconut milk

Cook's Tip
Adjust the dipping consistency by adding slightly less water than recommended; you can always stir in a little more at the last minute. Serve the sauce either warm or cold.

1 First make the peanut sauce. Heat the oil in a pan, add the chilli and garlic and cook for 1 minute, or until softened. Add the spices and cook for 1 minute.

2 Stir in the peanut butter and water, then cook, stirring constantly, for 2 minutes, or until combined.

3 Add the soy sauce, grated ginger, sugar, lime juice and coconut milk, then cook over a low heat, stirring frequently, until smooth and heated through. Transfer to a bowl.

4 Bring a pan of lightly salted water to the boil, add the potatoes and cook for 10–15 minutes, or until tender. Drain, then halve or thickly slice the potatoes, depending on their size.

5 Meanwhile, steam the broccoli and green beans for 4–5 minutes, or until tender but still crisp. Add the carrots 2 minutes before the end of the cooking time.

6 Arrange the cooked vegetables on a serving platter with the red pepper and sprouted beans. Garnish with watercress and serve with the peanut sauce.

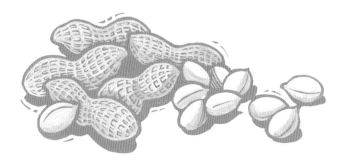

ROASTED PEPPER SAUCE WITH MALFATTI

A smoky red pepper and tomato sauce adds the finishing touch to spinach and ricotta dumplings. The Italians call these malfatti, *which means "badly made", because of their uneven shape. However, they still taste wonderful.*

SERVES 4

INGREDIENTS
500g/1¼lb young leaf spinach
1 onion, finely chopped
1 garlic clove, crushed
15ml/1 tbsp extra virgin olive oil
350g/12 oz/1½ cups ricotta cheese
3 eggs, beaten
50g/2oz/scant 1 cup undyed dried breadcrumbs
50g/2oz/½ cup plain (all-purpose) flour
50g/2 oz/⅔ cup freshly grated Parmesan cheese
freshly grated nutmeg
25g/1oz/2 tbsp butter, melted

FOR THE ROASTED PEPPER SAUCE
2 red (bell) peppers, seeded and quartered
30ml/2 tbsp extra virgin olive oil
1 onion, chopped
400g/14oz can chopped tomatoes
150ml/¼ pint/⅔ cup water
salt and ground black pepper

1 Make the sauce. Preheat the grill (broiler) and grill (broil) the pepper quarters, skin-side up, until they blister and blacken. Cool slightly, then peel off the skins and chop the flesh.

2 Heat the oil in a pan, add the onion and peppers and cook over a low heat, stirring occasionally, for 5 minutes.

3 Add the tomatoes and water, with salt and pepper to taste. Bring to the boil, lower the heat and simmer gently for 15 minutes.

4 Process the mixture in a food processor or blender, in batches if necessary, then return to the clean pan and set aside.

5 Trim any thick stalks from the spinach, wash it well if necessary, then blanch in a pan of boiling water for about 1 minute. Drain, refresh under cold water and drain again. Squeeze dry, then chop finely.

6 Put the onion, garlic, olive oil, ricotta, eggs and breadcrumbs in a bowl. Add the spinach and mix well. Stir in the flour and 5ml/1 tsp salt with half the Parmesan, then season to taste with pepper and nutmeg. Roll the mixture into 16 small logs and chill lightly.

7 Bring a large pan of water to the boil. Carefully drop in the malfatti, in batches, and cook them for 5 minutes. Remove with a fish slice (metal spatula) and toss with the melted butter.

8 To serve, reheat the sauce and divide it among four plates. Arrange four malfatti on each and sprinkle the remaining Parmesan over them. Serve immediately.

Fresh Tomato & Ginger Sauce with Tofu & Potato Rösti

In this recipe, the tofu is marinated in a mixture of tamari, honey and oil, flavoured with garlic and ginger. This marinade is then added to the fresh tomatoes to make a thick, creamy tomato sauce with a delicious tang, and the method makes sure that the tofu is infused with the same flavours.

Serves 4

Ingredients
425g/15oz tofu, cut into 1cm/½in cubes
4 large potatoes, about 900g/2lb total weight, peeled
sunflower oil, for frying
salt and ground black pepper
10ml/2 tsp sesame seeds, toasted

For the fresh tomato and ginger sauce
30ml/2 tbsp tamari or dark soy sauce
15ml/1 tbsp clear honey
2 garlic cloves, crushed
4cm/1½in piece of fresh root ginger, grated
5ml/1 tsp toasted sesame oil
15ml/1 tbsp olive oil
8 tomatoes, halved, seeded and chopped

1 For the sauce, mix together the tamari or dark soy sauce, honey, garlic, root ginger and toasted sesame oil in a shallow dish.

2 Add the tofu, then spoon the liquid over the tofu and leave to marinate in the refrigerator for at least 1 hour. Turn the tofu occasionally in the marinade to allow the flavours to infuse (steep).

3 To make the rösti, par-boil the potatoes for 10–15 minutes, until almost tender. Leave to cool, then grate coarsely. Season well with salt and freshly ground black pepper. Preheat the oven to 200°C/400°F/Gas 6.

4 Using a slotted spoon, remove the tofu from the marinade and reserve the marinade. Spread out the tofu on a baking sheet and bake, turning it occasionally, for 20 minutes, until golden and crisp on all sides.

5 Take a quarter of the potato mixture in your hands at a time and form into coarse patties.

6 Heat a frying pan with just enough oil to cover the base. Place the patties in the frying pan and flatten the mixture, using your hands or a spatula to form rounds about 1cm/½in thick.

7 Cook for about 6 minutes, or until golden and crisp underneath. Carefully turn the rösti over and cook for a further 6 minutes, or until golden brown in colour.

8 Meanwhile, complete the sauce. Heat the oil in a pan, add the reserved marinade and then the tomatoes and cook for 2 minutes, stirring constantly.

9 Reduce the heat and simmer, covered, for 10 minutes, stirring occasionally, until the tomatoes break down. Press the mixture through a sieve to make a thick, smooth sauce.

10 To serve, place a rösti on each of four warm serving plates. Arrange the tofu on top, spoon over the tomato sauce and sprinkle with sesame seeds.

QUICK TOMATO SAUCE WITH BAKED CHEESE POLENTA

This quick tomato sauce can be prepared from store-cupboard ingredients. The rich flavour of the sauce enhances baked polenta and provides a contrast in textures.

SERVES 4

INGREDIENTS
5ml/1 tsp salt
250g/9oz/2¼ cups quick-cook polenta
5ml/1 tsp paprika
2.5ml/½ tsp ground nutmeg
75g/3oz/¾ cup grated Gruyère cheese

FOR THE QUICK TOMATO SAUCE
30ml/2 tbsp olive oil
1 large onion, finely chopped
2 garlic cloves, crushed
2 × 400g/14oz cans chopped tomatoes
15ml/1 tbsp tomato purée (paste)
5ml/1 tsp sugar
salt and ground black pepper

1 Line a 28 × 18cm/11 × 7in baking tin (pan) with clear film (plastic wrap). Bring 1 litre/1¾ pints/4 cups water to the boil with the measured salt.

2 Pour in the quick-cook polenta in a steady stream and cook, stirring constantly, for 5 minutes. Beat in the paprika and nutmeg, then pour into the prepared tin and smooth the surface. Leave to cool.

3 To make the quick tomato sauce, heat the oil in a pan and cook the onion and garlic until soft. Add the chopped tomatoes, tomato purée and sugar. Season, and simmer for 20 minutes. Preheat the oven to 200°C/400°F/Gas 6.

4 Turn out the polenta on to a board, and cut into 5cm/2in squares. Place half the squares in a greased ovenproof dish. Spoon over half the tomato sauce and sprinkle with half the cheese. Repeat the layers. Bake for 25 minutes.

Cheddar Cheese Sauce with Cauliflower

Select a mature farmhouse Cheddar to give this popular family dish a full flavour, and season with plenty of freshly ground black pepper.

Serves 4

Ingredients
1.2kg/2½lb cauliflower florets (about 1 large head)
3 bay leaves

For the Cheddar cheese sauce
40g/1½oz/3 tbsp butter
45ml/3 tbsp plain (all-purpose) flour
450ml/¾ pint/scant 2 cups milk
50g/2oz/3 cups grated mature (sharp) Cheddar cheese
salt and ground black pepper

1 Preheat the oven to 180°C/350°F/Gas 4. Lightly grease a 30cm/12in round ovenproof dish.

2 Bring a large pan of lightly salted water to the boil. Add the cauliflower florets and cook for 7–8 minutes, or until just tender but still firm. Drain well.

3 To make the sauce, melt the butter in a heavy pan. Whisk in the flour until blended with the butter. Cook until smooth and bubbling, stirring constantly.

4 Gradually stir in the milk. Bring to the boil and continue cooking, stirring constantly, until the sauce is thickened and smooth. Remove the pan from the heat and stir in the grated cheese until it has melted. Season the sauce to taste with salt and pepper.

5 Place the bay leaves on the base of the prepared dish. Arrange the cauliflower florets on top in an even layer. Pour the cheese sauce evenly over the cauliflower.

6 Bake for 20–25 minutes, or until golden brown and bubbling. Serve immediately, straight from the dish.

Wild Mushroom Sauce with Polenta & Gorgonzola

The flavour of wild mushrooms combines well with mascarpone in this sauce to heighten the taste of the polenta. It's also a delicious topping for baked potatoes.

Serves 4–6

INGREDIENTS
900ml/1½ pints/3¾ cups milk
900ml/1½ pints/3¾ cups water
5ml/1 tsp salt
300g/11oz/2¾ cups polenta
50g/2oz/¼ cup butter
115g/4oz Gorgonzola cheese
fresh thyme sprigs, to garnish

FOR THE WILD MUSHROOM SAUCE
40g/1½oz/scant 1 cup dried porcini mushrooms
150ml/¼ pint/⅔ cup hot water
25g/1oz/2 tbsp butter
115g/4oz/1½ cups button (white) mushrooms, chopped
60ml/4 tbsp dry white wine
generous pinch of dried thyme
60ml/4 tbsp mascarpone cheese
salt and ground black pepper

COOK'S TIP
If available, use fresh porcini mushrooms instead of dried and do not soak. You would need about 175g/6oz fresh porcini for this recipe. They are also sold under the name ceps.

1 Pour the milk and water into a large pan. Add the salt and bring to the boil. Gradually add the polenta, stirring constantly. When the mixture is thick and smooth, lower the heat and simmer, stirring occasionally, for about 20 minutes.

2 Remove from the heat and stir in the butter and Gorgonzola. Spoon the polenta mixture into a shallow dish and level the surface. Let the polenta set until solid, then cut into wedges.

3 Meanwhile, make the sauce. Soak the porcini in the hot water for 15 minutes. Drain, reserving the liquid. Finely chop the porcini and strain the soaking liquid through a sieve lined with kitchen paper. Discard the kitchen paper.

4 Melt half the butter in a small pan. Sauté the chopped fresh mushrooms for about 5 minutes.

5 Add the wine, porcini and strained soaking liquid, with the dried thyme. Season to taste. Cook for a further 2 minutes. Stir in the mascarpone and simmer for a few minutes, until reduced by a third. Set aside to cool.

6 Heat a ridged griddle pan or grill (broiler), and cook the polenta until crisp. Brush with melted butter and serve hot with the sauce. Garnish with thyme.

SALSAS

"Salsa" is simply translated as "sauce", but since the sauces we refer to as salsas originated in the rich, colourful tradition of Mexican cooking, they have a very different style from the familiar types of classic sauces covered in other chapters. They're perfect for summer eating, and an ideal choice to accompany foods cooked on the barbecue. Fresh, colourful chillies are finely chopped and tossed imaginatively with fruits, vegetables or herbs to create highly individual combinations that enliven any dish or simple meal, from fish to meat, and from vegetables to eggs. Salsas may be fiery-hot, or delicately spiced hot, sweet and sour, or just hot and sweet – depending on your taste and the food it will accompany. The most basic salsas are "crudo", which simply means raw, so the ingredients take no more preparation than fine chopping or whizzing in a blender to combine. The most typical Mexican salsa crudo would have chillies, onions, tomatoes or (bell) peppers with fresh coriander (cilantro), for a simple, vibrant, zesty mix. Others can be more elaborate, sometimes simmered to soften ingredients and mingle flavours, or with the addition of exotic fruits or spices. Above all, salsas are an opportunity to show your creative flair – try some of these varied recipes, then start experimenting with your own.

SALSA VERDE

There are many versions of this classic green salsa. Try this one drizzled over chargrilled squid, or with baked potatoes served with a green salad.

SERVES 4

INGREDIENTS
2–4 green chillies, halved and seeded
8 spring onions (scallions), trimmed
2 garlic cloves, halved
50g/2oz salted capers
fresh tarragon sprig
bunch of fresh parsley
grated rind and juice of 1 lime
juice of 1 lemon
90ml/6 tbsp olive oil
about 15ml/1 tbsp green Tabasco sauce
ground black pepper

1 Place the chillies, spring onions and garlic in a food processor and pulse briefly. Rub the excess salt off the capers. Add them, with the tarragon and parsley, to the food processor and pulse again until the ingredients are quite finely chopped.

2 Transfer the mixture to a bowl. Mix in the lime rind and juice, lemon juice and olive oil, stirring lightly so the citrus juice and oil do not emulsify. Add green Tabasco sauce, a little at a time, and black pepper to taste.

3 Chill the salsa in the refrigerator until ready to serve, but do not prepare it more than 8 hours in advance.

TOMATO SALSA

This simple side dish is very versatile and really enhances a wide range of hot and cold dishes and is the perfect accompaniment to a meat-based barbecue.

SERVES 6

INGREDIENTS
6 medium tomatoes
1 green Kenyan chilli
2 spring onions (scallions), chopped
10cm/4in length cucumber, diced
30ml/2 tbsp lemon juice
30ml/2 tbsp fresh coriander (cilantro), chopped
15ml/1 tbsp fresh parsley, chopped
salt and ground black pepper

1 Cut a small cross in the stalk end of each tomato. Place in a bowl and cover with boiling water.

2 After 30 seconds or as soon as the skins split, drain and immediately plunge into cold water. Gently slide off the skins. Quarter the tomatoes, remove and discard the seeds and dice the flesh.

3 Cut the chilli in half lengthways, remove the stalk, seeds and the membrane, and chop the flesh finely.

4 Mix together all the ingredients and season to taste with salt and pepper, then transfer to a serving bowl. Cover with clear film (plastic wrap) and chill in the refrigerator for 1–2 hours before serving.

CORIANDER PESTO SALSA

This aromatic salsa is delicious drizzled over fish and chicken, tossed with pasta ribbons or used to dress a fresh avocado and tomato salad.

SERVES 4

INGREDIENTS
50g/2oz/1 cup fresh coriander (cilantro) leaves
15g/½oz/¼ cup fresh parsley
2 fresh red chillies
1 garlic clove
50g/2oz/½ cup shelled pistachio nuts
25g/1oz/⅓ cup finely grated Parmesan cheese, plus extra to garnish
90ml/6 tbsp olive oil
juice of 2 limes
salt and ground black pepper

1 Process the fresh coriander and parsley in a food processor or blender until finely chopped.

2 Halve the chillies lengthways and remove their seeds. Add to the herbs, together with the garlic, and process until finely chopped.

3 Add the pistachio nuts to the herb mixture and pulse the power until they are coarsely chopped. Stir in the Parmesan, olive oil and lime juice.

4 Add salt and pepper to taste. Spoon the mixture into a serving bowl, cover and chill until ready to serve, garnished with Parmesan.

VARIATION
Any number of different herbs or nuts may be used to make a similar salsa to this one – try a mixture of rosemary and parsley, or add a handful of pitted black olives.

Sweet Pepper Salsa

Roasting peppers enhances their sweet flavour, making them perfect for salsas. This is delicious served with poached salmon and also goes well with chicken.

SERVES 4

INGREDIENTS
1 red (bell) pepper
1 yellow (bell) pepper
5ml/1 tsp cumin seeds
1 fresh red chilli, seeded
30ml/2 tbsp chopped fresh coriander (cilantro) leaves, plus extra to garnish
30ml/2 tbsp olive oil
15ml/1 tbsp red wine vinegar
salt and ground black pepper

1 Preheat the grill (broiler) to medium. Place the peppers on a baking sheet and grill (broil) them for 8–10 minutes, turning frequently, until their skins have blackened and are blistered.

2 Place the peppers in a bowl and cover with a clean dishtowel. Leave for 5 minutes so that the steam helps to lift the skin away from the flesh. Remove the dishtowel.

3 Meanwhile, place the cumin seeds in a small frying pan. Heat gently, stirring, until the seeds start to splutter and release their aroma. Remove the pan from the heat, then tip out the seeds into a mortar and crush them lightly with a pestle.

4 When the peppers are cool enough to handle, pierce a hole in the base of each and squeeze out all of the juices into a bowl. Peel, core and seed the peppers, then process the flesh and juices in a blender or food processor with the chilli and coriander until finely chopped.

5 Stir in the oil, vinegar and cumin with salt and pepper to taste. Serve the salsa at room temperature, garnished with coriander.

DOUBLE CHILLI SALSA

This is a scorchingly hot salsa for only the very brave. Serve it on the side or spread it sparingly on to cooked meats and burgers for a real kick.

SERVES 4–6

INGREDIENTS
6 habanero chillies or Scotch bonnets
2 ripe tomatoes
4 standard green jalapeño chillies
30ml/2 tbsp chopped fresh parsley
30ml/2 tbsp olive oil
15ml/1 tbsp balsamic or sherry vinegar
salt

1 Skewer a habanero or Scotch bonnet chilli on to a metal fork and hold it in a gas flame for 2–3 minutes, turning the chilli until the skin blackens and blisters. Repeat with all the habaneros or Scotch bonnets, then set aside until cool.

2 Skewer the tomatoes, one at a time, and hold them in the gas flame for 1–2 minutes, or until the skins wrinkle. Slip off the skins and halve. Use a teaspoon to scoop out and discard the seeds. Finely chop the flesh.

3 Rub the skins off the cooled chillies with a clean dishtowel. Do not touch the chillies with your hands: use a fork to hold them and slice them open with a sharp knife. Scrape out and discard the seeds, then finely chop the flesh.

4 Halve the jalapeño chillies, remove their seeds and finely slice them widthways into tiny strips.

5 Mix together both types of chilli, the tomatoes and chopped parsley. Mix the olive oil, vinegar and salt, pour this over the salsa, cover the dish and chill.

Chilli & Coconut Salsa

A sweet-and-sour salsa, spiked with chillies, that goes particularly well with fish, whether grilled or cooked on the barbecue – a tropical treat.

SERVES 6–8

INGREDIENTS
1 small coconut
1 small pineapple
2 fresh green Kenyan chillies
5cm/2in piece of lemon grass
60ml/4 tbsp natural (plain) yogurt
2.5ml/½ tsp salt
30ml/2 tbsp chopped fresh coriander (cilantro),
  plus extra sprigs to garnish

1 Puncture two of the coconut eyes with a screwdriver and drain the milk out from the shell.

2 Crack the coconut shell, prise away the flesh, and then coarsely grate the coconut into a medium-size bowl.

3 Cut the rind from the pineapple with a sharp knife and remove the eyes with a potato peeler. Finely chop the flesh and add to the coconut together with any juice.

4 Halve the chillies lengthways and remove the stalks, seeds and membrane. Chop very finely and stir into the coconut mixture. Finely chop the lemon grass and stir it in.

5 Add the remaining ingredients and stir well. Spoon into a serving dish and garnish with coriander sprigs.

Fiery Citrus Salsa

This very unusual salsa makes a fantastic marinade for shellfish, and it is also delicious drizzled over all kinds of meat cooked on the barbecue.

Serves 4

Ingredients
1 orange
1 green apple
2 fresh red chillies, halved and seeded
1 garlic clove
8 fresh mint leaves
juice of 1 lemon
salt and ground black pepper

1 Slice the bottom off the orange so that it will stand firmly on a chopping board. Using a sharp knife, remove the peel by slicing from the top to the bottom of the orange.

2 Hold the orange in one hand over a bowl. Slice towards the middle of the fruit, to one side of a segment, and then gently twist the knife to ease the segment away from the membrane and out of the orange. Remove all the segments. Squeeze any juice from the remaining membrane into the bowl.

3 Peel the apple, slice it into wedges and remove the core. Place the chillies in a blender or food processor with the orange segments and juice, apple wedges, garlic and fresh mint. Process for a few seconds until smooth. Then, with the motor running, gradually pour the lemon juice into the mixture.

4 Season to taste with a little salt and ground black pepper. Pour the salsa mixture into a bowl or small jug (pitcher) and serve immediately.

Pineapple & Passion Fruit Salsa

Pile this sweet, fruity salsa into brandy snap baskets or meringue nests for a luxurious dessert. It's also great served with amaretti for dipping.

Serves 6

Ingredients
1 small fresh pineapple
2 passion fruit
150ml/¼ pint/⅔ cup Greek (US strained plain) yogurt
30ml/2 tbsp light muscovado (brown) sugar

1 Cut off the top and bottom of the pineapple so that it will stand firmly on a chopping board. Using a large, sharp knife, slice off the peel.

2 Use a small, sharp knife carefully to cut out the eyes. Slice the peeled pineapple and use a small pastry cutter to remove the tough core. Discard the core and finely chop the flesh.

3 Cut the passion fruit in half and use a spoon to scoop out the seeds and pulp into a bowl.

4 Stir in the chopped pineapple and the Greek yogurt. Cover with clear film (plastic wrap) and chill in the refrigerator until required. Stir in the muscovado sugar just before serving the salsa.

Variation
For a richer mixture, you can substitute lightly whipped double (heavy) cream for the Greek (US strained plain) yogurt.

BARBECUE CORN SALSA

Serve this succulent salsa with smoked meats or a juicy grilled gammon or ham steak. It is also good with oily fish, such as mackerel and sardines.

SERVES 4

INGREDIENTS
2 corn cobs
30ml/2 tbsp melted butter
4 tomatoes
6 spring onions (scallions), finely chopped
1 garlic clove, finely chopped
30ml/2 tbsp fresh lemon juice
30ml/2 tbsp olive oil
red Tabasco sauce, to taste
salt and ground black pepper
spring onion (scallion) slices, to garnish

1 Remove the husks and silky threads covering the corn cobs. Brush the cobs with the melted butter and cook on the barbecue or under the grill (broiler) for about 20–30 minutes, turning occasionally, until tender and tinged brown.

2 To remove the kernels, stand the cob upright on a chopping board and use a large, heavy knife to slice down the length of the cob.

3 Skewer the tomatoes in turn on a metal fork and hold in a gas flame for 1–2 minutes, turning, until the skin splits. Slip off the skin and dice the flesh.

4 Mix the spring onions and garlic with the corn and tomato in a small bowl. Mix the lemon juice, olive oil and Tabasco together. Season to taste. Pour this over the salsa and stir well. Cover the salsa and leave to infuse (steep) at room temperature for 1–2 hours before serving, garnished with slices of spring onion.

PLANTAIN SALSA

Here is a summery salsa which is perfect for lazy outdoor eating. Serve with meat or fish cooked on the barbecue or with taco chips for dipping.

SERVES 4

INGREDIENTS
knob (pat) of butter
4 ripe plantains
handful of fresh coriander (cilantro), plus extra to garnish
30ml/2 tbsp olive oil
5ml/1 tsp cayenne pepper
salt and ground black pepper

1 Preheat the oven to 200°C/400°F/Gas 6. Grease four pieces of foil, each measuring roughly 15 × 20cm/6 × 8in, with the knob of butter.

2 Peel the plantains and place one on each piece of buttered foil. Carefully fold the pieces of foil over the plantains to enclose them completely, sealing the edges tightly to form four parcels.

3 Bake the plantain for 25 minutes, or until tender. Alternatively, the plantain may be cooked in the embers of a charcoal barbecue.

4 Leave the parcels to cool slightly, then remove the plantains, discarding any liquid, and place in a food processor or blender.

5 Process the plantains with the coriander until fairly smooth. Stir in the olive oil, cayenne pepper and season with salt and pepper to taste.

6 Serve immediately, as the salsa will discolour and over-thicken if left to cool for too long. Garnish with torn coriander leaves.

Roasted Pepper & Ginger Salsa

Chargrilling to remove the skins will take away any bitterness from the peppers and soften the flesh. Serve the salsa with grilled vegetable kebabs.

SERVES 6

INGREDIENTS
1 large red (bell) pepper
1 large yellow (bell) pepper
1 large orange (bell) pepper
2.5ml/½ tsp coriander seeds
5ml/1 tsp cumin seeds
2.5cm/1in piece of fresh root ginger, chopped
1 small garlic clove, chopped
30ml/2 tbsp lime or lemon juice
1 small red onion, finely chopped
30ml/2 tbsp fresh coriander (cilantro), chopped
5ml/1 tsp fresh thyme, chopped
salt and ground black pepper

1 Preheat the grill (broiler) to hot. Quarter the peppers and remove the stalk, seeds and membranes. Grill (broil) the quarters, skin-side up, until charred and blistered. Rub off the skins and slice the flesh very finely.

2 Gently dry-fry the coriander and cumin seeds over a medium heat for 30 seconds–1 minute, shaking the pan to make sure they don't scorch.

3 Crush the spices in a mortar with a pestle. Add the ginger and garlic and continue to work to a pulp. Work in the lime or lemon juice.

4 Mix together the peppers, spice mixture, onion and herbs. Season to taste with salt and ground black pepper, and spoon into a serving bowl. Chill for about 1–2 hours before serving as an accompaniment to grilled meats or kebabs.

Mango, Passion Fruit & Red Onion Salsa

A very simple tropical salsa, which is livened up by the addition of passion fruit pulp. This salsa goes well with salmon and all kinds of poultry.

SERVES 4

INGREDIENTS
1 large ripe mango
1 red onion
2 passion fruit
6 large fresh basil leaves
juice of 1 lime, to taste
sea salt

1 Holding the mango upright on a chopping board, use a large knife to slice the flesh away from each side of the large flat stone (pit) in two portions.

2 Using a smaller knife, trim away any flesh still clinging to the top and bottom of the stone.

3 Score the flesh of the mango halves deeply, taking care to avoid cutting through the skin: make parallel incisions about 1cm/½in apart; turn and cut lines in the opposite direction.

4 Carefully turn the skin inside out so the flesh stands out. Slice the dice away from the skin. Place in a bowl.

5 Finely chop the red onion and place it in the bowl with the mango. Halve the passion fruit, scoop out the seeds and pulp with a spoon, and add to the mango mixture in the bowl.

6 Tear the basil leaves coarsely and stir them into the mixture with lime juice and a little sea salt to taste. Mix well and serve the salsa immediately.

Berry Salsa

This unusual, richly coloured fruit salsa is the perfect choice for a summer al fresco meal, to serve with fish or poultry, especially if they are cooked on the barbecue.

SERVES 4

INGREDIENTS
1 fresh jalapeño chilli
½ red onion, minced
2 spring onions (scallions), chopped
1 tomato, finely diced
1 small yellow (bell) pepper, seeded and finely chopped
45ml/3 tbsp chopped fresh coriander (cilantro)
1.5ml/¼ tsp salt
15ml/1 tbsp raspberry vinegar
15ml/1 tbsp fresh orange juice
5ml/1 tsp clear honey
15ml/1 tbsp olive oil
175g/6oz/1½ cups strawberries, hulled
175g/6oz/1½ cups blueberries or blackberries
200g/7oz/generous 1 cup raspberries

1 Wearing rubber gloves, finely chop the chilli (discard the seeds and membrane if you like a less hot flavour). Place the chilli in a medium-size bowl. Add the red onion, spring onions, tomato, yellow pepper and coriander, and stir to blend.

2 In a small bowl, whisk together the salt, vinegar, orange juice, honey and olive oil. Pour over the jalapeño mixture and stir well.

3 Coarsely chop the strawberries. Add to the mixture with the other berries and stir to blend. Leave to stand at room temperature for 3 hours, then serve.

Mixed Melon Salsa

A combination of two very different melons gives this salsa an exciting flavour and texture. Try it with thinly sliced prosciutto or smoked salmon.

Serves 10

Ingredients
1 small orange-fleshed melon, such as Charentais
1 large wedge watermelon
2 oranges

1 Cut the orange-fleshed melon into quarters and remove and discard the seeds with a spoon. Use a large, sharp knife to cut off the skin. Dice the melon flesh into even pieces.

2 Pick out the seeds from the watermelon and discard, then remove the skin. Dice the flesh into small chunks.

3 Use a zester to pare long strips of rind from both oranges. Halve the oranges and squeeze out all their juice.

4 Mix both types of the melon and the orange rind and juice together in a bowl. Chill for about 30 minutes and serve.

VARIATIONS
• Other varieties of melon can be used for this exceptionally low-fat and refreshing salsa. Try cantaloupe, Galia or Ogen.
• For a slightly sharper flavour, substitute a large ruby grapefruit for the oranges. For a sweeter flavour, use an Ugli fruit.

Orange, Tomato & Chive Salsa

Fresh chives and sweet oranges provide a refreshing combination of flavours. This salsa can be used to cool down spicy meat or poultry.

SERVES 4

INGREDIENTS
2 large oranges
1 beefsteak tomato
bunch of fresh chives, chopped
1 garlic clove, thinly sliced
30ml/2 tbsp olive oil
sea salt

1 Slice the bottom off one orange so that it will stand firmly on a chopping board. Using a sharp knife, slice off the peel from the top to the bottom of the orange.

2 Hold the orange over a bowl. Slice towards the middle of the fruit, to one side of a segment, and then twist the knife to ease the segment away from the membrane. Repeat to remove all of the segments. Squeeze any juice from the membrane. Prepare the second orange in the same way. Chop the orange segments and place them in the bowl with the collected juice.

3 Halve the tomato and use a teaspoon to scoop the seeds into the bowl. Dice the flesh and add it to the bowl. Stir in the chives and garlic. Pour the olive oil over, season with sea salt to taste and stir well to mix. Serve within 2 hours.

Aromatic Peach & Cucumber Salsa

Angostura bitters add an unusual and very pleasing flavour to this salsa. The distinctive, sweet taste of the mint complements chicken and other meat dishes.

SERVES 4

INGREDIENTS
2 peaches
1 mini cucumber
2.5ml/½ tsp angostura bitters
15ml/1 tbsp olive oil
10ml/2 tsp fresh lemon juice
30ml/2 tbsp chopped fresh mint
salt and ground black pepper

1 Using a small, sharp knife, carefully score a line right around the centre of each peach, taking care to cut just through the skin.

2 Bring a large pan of water to the boil. Add the peaches and blanch them for 1 minute. Drain and briefly refresh in cold water. Peel off and discard the skins. Halve the peaches and remove their stones (pits). Dice the flesh and place in a bowl.

3 Trim the ends off the cucumber, then finely dice the flesh and stir it into the peaches. Stir the angostura bitters, olive oil and lemon juice together and then stir this dressing into the peach mixture. Stir in the mint with salt and pepper to taste. Chill and serve within 1 hour.

DIPS

Far from being just for parties, dips are for any occasion, any time of day and any season. They are an opportunity for informal eating, an appetite teaser and a very healthy way to snack. They're also a good choice for packed lunches and picnics, as they travel well and can be served in so many ways. Hot or cold, dips are a very versatile food; they are invariably quick to make and uncomplicated, so they're easily rustled up at a moment's notice. For a satisfying treat, try a warm, creamy cheese Fonduta with crusty bread for dipping, or Hot Chilli Bean Dip. As a light, refreshing summer snack, Blue Cheese Dip with fresh crudités or creamy Guacamole will fit the bill. For parties, choose a selection of different dips for variety, so there's something for everyone's taste. Serve your favourite dips with raw vegetable crudités such as carrot, cucumber or celery sticks, raw mushrooms or cauliflower florets. Cooked vegetables such as asparagus, artichokes or deep-fried mushrooms are just incomplete without a creamy or tangy savoury dip, and dipped strips of pitta bread, breadsticks and taco chips, are perfect for easy snacking.

BASIL & LEMON MAYONNAISE

This fresh mayonnaise is flavoured with lemon and two types of basil. Serve as a dip with potato wedges or crudités, or as an accompaniment to salads.

SERVES 4

INGREDIENTS
2 large (US extra large) egg yolks
15ml/1 tbsp lemon juice
150ml/¼ pint/⅔ cup olive oil
150ml/¼ pint/⅔ cup sunflower oil
handful of green basil leaves
handful of dark opal (purple) basil leaves
4 garlic cloves, crushed
salt and ground black pepper
green and dark opal basil leaves and sea salt, to garnish

1 Place the egg yolks and lemon juice in a food processor or blender and process them briefly together.

2 Stir the two oils together in a jug (pitcher). With the machine running, pour in the oil very slowly, a drop at a time. Once half the oil has been added, the remainder can be incorporated more quickly. Continue processing the mixture to form a thick and creamy mayonnaise.

3 Tear both types of basil into small pieces and stir into the mayonnaise with the crushed garlic and seasoning. Transfer to a serving dish, cover and chill until ready to serve, garnished with basil leaves and sea salt.

SAFFRON DIP

*Serve this mild dip with fresh vegetable crudités – it is particularly good with florets
of cauliflower – or as an accompaniment to mushrooms cooked in breadcrumbs.*

SERVES 4

INGREDIENTS
15ml/1 tbsp boiling water
small pinch of saffron threads
200g/7oz/scant 1 cup fromage frais (farmer's cheese)
10 fresh chives
10 fresh basil leaves
salt and ground black pepper

1 Pour the boiling water into a small container and add the saffron threads. Leave
to infuse (steep) for 3 minutes.

2 Beat the fromage frais with a fork until it is completely smooth, then stir in the
infused saffron liquid.

3 Use a pair of kitchen scissors to snip the chives into the dip. Tear the basil leaves
into small pieces and stir them in. Season with salt and pepper to taste. Serve
the dip immediately.

VARIATION
*Omit the saffron and add a squeeze of lemon juice
instead. A pinch of turmeric gives a good colour.*

MELLOW GARLIC DIP

Two whole heads of garlic may seem like a lot, but roasting transforms the flesh to a tender, sweet and mellow pulp. Serve with crunchy breadsticks and crisps. For a low-fat version of this dip, use reduced-fat mayonnaise and low-fat yogurt.

SERVES 4

INGREDIENTS
2 whole garlic heads
15ml/1 tbsp olive oil
60ml/4 tbsp mayonnaise
75ml/5 tbsp Greek (US strained plain) yogurt
5ml/1 tsp wholegrain mustard
salt and ground black pepper

1 Preheat the oven to 200°C/400°F/Gas 6. Separate the garlic cloves and place them in a small roasting pan. Pour the olive oil over the garlic cloves and turn them with a spoon to coat them evenly. Roast them for 20–30 minutes, or until tender and softened. Leave to cool for 5 minutes.

2 Trim off the root end of each roasted garlic clove. Peel the garlic cloves, discarding the skins, then place them on a chopping board and sprinkle with salt. Mash with a fork until puréed.

3 Place the garlic in a small bowl and stir in the mayonnaise, yogurt and wholegrain mustard.

4 Taste and adjust the seasoning, then spoon the dip into a bowl. Cover and chill until ready to serve.

Blue Cheese Dip

This dip can be mixed up in next to no time and is delicious served with pears, or with fresh vegetable crudités. This is a very thick dip to which you can add a little more yogurt, or stir in a little milk, for a softer consistency.

SERVES 4

INGREDIENTS
150g/5oz blue cheese, such as Stilton or Danish blue
150g/5oz/⅔ cup soft cheese
75ml/5 tbsp Greek (US strained plain) yogurt
salt and ground black pepper

1 Crumble the blue cheese into a bowl. Using a wooden spoon, beat the cheese to soften it.

2 Add the soft cheese and beat well with a wooden spoon to blend the two cheeses together.

3 Gradually beat in the Greek yogurt, adding enough to give you the consistency you prefer.

4 Season with lots of black pepper and a little salt. Chill the dip until you are ready to serve it.

VARIATION
For an extra rich dip, substitute 300g/11oz/1⅓ cups Dolcelatte Torta for both cheeses.

Squash & Parmesan Dip

The rich, nutty flavour of butternut squash is enhanced by roasting. Serve this unusual, creamy dip with Melba toast or cheese straws.

SERVES 4

INGREDIENTS
1 butternut squash
15g/¹⁄₂oz/1 tbsp butter
4 garlic cloves, unpeeled
30ml/2 tbsp freshly grated Parmesan cheese
45–75ml/3–5 tbsp double (heavy) cream
salt and ground black pepper

1 Preheat the oven to 200°C/400°F/Gas 6. Halve the butternut squash, then scoop out and discard the seeds.

2 Use a small, sharp knife to score the flesh in a deep criss-cross pattern: cut as close to the skin as possible, without cutting through it.

3 Arrange both halves in a small roasting pan and dot them with the butter. Sprinkle the butternut squash with salt and ground black pepper and roast near the top of the oven for 20 minutes.

4 Tuck the unpeeled garlic cloves around the squash in the roasting pan and continue roasting for a further 20 minutes, until the butternut squash is tender and softened.

5 Scoop the flesh out of the squash shells and place it in a food processor or blender. Slip the garlic cloves out of their skins and add to the squash. Process until smooth.

6 With the motor running, add all but 15ml/1 tbsp of the Parmesan cheese and then the cream. Check the seasoning and spoon the dip into a serving bowl; it is at its best served warm. Sprinkle the reserved cheese over the top. If you don't have a food processor or blender, mash the squash in a bowl using a potato masher, then beat in the cheese and cream with a wooden spoon.

THOUSAND ISLAND DIP

This variation on the classic dressing is far removed from the original version, but can be served in the same way – with grilled king prawns laced on to bamboo skewers.

SERVES 4

INGREDIENTS
4 sun-dried tomatoes in oil
4 fresh tomatoes
150g/5oz/⅔ cup soft cheese
60ml/4 tbsp mayonnaise
30ml/2 tbsp tomato purée (paste)
30ml/2 tbsp chopped fresh parsley
grated rind and juice of 1 lemon
red Tabasco sauce, to taste
5ml/1 tsp Worcestershire or soy sauce
salt and ground black pepper

1 Drain the sun-dried tomatoes on kitchen paper to remove the excess oil, then finely chop them.

2 Skewer each fresh tomato, in turn, on a metal fork and hold in a gas flame for about 1–2 minutes, or until the skin wrinkles and splits. Leave to cool, then slip off and discard the skins. Halve the tomatoes and scoop out the seeds with a teaspoon. Finely chop the tomato flesh and set aside.

3 Beat the soft cheese in a bowl, then gradually beat in the mayonnaise and tomato purée to a smooth mixture.

4 Stir in the chopped parsley and sun-dried tomatoes, then add the chopped fresh tomatoes and their seeds, and mix well.

5 Add the lemon rind and juice, and Tabasco sauce to taste. Stir in the Worcestershire or soy sauce and salt and pepper to taste.

6 Transfer the dip to a serving bowl, cover with clear film (plastic wrap) and chill in the refrigerator until ready to serve.

GUACAMOLE

This is quite a fiery version of the popular Mexican dish, although probably nowhere near so hot as the dish you would be served in Mexico, where it often seems that heat knows no bounds. Serve it as a snack with tortilla chips or breadsticks.

SERVES 4

INGREDIENTS
2 ripe avocados
2 tomatoes, peeled, seeded and finely chopped
6 spring onions (scallions), finely chopped
1–2 fresh chillies, seeded and finely chopped
30ml/2 tbsp fresh lime or lemon juice
15ml/1 tbsp chopped fresh coriander (cilantro)
salt and ground black pepper
fresh coriander (cilantro) sprigs, to garnish

1 Cut the avocados in half and remove the stones (pits) and discard. Scoop the flesh into a large bowl and mash it coarsely with a large fork.

2 Add the tomatoes, spring onions, chillies, lime or lemon juice and coriander. Mix well and season with salt and ground black pepper to taste. Serve as soon as possible, garnished with fresh coriander.

COOK'S TIP
Unless you are going to serve the dip immediately, cover the surface closely with a piece of clear film (plastic wrap) to prevent browning. If the surface should still start to brown, stir lightly before serving.

Spiced Carrot Dip

This is a delicious dip with a sweet and spicy flavour. Serve wheat crackers or fiery tortilla chips as accompaniments for dipping. It also makes a delicious topping for baked potatoes and goes well with salad vegetables.

SERVES 4

INGREDIENTS
1 onion
3 carrots, plus extra to garnish
grated rind and juice of 2 oranges
15ml/1 tbsp hot curry paste
150ml/¼ pint/⅔ cup natural (plain) yogurt
handful of fresh basil leaves
15–30ml/1–2 tbsp fresh lemon juice, to taste
red Tabasco sauce, to taste
salt and ground black pepper

1 Finely chop the onion. Peel and grate the carrots. Place the onion, carrots, orange rind and juice, and curry paste in a small pan. Bring to the boil, cover and simmer for 10 minutes.

2 Remove from the heat and leave the mixture to cool slightly, then process in a blender until smooth. Leave to cool completely.

3 Stir in the yogurt. Tear the basil leaves into small pieces and add most of them to the carrot mixture.

4 Add the lemon juice, Tabasco and seasoning. Serve within a few hours at room temperature, garnished with grated carrot and basil.

CREAMY AUBERGINE DIP

Spread this velvet-textured dip thickly on to toasted rounds of rustic bread, then top them with slivers of sun-dried tomato to make wonderful, Italian-style crostini. It's also great served with warm pitta bread or naan.

SERVES 4

INGREDIENTS
1 large aubergine (eggplant)
30ml/2 tbsp olive oil
1 small onion, finely chopped
2 garlic cloves, finely chopped
60ml/4 tbsp chopped fresh parsley
75ml/5 tbsp crème fraîche
red Tabasco sauce, to taste
juice of 1 lemon, to taste
salt and ground black pepper

COOK'S TIP
Rather than grilling (broiling), the aubergine can be roasted in the oven at 200°C/400°F/Gas 6 for 20 minutes, or until tender, if you like.

1 Preheat the grill (broiler) to medium. Place the whole aubergine on a non-stick baking sheet and grill (broil) it for 20–30 minutes under a medium-high heat, turning occasionally, until the skin is blackened and wrinkled and the aubergine feels soft when squeezed.

2 Remove from the oven, cover the aubergine with a clean dishtowel and leave it to cool for about 5 minutes.

3 Heat the olive oil in a large, heavy frying pan, add the onion and garlic and cook over a low heat, stirring occasionally, for 5 minutes, until they are softened, but not browned.

4 Peel the skin from the aubergine. Mash the flesh with a large fork or potato masher to make a pulpy purée.

5 Stir in the onion and garlic, parsley and crème fraîche. Add Tabasco, lemon juice and salt and pepper to taste.

6 Transfer the dip to a serving bowl and serve warm or leave to cool and serve at room temperature.

Hot Chilli Bean Dip

Make this one as hot as you like – the sour cream helps to balance the heat of the chillies. Serve it with tortilla chips or vegetable crudités.

Serves 4

Ingredients

275g/10oz/1½ cups dried pinto beans, soaked overnight and drained
1 bay leaf
45ml/3 tbsp sea salt
15ml/1 tbsp vegetable oil
1 small onion, sliced
1 garlic clove, finely chopped
2–4 canned hot green chillies (optional)
75ml/5 tbsp sour cream, plus extra to garnish
2.5ml/½ tsp ground cumin
hot pepper sauce, to taste
15ml/1 tbsp chopped fresh coriander (cilantro)

Variation

To save time, use 2½ × 400g/14oz cans beans instead of the dried beans.

---

1 Place the beans in a large pan. Add fresh cold water to cover and the bay leaf. Bring to a boil, then cover and simmer for 30 minutes.

2 Add the sea salt and continue simmering for about 30 minutes, or until the beans are tender. (The beans may take up to 30 minutes longer to cook, depending on how long they have been stored.)

3 Drain the cooked beans, reserving 120ml/4fl oz/½ cup of the liquid. Leave both to cool slightly. Discard the bay leaf.

4 Heat the oil in a non-stick frying pan. Add the onion and garlic and cook over low to medium heat, stirring occasionally, for 8–10 minutes, or until just softened and translucent.

5 Combine the beans, onion and garlic mixture, chillies, if using, and the reserved cooking liquid in a food processor or blender. Process until the mixture forms a coarse purée.

6 Transfer to a bowl and stir in the sour cream, cumin and hot pepper sauce to taste. Stir in the chopped coriander, garnish with extra sour cream and serve the dip warm.

CANNELLINI BEAN DIP

This soft bean dip or pâté is good spread on wheaten crackers or toasted muffins. Alternatively, it can be served with wedges of tomato and a crisp green salad.

SERVES 4

INGREDIENTS
400g/14oz can cannellini beans
grated rind and juice of 1 lemon
30ml/2 tbsp olive oil
1 garlic clove, finely chopped
30ml/2 tbsp chopped fresh parsley
red Tabasco sauce, to taste
salt and ground black pepper
cayenne pepper, to garnish

1 Drain the beans in a sieve and rinse them well under cold water. Drain well and transfer to a bowl.

2 Use a potato masher to purée the beans coarsely, then stir in the lemon rind, juice and olive oil. Stir in the chopped garlic and parsley. Add Tabasco sauce, salt and pepper to taste.

3 Spoon the mixture into a small bowl and dust lightly with cayenne pepper. Chill in the refrigerator until ready to serve.

VARIATION
Canned or cooked butter (lima) beans or kidney beans can also be used for this dip.

HUMMUS

This nutritious dip can be served with vegetable crudités or packed into salad-filled pitta, but it is best spread thickly on hot buttered toast.

SERVES 4

INGREDIENTS
400g/14oz can chickpeas, drained
2 garlic cloves
30ml/2 tbsp tahini or smooth peanut butter
60ml/4 tbsp olive oil
juice of 1 lemon
2.5ml/½ tsp cayenne pepper
15ml/1 tbsp sesame seeds
sea salt

1 Rinse the chickpeas well under cold running water, drain thoroughly and place in a food processor or blender with the garlic and a good pinch of sea salt. Process until very finely chopped.

2 Add the tahini or peanut butter and process until fairly smooth. With the motor still running, gradually pour in the oil and lemon juice.

3 Stir in the cayenne pepper and add more salt to taste. If the mixture is too thick, stir in a little cold water. Transfer the purée to a serving bowl.

4 Heat a small non-stick pan and add the sesame seeds. Cook them over a low heat, shaking the pan constantly, for 2–3 minutes, until they are golden brown in colour. Leave them to cool, then sprinkle them over the purée to garnish. Serve the dip at room temperature.

TZATZIKI

This classic Greek dip is a cooling mix of yogurt, cucumber and mint, perfect for a hot summer's day. Serve it with strips of lightly toasted pitta bread.

SERVES 4

INGREDIENTS
1 mini cucumber
4 spring onions (scallions)
1 garlic clove
200ml/7fl oz/scant 1 cup Greek (US strained plain) yogurt
45ml/3 tbsp chopped fresh mint
salt and ground black pepper
fresh mint sprig, to garnish (optional)

1 Trim the ends from the cucumber, then cut it into 5mm/¼in dice. Set aside. Trim the spring onions and garlic, then chop both very finely.

2 Beat the yogurt until smooth, if necessary, then gently stir in the cucumber, onions, garlic and mint.

3 Add salt and plenty of ground black pepper to taste, then transfer the mixture to a serving bowl. Chill until ready to serve and then garnish with a small mint sprig, if you like.

COOK'S TIP
Choose Greek-style yogurt for this dip – it has a higher fat content than most yogurts, but this gives it a deliciously rich, creamy texture.

SOUR CREAM COOLER

This refreshing dip makes the perfect accompaniment to hot and spicy Mexican dishes. Alternatively, serve it as a snack with the fieriest tortilla chips you can find.

SERVES 2

INGREDIENTS
1 small yellow (bell) pepper
2 small tomatoes
30ml/2 tbsp chopped fresh parsley, plus extra to garnish
150ml/¼ pint/⅔ cup sour cream
grated lemon rind, to garnish

1 Halve the yellow pepper lengthways. With a sharp knife, remove the core and scoop out the seeds, then cut the flesh into tiny dice.

2 Cut the tomatoes in half, then use a teaspoon to scoop out and discard the seeds. Cut the tomato flesh into tiny dice.

3 Pour the sour cream into a bowl. Stir the pepper and tomato dice and the chopped parsley into the sour cream and mix well.

4 Spoon the dip into a small bowl, cover with clear film (plastic wrap) and chill in the refrigerator until required. Garnish with grated lemon rind and parsley just before serving.

COOK'S TIP
Use finely diced avocado or cucumber in place of the (bell) pepper or tomato.

SATAY DIP

This is a deliciously pungent sauce that tastes great served with spicy chicken on skewers but is equally good as a dip for crisp vegetables.

SERVES 6

INGREDIENTS
150g/5oz/generous 1 cup roasted, unsalted peanuts
45ml/3 tbsp vegetable oil
1 small onion, coarsely chopped
2 garlic cloves, crushed
1 fresh red chilli, seeded and chopped
2.5cm/1in piece of fresh root ginger, peeled and chopped
5cm/2in piece of lemon grass, coarsely chopped
2.5ml/½ tsp ground cumin
45ml/3 tbsp chopped fresh coriander (cilantro) stalks
15ml/1 tbsp sesame oil
175ml/6fl oz/¾ cup coconut milk
30ml/2 tbsp thick soy sauce (kecap manis)
10ml/2 tsp lime juice
salt and ground black pepper
lime wedges and chives, to garnish

1 Rub the husks from the peanuts in a clean dishtowel. Place the nuts in a food processor or blender with 30ml/2 tbsp vegetable oil and process to a smooth paste. Transfer to a bowl.

2 Place the next seven ingredients in the food processor or blender and process to a fairly smooth paste.

3 Heat the remaining vegetable oil with the sesame oil in a frying pan and add the onion paste. Cook over a low heat for 10–15 minutes, stirring occasionally.

4 Stir in the peanuts, coconut milk, soy sauce and lime juice and heat through, stirring constantly.

5 Add salt and ground black pepper to taste, then spoon the mixture into small bowls or saucers. Serve warm, garnished with lime wedges and chives.

Red Onion Raita

Raita is a traditional Indian side dish served as an accompaniment for hot curries.
It is also delicious served with poppadums as a dip.

Serves 4

Ingredients
5ml/1 tsp cumin seeds
1 small garlic clove
1 small fresh green chilli
1 large red onion
150ml/¼ pint/⅔ cup natural (plain) yogurt
30ml/2 tbsp chopped fresh coriander (cilantro), plus extra to garnish
2.5ml/½ tsp sugar
salt

1 Heat a small frying pan and dry-fry the cumin seeds, shaking the pan frequently, for 1–2 minutes, until they release their aroma and begin to pop.

2 Transfer the seeds to a mortar and lightly crush them with a pestle or flatten them with the heel of a heavy-bladed knife.

3 Finely chop the garlic. Cut the chilli in half lengthways and scrape out the seeds and membranes, then chop the flesh finely, along with the red onion.

4 Place the natural yogurt in a bowl and add the garlic, chilli and red onion, along with the crushed cumin seeds and fresh coriander. Stir to combine.

5 Add sugar and salt to taste. Spoon the raita into a small bowl, cover with clear film (plastic wrap) and chill in the refrigerator until ready to serve. Garnish with extra coriander before serving.

VARIATION
Red onions have a milder, sweeter flavour than most other varieties, but you could also use a Vidalia onion or 2–3 shallots. However, the attractive colouring of the dip will be lost.

Lemon & Coconut Dhal

A deliciously warm, spicy dish, this can be served either as a dip with poppadums or naan bread or as an accompaniment to an Indian-style main dish.

SERVES 8

INGREDIENTS
30ml/2 tbsp sunflower oil
5cm/2in piece of fresh root ginger, finely chopped
1 onion, finely chopped
2 garlic cloves, finely chopped
2 small fresh red chillies, seeded and finely chopped
5ml/1 tsp cumin seeds
150g/5oz/⅔ cup red lentils
250ml/8fl oz/1 cup water
15ml/1 tbsp hot curry paste
200ml/7fl oz/scant 1 cup coconut cream
juice of 1 lemon
handful of fresh coriander (cilantro) leaves
25g/1oz/¼ cup flaked (sliced) almonds
salt and ground black pepper

VARIATION
Try making this dhal with yellow split peas: they take longer to cook and a little extra water has to be added but the result is equally tasty.

1 Heat the oil in a large, shallow pan. Add the chopped ginger, onion, garlic, chillies and cumin seeds. Cook over a low heat, stirring occasionally, for about 5 minutes, until softened but not coloured.

2 Stir the lentils, water and curry paste into the pan. Bring to the boil, cover and cook gently over a low heat for 15–20 minutes, stirring the mixture occasionally, until the lentils are just tender but not yet broken.

3 Stir in all but 30ml/2 tbsp of the coconut cream. Bring to the boil and cook, uncovered, for a further 15–20 minutes, or until thick and pulpy. Remove from the heat, then stir in the lemon juice and the whole coriander leaves. Season with salt and pepper to taste.

4 Heat a large frying pan and dry-fry the flaked almonds for 1–2 minutes on each side, until golden brown. Stir about three-quarters of the toasted almonds into the dhal.

5 Transfer the dhal to a serving bowl and swirl in the remaining coconut cream. Sprinkle the reserved almonds on top and serve warm.

FONDUTA

This delicious cheese dip needs only some warm ciabatta bread or focaccia, a crisp salad and some robust red wine to complete the meal.

SERVES 4

INGREDIENTS
225g/8oz/2 cups diced Fontina or Gruyère cheese
250ml/8fl oz/1 cup milk
15g/½oz/1 tbsp butter
2 eggs, lightly beaten
ground black pepper

1 Put the cheese in a bowl with the milk and leave to soak for 2–3 hours. Transfer to a double boiler or a heatproof bowl set over a pan of simmering water.

2 Add the butter and eggs and cook gently, stirring until the cheese has melted to a smooth sauce with the consistency of custard.

3 Remove from the heat and season with pepper. Transfer to a serving dish and serve immediately.

COOK'S TIP
Be careful not to overheat the sauce, or the eggs might curdle. A very gentle heat will produce a lovely smooth sauce.

Spicy Tuna Dip

A piquant dip, delicious served with breadsticks – use more oil to turn it into a sauce, less for filling hard-boiled eggs, tomatoes or celery sticks.

Serves 6

Ingredients
90g/3¼oz can tuna in oil
good quality, light olive oil
3 hard-boiled eggs
75g/3oz/¾ cup pitted green olives
50g/2oz can anchovy fillets, drained
45ml/3 tbsp capers, drained
10ml/2 tsp Dijon mustard
ground black pepper
fresh parsley sprigs, to garnish

1 Drain the oil from the tuna into a small bowl and supplement the quantity to 90ml/6 tbsp with olive oil.

2 Halve the hard-boiled eggs, remove the yolks and then place in a food processor or blender. Discard the whites or use in another dish.

3 Reserve a few olives for garnishing, then add the rest to the processor or blender together with the remaining ingredients. Process together until smooth. Season with pepper to taste. Spoon into a bowl and garnish with the reserved olives and the parsley sprigs.

TAHINI YOGURT DIP WITH SESAME SEED FALAFEL

Sesame seeds are used to give a crunchy coating to these spicy bean patties. Serve with the tahini yogurt dip and warm pitta bread as a light lunch or supper dish.

SERVES 4

INGREDIENTS
250g/9oz/1⅓ cups dried chickpeas
2 garlic cloves, crushed
1 fresh red chilli, seeded and thinly sliced
5ml/1 tsp ground coriander
5ml/1 tsp ground cumin
15ml/1 tbsp chopped fresh mint
15ml/1 tbsp chopped fresh parsley
2 spring onions (scallions), finely chopped
1 large (US extra large) egg, beaten
sesame seeds, for coating
sunflower oil, for frying
salt and ground black pepper

FOR THE TAHINI YOGURT DIP
30ml/2 tbsp light tahini
200g/7oz/scant 1 cup natural (plain) live yogurt
5ml/1 tsp cayenne pepper, plus extra for sprinkling
15ml/1 tbsp chopped fresh mint
1 spring onion (scallion), thinly sliced

VARIATION
The dip is also marvellous served with vegetable crisps (chips).

1 Place the chickpeas in a bowl, cover with cold water and leave to soak overnight. Drain and rinse the chickpeas, then place in a pan and cover with cold water. Bring to the boil and boil rapidly for 10 minutes, then reduce the heat and simmer for 1½–2 hours, or until tender.

2 Meanwhile, make the tahini yogurt dip. Mix together the tahini, yogurt, cayenne pepper and mint in a small bowl. Sprinkle the spring onion and extra cayenne pepper on top and chill until required.

3 Combine the chickpeas with the garlic, chilli, ground spices, herbs, spring onions and seasoning, then mix in the egg. Place in a food processor and process until the mixture forms a coarse paste. If the paste seems too soft, chill it for 30 minutes.

4 Form the chilled chickpea paste into 12 patties with your hands, then roll each one in the sesame seeds to coat thoroughly.

5 Heat enough oil to cover the base of a large frying pan. Cook the falafel, in batches if necessary, for 6 minutes, turning once. Serve immediately with the tahini yogurt dip.

RELISHES
& CHUTNEYS

It's a myth that preserving is an art. The preparation of a simple chutney or relish is within the reach of any cook, and it's certainly a worthwhile task. When you line up the jars on your kitchen shelf – and maybe even give a few jars as gifts – you'll feel a real glow of satisfaction. Once you open the jar, the benefits are even more evident: a spoonful of fruity, spicy chutney or relish can lift the appetite and transform the flavour of the plainest hunk of bread and cheese or meat into a tasty lunch. If your taste is for the exotic, Indian curries are traditionally accompanied by a spoonful of fruity chutney, often made with mangoes and spiced with chilli or ginger. Almost any cooked meat will benefit from a spicy spoonful of rich chutney on the side – every burger needs its relish, and even a plateful of fresh oysters can be lifted to another level by adding a spoonful of Bloody Mary Relish. The flavour of most chutneys and relishes improves with keeping, so, however tempting it may be to open the jars, store them carefully for 3–4 weeks before doing so to enjoy them at their best.

GINGER, DATE & APPLE CHUTNEY

Serve this rich, spicy chutney with cold sliced meats or pies. Make it well ahead to allow time for the warming flavours to mature, and store in airtight jars.

MAKES ABOUT 1.3–1.6KG/3–3½LB

INGREDIENTS
450g/1lb cooking apples
450g/1lb/3¼ cups dates, stoned (pitted)
225g/8oz/1 cup dried apricots
115g/4oz glacé (candied) ginger, chopped
1–2 garlic cloves, crushed
225g/8oz/1⅓ cups sultanas (golden raisins)
225g/8oz/1 cup light muscovado (brown) sugar
5ml/1 tsp salt
300ml/½ pint/1¼ cups white malt vinegar

1 Peel, core and chop the apples into small chunks. Coarsely chop the dates and dried apricots.

2 Put all the fruit together in a large pan, with all the remaining ingredients. Cover and simmer gently for 10–15 minutes, or until the fruit is tender and the liquid is well reduced.

3 Spoon into clean screw-top jars. Seal the jars and label them. Store in a cool place for 4 weeks before using.

Curried Fruit Chutney

A piquant fruit chutney that is delicious with cold sliced turkey and ham, this a great choice for traditional Christmas catering, but is also wonderful in the summer.

MAKES ABOUT 1.2KG/2½LB

INGREDIENTS
225g/8oz/1 cup dried apricots
225g/8oz/1⅓ cups dried peaches
225g/8oz/1⅓ cups dates, stoned (pitted)
225g/8oz/1⅓ cups raisins
1–2 garlic cloves, crushed
225g/8oz/1 cup light muscovado (brown) sugar
300ml/½ pint/1¼ cups white malt vinegar
300ml/½ pint/1¼ cups water
5ml/1 tsp salt
10ml/2 tsp mild curry powder

1 Put all the ingredients in a large pan, cover and simmer very gently for about 10–15 minutes, or until tender.

2 Leave to cool slightly, then transfer the mixture to a food processor, in batches, and chop or mince (grind) coarsely.

3 Spoon into clean screw-top jars. Seal the jars and label them. Store in a cool place for 4 weeks before using.

CRANBERRY & ORANGE RELISH

This colourful, festive relish is excellent served with roast turkey, goose or duck. It is also the perfect accompaniment to traditional cold game pies.

MAKES ABOUT 450G/1LB

INGREDIENTS
225g/8oz/2 cups fresh cranberries
1 onion, finely chopped
150ml/¼ pint/⅔ cup port
115g/4oz/generous ½ cup caster (superfine) sugar
finely grated rind and juice of 1 orange
2.5ml/½ tsp English (hot) mustard powder
1.5ml/¼ tsp ground ginger
1.5ml/¼ tsp ground cinnamon
5ml/1 tsp cornflour (cornstarch)
50g/2oz/scant ½ cup raisins

1 Put the cranberries, onion, port and sugar in a pan. Cook the mixture gently for 10 minutes, or until tender.

2 Mix the orange juice, mustard powder, ginger, cinnamon and cornflour together. Stir them into the cranberries.

3 Add the raisins and orange rind. Allow to thicken over the heat, stirring, and then simmer for 2 minutes. Cool, cover and chill ready for serving.

ANCHOVY & PARSLEY RELISH

This is a fabulous combination for a flavourful relish to serve as a topping for fresh vegetables. Serve these fresh-tasting nibbles as an appetizer or with drinks.

MAKES ABOUT 225G/8OZ

INGREDIENTS
50g/2oz/1 cup flat leaf parsley leaves
50g/2oz/½ cup black olives, pitted
25g/1oz/½ cup sun-dried tomatoes
4 canned anchovy fillets, drained
50g/2oz red onion, finely chopped
25g/1oz small pickled capers, rinsed
1 garlic clove, finely chopped
15ml/1 tbsp olive oil
juice of ½ lime
1.5ml/¼ tsp ground black pepper
a selection of cherry tomatoes, radishes, celery and cucumber, to serve

1 Coarsely chop the parsley, black olives, sun-dried tomatoes and anchovy fillets and mix in a bowl with the red onion, capers, garlic, olive oil, lime juice and ground black pepper.

2 Halve the cherry tomatoes and radishes, chop the celery into bitesize chunks and cut the cucumber into 1cm/½in slices. Top each of the prepared vegetables with a generous amount of relish and serve immediately.

PICKLED PEACH & CHILLI CHUTNEY

This is a really spicy, rich chutney that is great served with cold roast meats, such as ham, pork or turkey. It is also good with a strong farmhouse Cheddar cheese.

MAKES ABOUT 450G/1LB

INGREDIENTS
475ml/16fl oz/2 cups cider vinegar
275g/10oz/1¼ cups light muscovado (brown) sugar
225g/8oz/1½ cups stoned (pitted) and finely chopped dried dates
5ml/1 tsp ground allspice
5ml/1 tsp ground mace
450g/1lb ripe peaches, stoned (pitted)
3 onions, thinly sliced
4 fresh red chillies, seeded and finely chopped
4 garlic cloves, crushed
5cm/2in piece of fresh root ginger, finely grated
5ml/1 tsp salt

1 Place the vinegar, sugar, chopped dates and spices in a large, heavy pan and bring to the boil, stirring occasionally.

2 Cut the peaches into small chunks. Add to the pan with all the remaining ingredients and return the mixture to the boil. Lower the heat and simmer for 40–50 minutes, or until thick. Stir frequently to prevent the mixture from burning on the base of the pan.

3 Spoon the chutney into clean, sterilized jars and seal. When cold, store the jars in the refrigerator and use within 2 months.

COOK'S TIP
To test the consistency of the finished chutney before bottling, spoon a little of the mixture on to a plate: the chutney is ready once it holds its shape.

Nectarine Relish with Chilli & Rosemary

This sweet and tangy fruit relish goes very well with hot roast meats and game birds, such as pork, chicken, guinea fowl and pheasant.

Makes about 450g/1lb

Ingredients
45ml/3 tbsp olive oil
2 Spanish (Bermuda) onions, thinly sliced
1 fresh green chilli, seeded and finely chopped
5ml/1 tsp finely chopped fresh rosemary
2 bay leaves
450g/1lb nectarines, stoned (pitted) and diced
150g/5oz/1 cup raisins
10ml/2 tsp crushed coriander seeds
350g/12 oz/1½ cups demerara (raw) sugar
200ml/7fl oz/scant 1 cup red wine vinegar

1 Heat the oil in a large, heavy pan. Add the sliced onions, chopped chilli, rosemary and bay leaves. Cook, stirring frequently, for 15–20 minutes, or until the onions are soft but not browned.

2 Add all the remaining ingredients and gradually bring to the boil, stirring frequently. Lower the heat and simmer for 1 hour, or until the relish is thick and sticky, stirring occasionally.

3 Remove and discard the bay leaves. Spoon into sterilized jars, and seal. Cool, then chill. The relish will keep in the refrigerator for up to 5 months.

Variation
You can substitute small, white-fleshed peaches for the nectarines. Peel them by blanching briefly in hot water, then rinsing in cold water – the skins should slip off easily.

Papaya & Lemon Relish

This chunky relish is best made with a firm, unripe papaya. Leave for a week before eating to allow all the flavours to mellow. Store unopened jars in a cool place.

MAKES ABOUT 450G/1LB

INGREDIENTS
1 large unripe papaya
1 onion, thinly sliced
40g/1½oz/⅓ cup raisins
250ml/8fl oz/1 cup red wine vinegar
juice of 2 lemons
150ml/¼ pint/⅔ cup elderflower cordial
150g/5oz/¾ cup golden granulated sugar
1 cinnamon stick
1 fresh bay leaf
2.5ml/½ tsp hot paprika
2.5ml/½ tsp salt

1 Peel the papaya and cut in half lengthways. Remove the seeds with a teaspoon. Use a sharp knife to cut the flesh into small chunks and place them in a pan. Add the onion slices and raisins, then stir in the red wine vinegar. Bring the liquid to the boil, then immediately lower the heat and simmer gently for 10 minutes.

2 Add all the remaining ingredients to the pan and bring to the boil, stirring constantly. Check that all the sugar has dissolved, then lower the heat and simmer for 50–60 minutes, or until the relish is thick and syrupy.

3 Remove and discard the bay leaf. Ladle the relish into hot, sterilized jars. Seal and label, then store in a cool, dark place for 1 week before using. Keep the relish chilled after opening.

PIQUANT PINEAPPLE RELISH

This fruity sweet-and-sour relish is excellent served with grilled chicken, gammon or bacon. It also has a special affinity with pork chops cooked on the barbecue.

SERVES 4

INGREDIENTS

400g/14oz can crushed pineapple in natural juice
30ml/2 tbsp light muscovado (brown) sugar
30ml/2 tbsp wine vinegar
1 garlic clove, finely chopped
4 spring onions (scallions), finely chopped
2 fresh red chillies, seeded and chopped
10 fresh basil leaves, finely shredded
salt and ground black pepper

1 Drain the pineapple well and reserve 60ml/4 tbsp of the juice. Set the pineapple pieces aside.

2 Place the reserved juice in a small pan with the sugar and wine vinegar, then heat gently, stirring, until the sugar has completely dissolved. Remove the pan from the heat and season with salt and pepper to taste. Leave to cool slightly.

3 Place the pineapple, garlic, spring onions and chillies in a bowl. Mix well and stir in the juice. Leave to cool for 5 minutes, then stir in the basil and serve.

COOK'S TIP
This relish tastes extra special when made with chopped, fresh pineapple. Reserve 60ml/4 tbsp juice when chopping the pineapple.

Spicy Corn Relish

Serve this simple spicy relish with bowls of Red Onion Raita, Sweet Mango Relish and a plateful of crisp onion bhajis for a fabulous Indian-style appetizer.

SERVES 4

INGREDIENTS
30ml/2 tbsp vegetable oil
1 large onion, chopped
1 fresh red chilli, seeded and chopped
2 garlic cloves, chopped
5ml/1 tsp black mustard seeds
10ml/2 tsp hot curry powder
320g/11¼oz can corn, drained
grated rind and juice of 1 lime
45ml/3 tbsp chopped fresh coriander (cilantro)
salt and ground black pepper

1 Heat the oil in a large, heavy frying pan and cook the onion, chilli and garlic over a high heat for 5 minutes, until the onions are just beginning to brown.

2 Stir in the mustard seeds and curry powder, then cook for 2 minutes more, stirring constantly, until the seeds start to splutter and give off their aroma and the onions are browned.

3 Remove the onion and spice mixture from the heat and leave to cool completely. Transfer the mixture to a glass bowl.

4 Add the drained corn to the bowl containing the onion mixture and stir to mix. Add the lime rind and juice, coriander and seasoning. Mix well, then cover and serve at room temperature.

COOK'S TIP
Use frozen rather than canned corn, as the kernels are plump and moist.

Sweet Mango Relish

Stir a spoonful of this relish into soups and stews for added flavour or serve it with a wedge of Cheddar cheese and chunks of crusty bread.

MAKES 750ML/1¼ PINTS/3 CUPS

INGREDIENTS
2 large mangoes
1 cooking apple, peeled and chopped
2 shallots, chopped
4cm/1½in piece of fresh root ginger, chopped
2 garlic cloves, crushed
115g/4oz/⅔ cup small sultanas (golden raisins)
2 star anise
5ml/1 tsp ground cinnamon
2.5ml/½ tsp dried chilli flakes
2.5ml/½ tsp salt
175ml/6fl oz/¾ cup cider vinegar
130g/4½oz/generous ½ cup light muscovado (brown) sugar

1 One at a time, hold the mangoes upright on a chopping board and use a large knife to slice the flesh away from each side of the stone (pit). Using a smaller knife, carefully trim away any flesh still clinging to the top and bottom of the stone.

2 Score the flesh of the mango halves deeply, without cutting through the skin: make parallel incisions about 1cm/½in apart, then turn and cut in the opposite direction. Carefully turn the skin inside out and slice the dice away from the skin.

3 Place the diced mango, chopped apple, shallots, ginger, garlic and sultanas in a large, heavy pan. Add the star anise, cinnamon, chilli, salt, vinegar and sugar. Bring to the boil, stirring constantly, until the sugar has dissolved. Reduce the heat and simmer gently for a further 4 minutes, stirring occasionally, until the chutney has reduced and thickened.

4 Leave to cool for about 5 minutes, then ladle into warm, sterilized jars. Cool completely, cover and label. Store in the refrigerator for up to 2 months..

CHILLI & BASIL RELISH

This spicy relish will keep for at least a week in the refrigerator. Serve it at barbecues with sausages, chicken, steak or burgers in a sesame bun.

SERVES 8

INGREDIENTS
6 tomatoes
30ml/2 tbsp olive oil
1 onion, coarsely chopped
1 red (bell) pepper, seeded and chopped
2 garlic cloves, chopped
5ml/1 tsp ground cinnamon
5ml/1 tsp chilli flakes
5ml/1 tsp ground ginger
5ml/1 tsp salt
2.5ml/½ tsp ground black pepper
75g/3oz/6 tbsp light muscovado (brown) sugar
75ml/5 tbsp cider vinegar
handful of fresh basil leaves, chopped

COOK'S TIP
This relish thickens slightly on cooling, so do not worry if the mixture seems a little runny at the end of step 6.

1 Skewer each of the tomatoes, in turn, on a metal fork and hold in a gas flame for 1–2 minutes, turning, until the skin splits and wrinkles. Slip off the tomato skins, then coarsely chop the flesh.

2 Heat the olive oil in a heavy pan. Add the chopped onion, red pepper and garlic to the pan.

3 Cook gently for 5–8 minutes, or until the pepper is softened. Add the chopped tomatoes, cover and cook for a further 5 minutes, until the tomatoes release their juices.

4 Stir in the cinnamon, chilli flakes, ginger, salt, pepper, sugar and vinegar. Bring gently to the boil, stirring, until the sugar dissolves.

5 Simmer, uncovered, for 20 minutes, or until the mixture is pulpy. Stir in the basil leaves and check the seasoning.

6 Leave to cool completely, then transfer to a glass jar or a plastic container with a tightly fitting lid. Store, covered, in the refrigerator.

BLOODY MARY RELISH

Serve this perfect party relish with sticks of crunchy cucumber or, on a really special occasion, with freshly shucked oysters as a dinner party appetizer.

SERVES 2

INGREDIENTS
4 ripe tomatoes
1 celery stalk
1 garlic clove
2 spring onions (scallions)
45ml/3 tbsp tomato juice
Worcestershire sauce, to taste
red Tabasco sauce, to taste
10ml/2 tsp horseradish sauce
15ml/1 tbsp vodka
juice of 1 lemon
salt and ground black pepper

1 Halve the tomatoes, celery and garlic. Trim the spring onions. Process the vegetables in a food processor or blender until very finely chopped. Transfer the mixture to a bowl.

2 Stir in the tomato juice and add a few drops of Worcestershire sauce and Tabasco to taste.

3 Stir in the horseradish sauce, vodka and lemon juice. Season with salt and ground black pepper to taste.

TART TOMATO RELISH

The whole lime used in this recipe adds a pleasantly sour aftertaste. This is delicious served with grilled or roast pork or lamb and goes well with creamy cheeses.

SERVES 4

INGREDIENTS
1 lime
450g/1lb cherry tomatoes
115g/4oz/½ cup dark muscovado (molasses) sugar
105ml/7 tbsp white wine vinegar
5ml/1 tsp salt
2 pieces of preserved stem ginger, chopped

1 Slice the lime thinly, then chop it into small pieces; do not remove the rind. Place the whole tomatoes, sugar, vinegar, salt, ginger and lime together in a pan.

2 Bring to the boil, stirring until the sugar dissolves, then simmer rapidly for 45 minutes. Stir frequently until the liquid has evaporated and the relish is thickened and pulpy.

3 Leave the relish to cool for about 5 minutes, then spoon it into clean jars. Cool completely, cover and store in the refrigerator for up to 1 month.

VARIATION
If you like, use ordinary tomatoes, coarsely chopped, in place of the cherry tomatoes used here.

TOFFEE ONION RELISH

Slow, gentle cooking reduces the onions to a soft, caramelized golden brown relish. It is ideal with a mature cheese in a ploughman's lunch and is great with quiche.

SERVES 4

INGREDIENTS
3 large onions
50g/2oz/¼ cup butter
30ml/2 tbsp olive oil
30ml/2 tbsp light muscovado (brown) sugar
30ml/2 tbsp pickled capers
30ml/2 tbsp chopped fresh parsley
salt and ground black pepper

1 Peel the onions and cut them in half vertically through the core, then slice them very thinly.

2 Heat the butter and oil together in a large, heavy pan. Add the sliced onions and sugar and cook very gently for about 30 minutes over a low heat, stirring occasionally, until the onions are reduced to a soft rich-brown, toffee-like mixture.

3 Coarsely chop the capers and stir into the browned onion mixture. Leave to cool completely and transfer to a bowl.

4 Stir in the chopped parsley and add salt and freshly ground black pepper to taste. Cover and chill until ready to serve.

VARIATION
Try making this recipe with red onions or shallots for a subtle variation in flavour.

Red Onion Marmalade

This is a rich and delicious marmalade, and makes a particularly good accompaniment to grilled salmon, especially when cooked on the barbecue.

SERVES 4

INGREDIENTS
5 red onions
50g/2oz/¼ cup butter
175ml/6fl oz/¾ cup red wine vinegar
50ml/2fl oz/¼ cup crème de cassis
50ml/2fl oz/¼ cup grenadine
50ml/2fl oz/¼ cup red wine
salt and ground black pepper

1 Remove the skins from the red onions and slice them finely. Melt the butter in a large, heavy pan and add the sliced onions. Sauté the onions for 5 minutes, or until golden brown.

2 Stir in the wine vinegar, crème de cassis, grenadine and wine and continue to cook for about 10 minutes, or until the liquid has almost entirely evaporated and the onions are glazed. Season well with salt and freshly ground black pepper.

COOK'S TIP
If serving this marmalade with salmon cooked on the barbecue, try to find fillets or steaks that are at least 2.5cm/1in thick. Brush the fish with olive oil, season with salt and ground black pepper, and cook on a medium barbecue for about 6–8 minutes, turning once during cooking. Keep the marmalade warm on the side of the barbecue.

OLD-FASHIONED PICKLE

This simple, old-fashioned pickle is absolutely delicious with cold meats or cheese, with a hunk of fresh crusty bread and butter on the side.

MAKES ABOUT 1.3–1.6KG/3–3½LB

INGREDIENTS
900g/2lb cucumbers, scrubbed and cut in 5mm/¼in slices
4 onions, very thinly sliced
30ml/2 tbsp salt
350ml/12fl oz/1½ cups cider vinegar
300g/11oz/generous 1½ cups sugar
30ml/2 tbsp mustard seeds
30ml/2 tbsp celery seeds
1.5ml/¼ tsp turmeric
1.5ml/¼ tsp cayenne

1 Put the sliced cucumbers and onions in a large bowl and sprinkle with the salt. Mix well. Cover loosely and leave to stand for 3 hours. Drain the vegetables. Rinse well under cold running water and then drain again.

2 Combine the remaining ingredients in a large, non-reactive saucepan and bring to the boil. Add the drained cucumbers and onions. Reduce the heat and simmer for 2–3 minutes. Do not boil, or the pickles will be limp.

3 Spoon the hot vegetables into warm, sterilized jars. Add enough of the liquid to come to 1cm/½in from the top and seal with a vinegar-proof lid. Leave to cool, then label; and store in a cool, dark place for at least 4 weeks before opening.

Apple & Red Onion Marmalade

This marmalade chutney is good enough to eat on its own. Serve it with good quality pork sausages for thoroughly modern hot dogs, or in a ham sandwich.

Makes about 450g/1lb

Ingredients
60ml/4 tbsp extra virgin olive oil
900g/2lb red onions, thinly sliced
75g/3oz/6 tbsp demerara (raw) sugar
2 Cox's Orange Pippin or other crisp, sweet apples
90ml/6 tbsp cider vinegar

1 Heat the olive oil in a large, heavy pan. Add the onions and cook over a low heat, stirring occasionally, for 5 minutes.

2 Stir in the demerara sugar and cook, uncovered, over a medium heat for about 40 minutes, stirring occasionally, or until the onions have softened.

3 Peel, core and grate the apples. Add them to the pan with the vinegar and continue to cook for 20 minutes, or until the chutney is thick and sticky.

4 Spoon into warm, sterilized jars and seal with vinegar-proof lids. (Proper preserving jars, such as Kilner (Mason) jars are ideal, as they are designed to seal securely with a ring gasket.) Leave to cool, then label and store in the refrigerator for up to 1 month.

CHRISTMAS CHUTNEY

This savoury mixture of spices and dried fruit takes its inspiration from mincemeat, and makes a delicious traditional addition to a seasonal buffet. Serve with cold meats.

MAKES ABOUT 1–1.6KG/2¼–3½LB

INGREDIENTS
450g/1lb cooking apples, peeled, cored and chopped
500g/1¼lb/3⅓ cups luxury mixed dried fruit
grated rind of 1 orange
30ml/2 tbsp mixed (apple pie) spice
150ml/¼ pint/⅔ cup cider vinegar
350g/12oz/1½ cups light muscovado (brown) sugar

1 Place the chopped apples, dried fruit and grated orange rind in a large, heavy pan. Stir in the mixed spice, cider vinegar and sugar. Heat the ingredients gently, stirring until all the sugar has dissolved.

2 Bring to the boil, then lower the heat and simmer the mixture for about 40–45 minutes, stirring occasionally, until thick.

3 Ladle into warm, sterilized jars, cover and seal. Keep in a cool dark place for 1 month before using. Store in the refrigerator after opening.

COOK'S TIP
Stir frequently towards the end of the cooking time, as it tends to catch on the base of the pan.

Fig & Date Chutney

This recipe is usually made with dried figs and dates, but fresh fruit provides a superb flavour and texture. It is the perfect accompaniment to all kinds of cheeses.

MAKES ABOUT 450G/1LB

INGREDIENTS
1 orange
5 large fresh figs, coarsely chopped
350g/12oz/2½ cups fresh dates, peeled, stoned (pitted) and chopped
2 onions, chopped
5cm/2in piece of fresh root ginger, peeled and finely grated
5ml/1 tsp dried crushed chillies
300g/11oz/generous 1½ cups golden granulated sugar
300ml/½ pint/1¼ cups spiced preserving vinegar
2.5ml/½ tsp salt

1 Finely grate the rind of the orange, then cut off the remaining pith. Cut between the membranes to separate the segments.

2 Place the orange segments in a large, heavy pan with the chopped figs and dates. Add the rind, then stir in the remaining ingredients. Bring to the boil, stirring until the sugar has dissolved, then lower the heat and simmer gently for 1 hour, or until thickened and pulpy, stirring frequently.

3 Spoon into hot sterilized jars. Seal while the chutney is still hot, and label when cold. Store in a cool dark place for at least 1 week before using. Keep opened jars in the refrigerator.

PINEAPPLE & MINT CHUTNEY

This refreshing, light fruit chutney has a wonderfully fresh flavour; it is good with rich meat dishes, particularly lamb, chicken or pork.

MAKES ABOUT 1KG/2¼LB

INGREDIENTS
250ml/8fl oz/1 cup raspberry vinegar
250ml/8fl oz/1 cup dry white wine
1 small pineapple, peeled and chopped
2 medium-size oranges, peeled and chopped
2 eating apples, peeled and chopped
1 red (bell) pepper, seeded and diced
1½ onions, finely chopped
60ml/4 tbsp clear honey
pinch of salt
1 whole clove
4 black peppercorns
30ml/2 tbsp chopped fresh mint

1 Combine the raspberry vinegar and white wine in a large pan and bring to the boil. Boil for 3 minutes.

2 Add the remaining ingredients, except the mint, and stir to blend. Simmer gently for about 30 minutes, stirring occasionally.

3 Transfer to a strainer set over a large bowl and drain, pressing down with the back of a spoon to extract the liquid. Remove and discard the clove and peppercorns. Set the fruit mixture aside in another bowl.

4 Return the strained juice to the pan and boil until reduced by two-thirds. Pour the liquid over the fruit mixture.

5 Stir in the mint and cover with clear film (plastic wrap). Leave to stand for about 6–8 hours before serving.

MANGO CHUTNEY

This classic chutney is frequently served with curries and Indian poppadums, but it is also delicious with baked ham or a traditional cheese ploughman's lunch.

MAKES ABOUT 450G/1LB

INGREDIENTS
3 firm green mangoes
150ml/¼ pint/⅔ cup cider vinegar
130g/4½ oz/generous ½ cup light muscovado (brown) sugar
1 small red finger chilli or jalapeño chilli, split
2.5cm/1in piece of fresh root ginger, peeled and finely chopped
1 garlic clove, finely chopped
5 cardamom pods, bruised
2.5ml/½ tsp coriander seeds, crushed
1 bay leaf
2.5ml/½ tsp salt

1 Peel the mangoes and cut the flesh off the stone (pit). Slice them lengthways, then cut into small chunks or wedges.

2 Place these in a large pan, add the vinegar and cover with a lid. Cook over a low heat for 10 minutes.

3 Stir in the muscovado sugar, chilli, ginger, garlic, bruised cardamom pods and coriander seeds. Add the bay leaf and salt. Gradually bring to the boil, stirring the mixture frequently.

4 Lower the heat and simmer, uncovered, for 30 minutes, or until the mixture is thick and syrupy. Remove the cardamom pods, if you like, and remove and discard the bay leaf.

5 Ladle the chutney into hot, sterilized jars. Leave to cool, then seal and label. Store in a cool, dark place for at least 1 week before eating. Keep in the refrigerator after opening.

Roasted Red Pepper & Chilli Jelly

The hint of chilli in this glowing red jelly makes it ideal for spicing up hot or cold roast meat. The jelly is also good stirred into sauces to add an extra kick.

MAKES ABOUT 900G/2LB

INGREDIENTS

8 red (bell) peppers, quartered and seeded
4 fresh red chillies, halved and seeded
1 onion, coarsely chopped
2 garlic cloves, coarsely chopped
250ml/8fl oz/1 cup water
250ml/8fl oz/1 cup white wine vinegar
7.5ml/1½ tsp salt
450g/1lb/2¼ cups preserving sugar
13g/⅓oz sachet (envelope) powdered pectin (about 25ml/1½ tbsp)

COOK'S TIP
It is not essential to use preserving sugar, but it produces less scum and so avoids the need to keep skimming the mixture. When buying preserving sugar, check that it does not already include any pectin – some brands do.

1 Place the peppers, skin-side up, on a rack in a grill (broiler) pan. Grill (broil) until the skins blister and blacken. Place in a plastic bag, seal the top and leave until cool enough to handle, then remove the skins.

2 Process the red peppers with the chillies, onion, garlic and water in a food processor or blender. Press the purée through a nylon sieve set over a bowl, pressing hard with a wooden spoon to extract as much juice as possible. There should be about 750ml/1¼ pints/3 cups.

3 Scrape the purée into a large, stainless steel pan. Add the vinegar and salt. Mix the sugar and pectin in a bowl, then stir into the liquid.

4 Heat gently until both the sugar and pectin have dissolved, then bring to a full rolling boil. Boil, stirring frequently, for exactly 4 minutes.

5 Remove the jelly from the heat and pour into warm, sterilized jars. Leave to cool and set, then cover. Keep opened jars in the refrigerator.

DRESSINGS
& MARINADES

The primary function of dressings and marinades is to add or balance flavour, and this can make all the difference to even the simplest foods. Both are usually based on a mix of oil and an acidic ingredient, such as vinegar or fruit juice, with aromatic additions, such as herbs, garlic or spices for a more individual flavour. Dressings are used to moisten foods, add variety and lift the flavour of any type of salad, from simple green leaves to substantial main meal salads. They are also of benefit to other foods, such as lightly cooked spears of asparagus, pak choi (bok choy), or crudités. Marinades are used not only to add flavour to foods, but can also tenderize meats or add moisture to dry foods, either before cooking or as a baste during cooking. A light Summer Herb Marinade makes the world of difference to the flavour of a simple piece of fish or meat, or try Peppered Citrus Marinade to add a delicious zip to meaty-textured monkfish. The tenderizing effect, caused by the acid content in marinades, is particularly beneficial for tough meats or poultry. A yogurt marinade has a tenderizing effect, too, with the added benefit of forming a deliciously tangy crust on the outside of grilled (broiled) food.

Avocado Dressing with Crudités & Breadsticks

This creamy-textured, delicately flavoured dressing is actually quite light, and also makes an excellent dressing for tomato and seafood salads.

MAKES ABOUT 450ML/³⁄₄ PINT/SCANT 2 CUPS

INGREDIENTS

30ml/2 tbsp wine vinegar
2.5ml/½ tsp salt, or to taste
4ml/¾ tsp ground white pepper
½ red onion, coarsely chopped
45ml/3 tbsp olive oil
1 large ripe avocado, halved and stoned (pitted)
15ml/1 tbsp fresh lemon juice
45ml/3 tbsp natural (plain) yogurt
45ml/3 tbsp water, or as needed
30ml/2 tbsp chopped fresh coriander (cilantro)
raw or briefly cooked cold vegetables and breadsticks, to serve

COOK'S TIP
This versatile dressing need not be limited to serving with crudités and salads. Serve it as a sauce with grilled (broiled) chicken or fish, or use it on sandwiches in place of mayonnaise or mustard, or to provide a cool contrast to any sort of spicy food.

1 Combine the vinegar and salt in a bowl and stir with a fork to dissolve. Stir in the pepper, chopped red onion and olive oil.

2 Scoop the avocado flesh into a food processor or blender. Add the lemon juice and onion mixture and process just enough to blend.

3 Add the yogurt and water and process until the mixture is smooth. If you like, add more water to thin. Adjust the seasoning according to taste.

4 Spoon the mixture into a bowl. Stir in the coriander. Serve immediately with the raw or briefly cooked cold vegetables and breadsticks. If you have to let the dressing stand, cover the bowl tightly with clear film (plastic wrap) to prevent the avocado from turning brown. Do not leave to stand for more than 1 hour.

LIME DRESSING WITH PAK CHOI

For this Thai recipe, the lime dressing is traditionally made using fish sauce, but vegetarians could use mushroom ketchup instead. Beware, this is a fiery dish.

SERVES 4

INGREDIENTS
6 spring onions (scallions)
2 pak choi (bok choy)
30ml/2 tbsp oil
3 fresh red chillies, cut into thin strips
4 garlic cloves, thinly sliced
15ml/1 tbsp crushed peanuts
salt

FOR THE LIME DRESSING
15–30ml/1–2 tbsp Thai fish sauce
30ml/2 tbsp lime juice
250ml/8fl oz/1 cup coconut milk

COOK'S TIP
Coconut milk is available in cans. Alternatively, creamed coconut is available in packets. To use creamed coconut, place about 115g/4oz in a jug (pitcher) and pour over 250ml/8fl oz/1 cup boiling water. Stir well until dissolved.

1 To make the dressing, blend together the fish sauce and lime juice in a bowl, and then stir in the coconut milk.

2 Cut the spring onions diagonally into slices, including all but the tips of the green parts. Keep the white parts separate from the green.

3 Using a large, sharp knife, cut the pak choi into very fine shreds. There is no need to discard the stalks.

4 Heat the oil in a wok and stir-fry the chillies for 2–3 minutes, or until crisp. Transfer to a plate using a slotted spoon. Stir-fry the garlic for 30–60 seconds, or until golden brown, and transfer to the plate with the chillies.

5 Stir-fry the white parts of the spring onions for 2–3 minutes and then add the green parts and stir-fry for 1 minute more. Add to the plate with the chillies and garlic.

6 Bring a large pan of salted water to the boil and add the shredded pak choi. Stir twice and then drain in a sieve or colander immediately.

7 Place the warmed pak choi in a large bowl, add the lime dressing and toss thoroughly to coat.

8 Spoon into a large serving bowl and sprinkle with the crushed peanuts and the stir-fried chilli mixture. Serve either warm or cold, as an accompaniment to rice dishes or as part of a salad.

CREAMY RASPBERRY DRESSING WITH ASPARAGUS

Old-fashioned raspberry vinegar gives this quick and easy dressing a refreshing, tangy fruit flavour – an ideal accompaniment to asparagus. You can cook the asparagus and make the dressing in advance, then chill in the refrigerator until required.

SERVES 4

INGREDIENTS
675g/1½lb thin asparagus spears
115g/4oz/1½ cups fresh raspberries, to garnish

FOR THE CREAMY RASPBERRY DRESSING
30ml/2 tbsp raspberry vinegar
2.5ml/½ tsp salt
5ml/1 tsp Dijon mustard
60ml/4 tbsp crème fraîche or natural (plain) yogurt
ground white pepper

COOK'S TIP
You can make your own raspberry vinegar by adding as many raspberries as you can to a 1 litre/ 1¾ pint/4 cup jug (pitcher) of red wine vinegar. Cover and leave to infuse (steep) for 1 week, then strain and pour into sterilized bottles.

1 Fill a tall pan with water about 10cm/4in deep and bring to the boil. Trim the tough ends of the asparagus spears.

2 Tie the asparagus spears into two bundles. Lower the bundles into the boiling water and cook for 3–5 minutes, or until just tender.

3 Remove the asparagus and immerse it in cold water to stop the cooking. Drain and untie the bundles. Pat dry. Chill for 1 hour.

4 To make the dressing, mix the vinegar and salt in a bowl and stir with a fork until dissolved. Stir in the mustard, crème fraîche or yogurt. Add pepper to taste. Place the asparagus on individual plates and drizzle the dressing across the middle of the spears. Garnish with fresh raspberries.

VARIATION
This dressing would also be delicious served with cold, cooked globe artichokes.

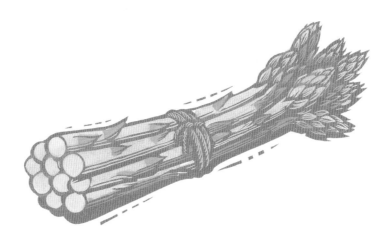

CORIANDER DRESSING WITH CHICKEN SALAD

Serve this salad warm to make the most of the wonderful flavour of chicken cooked on the barbecue and basted with a marinade of coriander, sesame and mustard, and finished with a matching dressing.

SERVES 6

INGREDIENTS
4 medium skinless, boneless chicken breast portions
225g/8oz mangetouts (snow peas)
2 heads decorative lettuce such as lollo rosso or oak leaf
3 carrots, cut into batons
175g/6oz/2¼ cups button (white) mushrooms, sliced
12 cherry tomatoes, halved
6 bacon rashers (strips), fried and chopped
15ml/1 tbsp chopped fresh coriander (cilantro), to garnish

FOR THE CORIANDER DRESSING
120ml/4fl oz/½ cup lemon juice
30ml/2 tbsp wholegrain mustard
250ml/8fl oz/1 cup olive oil
75ml/5 tbsp sesame oil
5ml/1 tsp coriander seeds, crushed

COOK'S TIP
If you have any spare dressing left over, store it in a screw-topped jar in the refrigerator for up to 4 days. Use the dressing for drizzling over other salads.

1 Mix all the dressing ingredients in a bowl. Place the chicken portions in a dish and pour over half the dressing. Marinate overnight in the refrigerator. Store the remaining dressing in the refrigerator.

2 Cook the mangetouts for about 2 minutes in boiling water, then drain and refresh in cold water.

3 Tear the lettuces into small pieces and mix with all the other salad ingredients and the bacon. Arrange in individual bowls.

4 Drain the chicken portions, reserving the marinade. Cook on a medium barbecue or under the grill (broiler) for 10–15 minutes, basting with the marinade and turning once, until cooked through.

5 Slice the chicken on the diagonal into thin pieces. Divide among the bowls of salad and add some of the dressing to each dish. Combine quickly and sprinkle some fresh coriander over each bowl. Serve immediately.

GINGER & LIME MARINADE FOR PRAWNS

This fragrant marinade will guarantee a mouth-watering aroma wafting from the kitchen, and is as delicious with chicken or pork as it is with prawns.

SERVES 4

INGREDIENTS
225g/8oz peeled raw tiger prawns (jumbo shrimp)
⅓ cucumber
15ml/1 tbsp sunflower oil
15ml/1 tbsp sesame seed oil
175g/6oz mangetouts (snow peas), trimmed
4 spring onions (scallions), diagonally sliced
30ml/2 tbsp chopped fresh coriander (cilantro), to garnish

FOR THE GINGER AND LIME MARINADE
15ml/1 tbsp clear honey
15ml/1 tbsp light soy sauce
15ml/1 tbsp dry sherry
2 garlic cloves, crushed
small piece of fresh root ginger, peeled and finely chopped
juice of 1 lime

1 Mix together the marinade ingredients, add the prawns and leave to marinate for 1–2 hours.

2 Prepare the cucumber. Slice it in half lengthways, scoop out the seeds, then slice each half neatly into crescents. Set aside.

3 Heat the sunflower and sesame oils in a large, heavy frying pan or wok. Drain the prawns (reserving the marinade) and stir-fry over a high heat for 4 minutes, or until they begin to turn pink. Add the mangetouts and the cucumber and stir-fry for 2 minutes more.

4 Stir in the reserved marinade, heat through, then stir in the spring onions and sprinkle with chopped fresh coriander to garnish.

PEPPERED CITRUS MARINADE FOR MONKFISH

Monkfish is a firm, meaty fish that cooks well on the barbecue and is always popular because there are no small bones. Serve with a green salad.

SERVES 4

INGREDIENTS
2 monkfish tails, about 350g/12oz each
1 lime
1 lemon
2 oranges
handful of fresh thyme sprigs
30ml/2 tbsp olive oil
15ml/1 tbsp mixed peppercorns, coarsely crushed
salt and ground black pepper

1 Using a sharp kitchen knife, remove any skin from the monkfish tails. Cut the fish carefully down one side of the backbone, sliding the knife between the bone and flesh, to remove the fillet on one side. Turn the fish and repeat on the other side, to remove the second fillet. Repeat on the second tail. Place the four fillets flat on a chopping board.

2 Cut two slices from each of the citrus fruits and arrange them over two of the fillets. Add a few sprigs of fresh thyme, and sprinkle with plenty of salt and ground black pepper. Finely grate the rind from the remaining fruit and sprinkle it over the fish. Lay the other two fillets on top and tie them firmly at intervals.

3 Squeeze the juice from the citrus fruits and mix it with the olive oil and more salt and pepper. Spoon the marinade over the fish. Cover with clear film (plastic wrap) and leave it to marinate in the refrigerator for about 1 hour, turning the fish occasionally and spooning the marinade over it.

4 Drain the monkfish, reserving the marinade, and sprinkle with the crushed peppercorns. Cook on a medium-hot barbecue or under the grill (broiler) for 15–20 minutes, basting with the marinade. Untie and cut in slices to serve.

Orange & Green Peppercorn Marinade for Bass

This is an excellent light marinade for using with whole fish. The cooked fish, in the lovely soft-coloured marinade, needs only a fresh herb sprig as a garnish.

SERVES 4

INGREDIENTS
1 medium whole sea bass, cleaned

FOR THE PEPPERCORN MARINADE
1 red onion
2 small oranges
90ml/6 tbsp light olive oil
30ml/2 tbsp cider vinegar
30ml/2 tbsp green peppercorns in brine, drained
30ml/2 tbsp chopped fresh parsley
salt and sugar, to taste

1 Check the weight of the fish. Using a sharp knife, make three or four deep, diagonal slashes on both sides of the sea bass.

2 Line an ovenproof dish with foil, leaving overhanging sides. Peel and slice the onion and oranges. Place half in the base of the dish, place the fish on top and cover with the remaining onion and orange.

3 Mix the remaining marinade ingredients and pour over the fish. Cover and leave to stand for 4 hours, occasionally spooning the marinade over the top.

4 Preheat the oven to 180°C/350°F/Gas 4. Fold the foil over the fish. Bake for 15 minutes per 450g/1lb, plus 15 minutes over. Serve with the juices.

SUMMER HERB MARINADE FOR SALMON

Make the best use of fresh-tasting summer herbs in this flavoursome marinade, which can also be used with other fish, as well as veal, chicken, pork or lamb.

SERVES 4

INGREDIENTS
4 salmon steaks or fillets, about 175g/6oz each

FOR THE HERB MARINADE
large handful of fresh herb sprigs, e.g. chervil, thyme, parsley, sage, chives,
  rosemary, oregano
90ml/6 tbsp olive oil
45ml/3 tbsp tarragon vinegar
1 garlic clove, crushed
2 spring onions (scallions), chopped
salt and ground black pepper

1 Discard any coarse stalks or damaged leaves from the herbs, then chop them very finely.

2 Add the chopped herbs to the remaining marinade ingredients in a large bowl. Stir to mix thoroughly.

3 Place the salmon steaks or fillets in the bowl and spoon the marinade over. Cover with clear film (plastic wrap) and set aside to marinate in a cool place for 4–6 hours.

4 Drain the fish when you are ready to cook it on the grill (broiler) or barbecue. Use the marinade to baste the fish occasionally during cooking.

Spicy Yogurt Marinade for Chicken

Plan this dish well in advance; the extra-long marinating time is necessary to develop a really mellow spicy flavour. It is a good choice for summer entertaining.

SERVES 6

INGREDIENTS
6 chicken pieces
juice of 1 lemon
5ml/1 tsp salt
fresh mint, lemon and lime, to garnish

FOR THE YOGURT MARINADE
5ml/1 tsp coriander seeds
10ml/2 tsp cumin seeds
6 cloves
2 bay leaves
1 onion, quartered
2 garlic cloves
5cm/2in piece of fresh root ginger, peeled and coarsely chopped
2.5ml/½ tsp chilli powder
5ml/1 tsp ground turmeric
150ml/¼ pint/⅔ cup natural (plain) yogurt

> COOK'S TIP
> *This marinade will also work well brushed over skewers of lamb or pork fillet (tenderloin) prior to grilling (broiling) or cooking on the barbecue.*

1 Skin the chicken pieces and make deep slashes in the fleshiest parts with a sharp knife. Sprinkle the lemon juice and salt over them and rub in.

2 Make the marinade. Spread the coriander and cumin seeds, cloves and bay leaves in the base of a large frying pan and dry-fry over a medium heat until the bay leaves are crispy.

3 Remove the pan from the heat and leave the spice mixture to cool, then grind it coarsely in a mortar with a pestle.

4 Finely mince (grind) the onion, garlic and ginger in a food processor or blender with the ground spices, chilli, turmeric and yogurt. Strain in the lemon juice from the chicken.

5 Arrange the chicken in a single layer in a roasting pan. Pour the marinade over, then cover and chill for 24–36 hours, turning the chicken pieces occasionally.

6 Preheat the oven to 200°C/400°F/Gas 6. Cook the chicken for 45 minutes, or until the juices run clear when the meat is pierced. Serve hot or cold, garnished with fresh mint and slices of lemon or lime.

LAVENDER BALSAMIC MARINADE FOR LAMB

Lavender is an unusual flavour to use with meat, but its heady, summery scent works well with lamb cooked on the barbecue. Use the flower heads as a garnish.

SERVES 4

INGREDIENTS
4 racks of lamb, with 3–4 cutlets (chops) each

FOR THE BALSAMIC MARINADE
1 shallot, finely chopped
45ml/3 tbsp chopped fresh lavender
15ml/1 tbsp balsamic vinegar
30ml/2 tbsp olive oil
15ml/1 tbsp lemon juice
handful of lavender sprigs
salt and ground black pepper

1 Place the racks of lamb in a large mixing bowl or wide dish and sprinkle the chopped shallot over them, then sprinkle with the chopped fresh lavender.

2 Beat together the balsamic vinegar, olive oil and lemon juice in a bowl, until well combined, then pour the mixture over the lamb. Season well with salt and ground black pepper and then turn the meat to coat evenly. If you like, leave to marinate for 1 hour. Alternatively, you can cook the lamb immediately.

3 Sprinkle a few lavender sprigs over the grill or on the coals of a medium-hot barbecue. Cook the lamb for 15–20 minutes, turning once and basting with any remaining marinade, until golden brown on the outside and still slightly pink in the centre. Just before serving, garnish with lavender flower heads.

COOK'S TIP
You can buy culinary lavender or pick it yourself, making sure that it is free from traffic pollution. As an alternative, you could use rosemary sprigs.

Red Wine & Juniper Marinade for Lamb

Juniper berries – probably best known for flavouring gin – have a pungent taste that is ideal to give a lift to lamb and also goes well with pork.

SERVES 4–6

INGREDIENTS
675g/1½lb boned leg of lamb, trimmed and cut into 2.5cm/1in cubes
2 carrots, cut into batons
225g/8oz baby onions or shallots
115g/4oz/1½ cups button (white) mushrooms
30ml/2 tbsp vegetable oil
150ml/¼ pint/⅔ cup stock
30ml/2 tbsp beurre manié
salt and ground black pepper

FOR THE RED WINE AND JUNIPER MARINADE
4 rosemary sprigs
8 dried juniper berries, lightly crushed
8 black peppercorns, lightly crushed
300ml/½ pint/1¼ cups red wine

1 Place the meat in a bowl, add the vegetables, rosemary, juniper berries and peppercorns, then pour over the wine. Cover and leave to marinate in a cool place for 4–5 hours, stirring once or twice during this time.

2 Remove the lamb and vegetables with a slotted spoon and set aside. Strain the marinade into a jug (pitcher).

3 Preheat the oven to 160°C/325°F/Gas 3. Heat the oil in a heavy pan and cook the meat and vegetables, in batches, until lightly browned. Transfer to a casserole and pour over the reserved marinade and stock. Cover and cook in the oven for 2 hours.

4 Twenty minutes before the end of cooking, stir in the beurre manié, then cover and return to the oven. Season to taste before serving.

Lemon & Rosemary Marinade for Lamb

Marinate the leg of lamb overnight in the refrigerator so that the flavours have plenty of time to penetrate the meat fully before roasting.

SERVES 6

INGREDIENTS
1.3–1.6kg/3–3½lb leg of lamb
2 garlic cloves, sliced
15ml/1 tbsp cornflour (cornstarch)

FOR THE LEMON AND ROSEMARY MARINADE
1 lemon, sliced
6 fresh rosemary sprigs
4 fresh lemon thyme sprigs
300ml/½ pint/1¼ cups dry white wine
60ml/4 tbsp olive oil
salt and ground black pepper

VARIATION
You can also use lemon and rosemary marinade for chicken pieces, but you must roast the meat without the marinade or it will become tough. Instead, use the marinade for making into gravy when the chicken is cooked.

1 Check the weight of the lamb. Make small cuts over the lamb surface. Insert a garlic piece in each. Place the lamb in a roasting pan, with the lemon slices and herbs sprinkled over it.

2 Mix together the white wine and olive oil in a jug (pitcher) and season with salt and pepper. Pour over the lamb. Cover with clear film (plastic wrap) and leave to marinate in a cool place for 4–6 hours or overnight in the refrigerator, turning occasionally.

3 Preheat the oven to 180°C/350°F/Gas 4, then roast the lamb for 25 minutes per 450g/1lb plus another 25 minutes. During cooking, baste the meat frequently with the marinade.

4 When the lamb is cooked, transfer to a warmed plate to rest. Drain the excess fat from the pan. Blend the cornflour with a little cold water and stir into the juices. Stir over a medium heat for 2–3 minutes, then adjust the seasoning. Carve the lamb and serve with the sauce.

CHINESE SESAME MARINADE FOR BEEF STRIPS

Toasted sesame seeds bring their distinctive smoky aroma to this Asian marinade, which also doubles as a delicious glaze on the finished dish.

SERVES 4

INGREDIENTS
450g/1lb rump (round) steak
30ml/2 tbsp sesame seeds
15ml/1 tbsp sesame oil
30ml/2 tbsp vegetable oil
115g/4oz/1½ cups small mushrooms, quartered
1 large green (bell) pepper, seeded and diced
4 spring onions (scallions), chopped diagonally

FOR THE CHINESE SESAME MARINADE
10ml/2 tsp cornflour (cornstarch)
30ml/2 tbsp rice wine or sherry
15ml/1 tbsp lemon juice
15ml/1 tbsp soy sauce
few drops Tabasco sauce
2.5cm/1in piece of fresh root ginger, peeled and grated
1 garlic clove, crushed

COOK'S TIP
This marinade would also be good with lean pork fillet (tenderloin) or chicken breast portions.

1 To make the marinade, blend the cornflour with the rice wine or sherry in a mixing bowl. Add the remaining marinade ingredients and mix well. Trim the steak and cut into thin strips about 1 × 5cm/½ × 2in. Stir into the marinade, cover and leave in a cool place for 3–4 hours.

2 Place the sesame seeds in a large frying pan or wok. Dry-fry over a medium heat, shaking the pan until the seeds are golden. Set aside.

3 Heat the sesame and vegetable oils in the frying pan. Drain the beef, reserving the marinade, and brown a few pieces at a time. Remove with a slotted spoon.

4 Add the mushrooms and green pepper and cook for 2–3 minutes, stirring constantly. Add the spring onions and cook for a further minute.

5 Return the beef to the pan, add the reserved marinade and stir over a medium heat for 2 minutes, or until heated through evenly coated with the glaze. Sprinkle with the toasted sesame seeds and serve immediately.

WINTER-SPICED ALE MARINADE FOR BEEF

This traditional northern European marinade can also be used in a casserole of beef or lamb pieces. It will imbue the meat with a lovely malty flavour.

SERVES 6

INGREDIENTS
1.3kg/3lb top rump beef

FOR THE WINTER-SPICED ALE MARINADE
1 onion, sliced
2 carrots, sliced
2 celery sticks, sliced
2–3 parsley stalks, lightly crushed
large fresh thyme sprig
2 bay leaves
6 cloves, lightly crushed
1 cinnamon stick
8 black peppercorns
300ml/½ pint/1¼ cups brown ale
45ml/3 tbsp vegetable oil
30ml/2 tbsp beurre manié
salt and ground black pepper

> COOK'S TIP
> *A rich, dark brown ale has the ideal flavour for this recipe, but the choice depends on your own taste.*

1 Put the meat in a plastic bag placed inside a large, deep bowl. Add the vegetables, herbs and spices, then pour the ale over. Seal the bag and leave in a cool place for 5–6 hours.

2 Remove the beef and set aside. Strain the marinade into a bowl, reserving the marinade and vegetables separately.

3 Preheat the oven to 160°C/325°F/Gas 3. Meanwhile, heat the oil in a flameproof casserole. Add the vegetables and cook over a medium heat, stirring occasionally, until lightly browned, then remove with a slotted spoon and set aside. Brown the beef all over in the remaining oil.

4 Return the vegetables to the casserole and pour the reserved marinade over the beef. Bring to the boil.

5 Cover the casserole and cook in the oven for 2½ hours. Turn the beef two or three times in the marinade during cooking.

6 To serve, remove the beef and slice neatly. Arrange on a plate with the vegetables. Gradually stir the beurre manié into the marinade and cook over a medium heat until thickened. Adjust the seasoning.

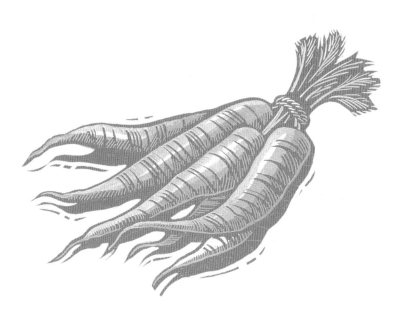

FRUIT SAUCES
& COULIS

Hot and cold fruit sauces can transform a simple scoop of ice cream or a piece of fruit into a complete dessert. A good range of sauces can increase your range of desserts three or four times over. Whether it's a tangy fruit coulis, a hot citrus sauce, a creamy banana mixture or a medley of summer berries, you can mix and match your favourite desserts with sauces to create a new dish every time. Try a generous drizzle of Passion Fruit & Strawberry Coulis over layered sundaes for a wonderfully indulgent treat, then next time spoon it over your favourite chocolate or fruit mousse. How about Hot Plum Sauce with Floating Islands, then perhaps serving the sauce with baked apples for another occasion? It's worth making the most of fruits in season to make deliciously fresh fruit coulis, to use in creative combinations at any time of year. Grilled pineapple is irresistible with a luscious spoonful of Papaya Sauce, or try Strawberry Sauce with Lemon Hearts for a special dinner party.

Papaya & Ginger Dip with Fresh Fruit

Sweet and smooth papaya teams up well with crème fraîche to make a luscious, tropical sweet dip that is very good with sweet biscuits or almost all types of fresh fruit for dipping. If fresh coconut is not available, you can substitute coconut strands and lightly toast them in a hot oven until golden before using.

Serves 6

Ingredients
2 ripe papayas
200ml/7fl oz/scant 1 cup crème fraîche
1 piece preserved stem ginger
fresh coconut, to decorate
papaya or other fresh fruit, to serve

Cook's Tip
Papaya, also known as pawpaw, originated in Malaysia and is now widely grown throughout the tropics in Asia, Africa and South America. Do not confuse it with the equally delicious, but quite different North American fruit called papaw.

1 Cut the papayas in half lengthways, then scoop out the seeds with a teaspoon and discard. Scoop out the flesh and process in a food processor or blender until it is completely smooth.

2 Stir in the crème fraîche and process until well blended. Transfer to a bowl. Finely chop the stem ginger and stir it in, then chill in the refrigerator until ready to serve.

3 Pierce a hole in two of the "eyes" of the coconut with a metal skewer and drain off the liquid. Put the coconut in a plastic bag. Hold it securely in one hand and hit it sharply with a hammer in a line all the way around the centre. Remove from the bag and lever the two halves apart.

4 Remove the shell from a piece of coconut, then snap the nut into pieces no
wider than 2.5cm/1in.

5 Use a swivel-bladed vegetable peeler to shave off 2cm/¾in lengths of coconut.
Sprinkle these over the dip. Serve the chilled dip with pieces of extra papaya or
other fresh fruit.

Passion Fruit & Strawberry Coulis with Yogurt Sundaes

Frozen yogurt makes a refreshing change from ice cream. Here, it is partnered with a delicious fresh fruit coulis that is simple to make. Fresh summer strawberries are unlikely to need sweetening, but some varieties may need a little sugar.

Serves 4

Ingredients
175g/6oz/1½ cups strawberries, hulled
  and halved
2 ripe peaches, stoned (pitted) and chopped
8 scoops (about 350g/12oz) vanilla or
  strawberry frozen yogurt

For the passion fruit and strawberry coulis
175g/6oz/1½ cups strawberries,
  hulled and halved
1 passion fruit
10ml/2 tsp icing (confectioners')
sugar (optional)

Cook's Tip
As the passion fruit ripens, its smooth shiny skin becomes wrinkled. However, it is a myth that the more wrinkled the fruit is, the sweeter it will be. The flesh is always slightly acidic and is very aromatic. The small, black, crunchy seeds are edible.

1 To make the coulis, purée the strawberries in a food processor or blender. Halve the passion fruit, scoop out the pulp and add it to the coulis. Sweeten with icing sugar if necessary.

2 Spoon half the remaining strawberries and half the chopped peaches into four tall sundae glasses.

3 Add a scoop of frozen yogurt. Set aside a few choice pieces of fruit for decoration, and use the rest to make a further layer on the top of each sundae. Top each with a final scoop of frozen yogurt.

4 Pour the passion fruit coulis over the final scoops of frozen yogurt and decorate the sundaes with the reserved strawberries and pieces of peach. Serve the sundaes immediately.

Lemon & Lime Sauce with Pancakes

This is a tangy, refreshing sauce and is a perfect foil for the pancakes. It is a much more interesting way to serve them than with a simple squeeze of lemon juice.

Serves 4

Ingredients
90g/3½oz/scant 1 cup plain (all-purpose) flour
pinch of salt
1 egg
300ml/½ pint/1¼ cups milk
vegetable oil, for frying
fresh lemon balm or mint, to decorate

For the lemon and lime sauce
1 lemon
2 limes
50g/2oz/¼ cup caster (superfine) sugar
25ml/1½ tbsp arrowroot
300ml/½ pint/1¼ cups water

1 First, make the sauce. Using a citrus zester, peel the rinds thinly from the lemon and limes taking care not to cut into the pith. Squeeze the juice from the fruit.

2 Place the rind in a pan, cover with water and bring to the boil. Drain through a sieve and reserve the rind.

3 In a small bowl, mix a little sugar with the arrowroot. Blend in enough water to give a smooth paste. Heat the remaining water, pour in the arrowroot mixture, and stir constantly until the sauce boils and thickens. Stir in the remaining sugar, the lemon and lime juice and reserved rind. Keep the sauce hot while you make the pancakes.

4 Sift the dry ingredients into a bowl and make a well in the centre. Add the egg and beat in with a wooden spoon. Beat in the milk, drawing in the flour to make a smooth batter.

5 Heat a little oil in a large, heavy frying pan. When hot, pour in a thin layer of batter and cook for 1–2 minutes, or until set. Toss the pancake or flip it over with a palette knife (metal spatula) and cook the other side until golden brown.

6 Transfer the pancake to a plate and keep it warm while you make the rest of the pancakes. As you make the pancakes, stack them interleaved with greaseproof (waxed) paper or baking parchment. Serve with the hot sauce and decorate with lemon balm or mint.

Hot Plum Sauce
with Floating Islands

The plum sauce can be made in advance, then reheated just before you cook the meringues. This makes an unusual dessert that is simpler to make than it looks. The fruity sauce is also healthier than the more traditional rich custard.

SERVES 4

INGREDIENTS
2 egg whites
30ml/2 tbsp concentrated apple juice syrup
freshly grated nutmeg, to serve

FOR THE HOT PLUM SAUCE
450g/1lb red plums
300ml/½ pint/1¼ cups apple juice

COOK'S TIP
It is best to use a metal or glass bowl for whisking egg whites, as it is essential that there should be no traces of grease. It is difficult to make sure that plastic bowls are completely greasefree. A copper bowl is perfect as there is a reaction between the egg white and the metal, which makes the whites really foamy. However, do not leave them standing in a copper bowl or they will turn grey.

---

1 To make the plum sauce, halve the plums and remove the stones (pits). Place them in a wide pan with the apple juice.

2 Bring to the boil, lower the heat and then cover with a lid and simmer gently for 15–20 minutes, or until the plums are tender.

3 Meanwhile, place the egg whites in a clean, dry, greasefree bowl and whisk them, preferably with an electric mixer, until they hold soft peaks.

4 Gradually whisk in the apple juice syrup, whisking until the meringue holds fairly firm peaks.

5 Using a tablespoon, scoop the meringue mixture into the gently simmering plum sauce. You may need to cook the "islands" in two batches.

6 Cover the pan and simmer gently for 2–3 minutes, or until the meringues are just set.

7 Transfer to individual bowls and serve the dessert immediately, sprinkled with a little freshly grated nutmeg.

BANANA SAUCE WITH CHOCOLATE CINNAMON CAKE

This sweet, creamy sauce makes a simple chocolate cake into a really luxurious dessert that is suitable for any special occasion.

SERVES 6

INGREDIENTS

90g/3½oz/7 tbsp unsalted (sweet) butter, at room temperature, plus extra for greasing
115g/4oz plain (semisweet) chocolate, finely chopped
15ml/1 tbsp instant coffee powder
5 eggs, separated
200g/7oz/1 cup granulated sugar
115g/4oz/1 cup plain (all-purpose) flour
10ml/2 tsp ground cinnamon

FOR THE BANANA SAUCE

4 ripe bananas
50g/2oz/¼ cup light muscovado (brown) sugar
15ml/1 tbsp fresh lemon juice
175ml/6fl oz/¾ cup whipping cream
15ml/1 tbsp rum (optional)

> VARIATION
> *For a special occasion, top the cake slices with a scoop of ice cream (rum and raisin, chocolate or vanilla) before adding the sauce. With this addition, the dessert will serve at least 8.*

1 Preheat the oven to 180°C/350°F/Gas 4. Grease a 20cm/8in round cake tin (pan) with a little butter.

2 Combine the chocolate and butter in a heatproof bowl set over a pan of simmering water or in the top of a double boiler. Stir until melted. Remove from the heat and stir in the coffee. Set aside.

3 Beat the egg yolks together with the granulated sugar until thick and lemon-coloured. Add the chocolate mixture and beat on low speed just to blend the mixture evenly.

4 Sift together the flour and ground cinnamon into a bowl. Beat the egg whites in a clean, greasefree bowl until they hold stiff peaks.

5 Fold a spoonful of whites into the chocolate mixture to lighten it. Fold in the remaining whites in three batches, alternating with the sifted flour.

6 Pour the mixture into the prepared tin. Bake the cake for 40–50 minutes, or until a skewer inserted in the centre comes out clean. Turn out the cake on to a wire rack to cool slightly.

7 Meanwhile, make the sauce. Preheat the grill (broiler). Slice the bananas into a shallow, heatproof dish. Add the muscovado sugar and lemon juice and stir to blend. Place under the grill and cook, stirring occasionally, for about 8 minutes, or until the sugar is caramelized and bubbling.

8 Transfer the bananas to a bowl and mash with a fork until almost smooth. Stir in the cream, and rum, if using. Cut the chocolate cake into slices and serve it warm, with the banana sauce.

Berry Sauce
with Baked Ricotta Cakes

The flavour of this fragrant fruity sauce contrasts well with these honey and vanilla-flavoured desserts. You can make the sauce with whatever fresh berries are in season or with your favourites at any time of year if you use frozen.

SERVES 4

INGREDIENTS
unsalted (sweet) butter, for greasing
250g/9oz/generous 1 cup ricotta cheese
2 egg whites, beaten
about 60ml/4 tbsp clear honey, plus extra to sweeten
few drops of vanilla essence (extract)
fresh mint leaves, to decorate (optional)

FOR THE RED BERRY SAUCE
450g/1lb/4 cups mixed fresh or frozen fruit, such as strawberries, raspberries, blackberries and cherries

COOK'S TIPS
• *The sauce can be made a day ahead. Chill until ready to use.*
• *Frozen fruit doesn't need extra water, as there will be ice crystals clinging to the berries.*

1 Preheat the oven to 180°C/350°F/Gas 4. Lightly grease four ramekins with a little butter.

2 Place the ricotta cheese in a bowl and break it up with a wooden spoon. Add the beaten egg whites, honey and vanilla essence and mix thoroughly until the mixture is smooth and well combined.

3 Spoon the ricotta mixture into the prepared ramekins and level the tops. Bake for 20 minutes or until the ricotta cakes are risen and golden.

4 Meanwhile, make the berry sauce. Reserve about a quarter of the fruit for decoration. Place the rest of the fruit in a pan, with a little water if the fruit is fresh, and heat gently until softened. Leave to cool slightly, then remove any cherry pits, if using cherries.

5 Press the fruit through a sieve, then taste and sweeten with honey if it is too tart. Serve the sauce, warm or cold, with the ricotta cakes. Decorate with the reserved berries and mint leaves, if using.

Papaya Sauce with Grilled Pineapple

As well as making a scrumptious dessert, this easy fruit sauce has a surprising, added bonus. Try it with savoury dishes, too. It tastes simply great with grilled chicken and game birds as well as with roast pork and lamb.

SERVES 6

INGREDIENTS
1 sweet pineapple
melted butter, for greasing and brushing
2 pieces drained preserved stem ginger in syrup, cut into fine batons
30ml/2 tbsp demerara (raw) sugar
pinch of ground cinnamon
30ml/2 tbsp preserved stem ginger syrup
fresh mint sprigs, to decorate

FOR THE PAPAYA SAUCE
1 ripe papaya, peeled and seeded
175ml/6fl oz/³⁄₄ cup apple juice

> VARIATION
> If you like, substitute half apple juice and half papaya nectar for the apple juice in the sauce.

1 Peel the pineapple and take spiral slices off the outside to remove the "eyes". Cut it crossways into six slices, each 2.5cm/1in thick.

2 Line a baking sheet with a sheet of foil, rolling up the sides to make a rim. Grease the foil with melted butter. Preheat the grill (broiler).

3 Arrange the pineapple slices on the baking sheet. Brush with butter, then top with the ginger batons, sugar and cinnamon. Drizzle over the stem ginger syrup. Grill (broil) for 5–7 minutes, or until the slices are lightly charred.

4 Cut a few slices from the papaya and set aside, then process the rest together with the apple juice in a food processor or blender.

5 Press the purée through a sieve placed over a bowl, then stir in any juices from cooking the pineapple.

6 Serve the pineapple slices with a little sauce drizzled around each plate. Decorate with the reserved papaya slices and the mint sprigs.

NECTARINE SAUCE WITH LATTICED PEACHES

Make this in summer when the fruits are in season, and enjoy the fresh flavour. The sauce is also delicious with ice cream and fresh fruit, such as raspberries.

SERVES 6

INGREDIENTS

FOR THE PASTRY
115g/4oz/1 cup plain (all-purpose) flour
45ml/3 tbsp butter or sunflower margarine
45ml/3 tbsp natural (plain) yogurt
30ml/2 tbsp orange juice
milk, for brushing

FOR THE FILLING
3 ripe peaches or nectarines
45ml/3 tbsp ground almonds
30ml/2 tbsp low-fat natural (plain) yogurt
finely grated rind of 1 small orange
1.5ml/¼ tsp natural almond essence (extract)

FOR THE NECTARINE SAUCE
1 ripe nectarine or peach
45ml/3 tbsp orange juice

COOK'S TIP
To peel peaches, blanch them in boiling water for about 30 seconds, then place in iced water. The skins will slip off easily.

1 For the pastry, sift the flour into a bowl and, using your fingertips, rub in the butter or margarine. Stir in the yogurt and orange juice to bind the mixture to a firm dough.

2 Roll out about half the pastry thinly and use a biscuit (cookie) cutter to stamp out rounds of about 7.5cm/3in in diameter, or slightly larger than the circumference of the peaches. Place on a lightly greased baking sheet.

3 For the filling, peel the peaches or nectarines, halve them and remove the stones (pits).

4 Mix together the almonds, yogurt, orange rind and almond essence. Spoon into each peach half and place, cut-side down, on the pastry rounds.

5 Roll out the remaining pastry thinly and cut into thin strips. Arrange the strips over the peaches to form a lattice, brushing with milk to secure firmly. Trim off the ends neatly.

6 Chill in the refrigerator for 30 minutes. Preheat the oven to 200°C/400°F/ Gas 6. Brush the tarts with milk, and bake for 15–18 minutes.

7 For the sauce, peel the nectarine or peach and remove the stone. Process to a purée in a food processor, with the orange juice. Serve the peaches hot, with the sauce spooned around.

LIME & CARDAMOM SAUCE WITH BANANAS

The warm spicy-sweet flavour of cardamom is offset by the tang of lime in this unusual sauce. Use the pale green or beige pods for the best flavour.

SERVES 4

INGREDIENTS
6 small bananas
25g/1oz/2 tbsp butter
vanilla ice cream, to serve

FOR THE LIME AND CARDAMOM SAUCE
25g/1oz/2 tbsp butter
seeds from 4 cardamom pods, crushed
50g/2oz/½ cup flaked (sliced) almonds
thinly pared rind and juice of 2 limes
50g/2oz/¼ cup light muscovado (brown) sugar
30ml/2 tbsp dark rum

COOK'S TIP
Crush the cardamom seeds in a mortar with a pestle or in a bowl with the end of a rolling pin. Do this just before using, to retain their essential flavour.

1 Peel the bananas and cut them in half lengthways. Melt the butter in a large, heavy frying pan over a low to medium heat. Add half the bananas and cook gently until the undersides are golden. Turn them carefully, using a fish slice or metal spatula.

2 As they cook, transfer the bananas to a heatproof serving dish and keep warm. Cook the remaining bananas in the same way.

3 To make the lime and cardamom sauce melt the butter, then add the cardamom seeds and almonds. Cook, stirring, until golden.

4 Stir in the lime rind and juice, then the sugar. Cook, stirring constantly, until the mixture is smooth, bubbling and slightly reduced. Stir in the rum.

5 Pour the hot sauce over the bananas and serve immediately, with scoops of vanilla ice cream.

STRAWBERRY SAUCE WITH LEMON HEARTS

This speedy, sweet sauce makes a delicious accompaniment for these delicate lemon and cheese hearts. It also tastes great with ice cream or mousse.

SERVES 4

INGREDIENTS
175g/6oz/¾ cup ricotta cheese
150ml/¼ pint/⅔ cup natural (plain) yogurt
15ml/1 tbsp sugar
finely grated rind of ½ lemon
30ml/2 tbsp lemon juice
10ml/2 tsp powdered gelatine
2 egg whites
oil, for greasing

FOR THE STRAWBERRY SAUCE
225g/8oz/2 cups fresh or frozen and thawed strawberries, plus extra to decorate
15ml/1 tbsp lemon juice

> VARIATION
> *Add a dash of Cointreau or Grand Marnier liqueur to the strawberry sauce.*

1 Put the ricotta in a bowl and beat well until smooth. Stir in the yogurt, sugar and lemon rind.

2 Place the lemon juice in a small bowl and sprinkle the gelatine over it. Place the bowl over a pan of barely simmering water and stir the mixture to dissolve the gelatine completely.

3 Beat the egg whites until they form soft peaks. Quickly stir the gelatine into the ricotta cheese mixture, mixing it in evenly, then immediately fold in the beaten egg whites.

4 Spoon the mixture into four lightly oiled, individual heart-shaped moulds and chill the moulds until set.

5 To make the sauce, place the strawberries and lemon juice in a food processor and process until smooth. Pour on to plates and top with turned-out hearts. Decorate with the extra strawberries.

RASPBERRY SAUCE WITH BAKED PEACHES

Peaches and raspberries are classic partners – a combination that's hard to beat for a sophisticated summer dessert. Try this sauce with a cool slice of honeydew or charentais melon for a fabulous summer appetizer.

SERVES 6

INGREDIENTS
45ml/3 tbsp unsalted (sweet) butter, at room temperature
50g/2oz/¼ cup caster (superfine) sugar
1 egg, beaten
50g/2oz/½ cup ground almonds
6 ripe peaches

FOR THE RASPBERRY SAUCE
175g/6oz/1 cup raspberries
15ml/1 tbsp icing (confectioners') sugar
15ml/1 tbsp fruit-flavoured brandy (optional)

> VARIATION
> Fresh nectarines can be used instead of peaches and Amaretto instead of fruit brandy.

1 Preheat the oven to 180°C/350°F/Gas 4. Beat the butter with the caster sugar until soft and fluffy. Beat in the egg. Add the ground almonds and beat just to blend well together.

2 Halve the peaches and remove the stones (pits). With a spoon, scrape out some of the flesh from each peach half, slightly enlarging the hollow left by the stone. Reserve the excess peach flesh to use in the sauce.

3 Place the peach halves on a baking sheet (secure with crumpled foil to keep them steady). Using a teaspoon, fill the hollow in each peach half with the butter and almond mixture.

4 Bake for about 30 minutes, or until the almond filling is puffed and golden, and the peaches are very tender.

5 For the sauce, combine all the ingredients in a food processor or blender. Add the reserved peach flesh. Process until smooth. Press through a strainer set over a bowl to remove fibres and seeds.

6 Let the peaches cool. Place two halves on each plate and spoon the sauce over them. Serve immediately.

CUSTARDS, CHOCOLATE & OTHER SAUCES

Sweet sauces can transform an ordinary dessert into a triumphant finale to any meal, adding that special touch that makes all the difference. Whether a traditional custard, a rich chocolate sauce or a sophisticated combination of maple syrup and orange liqueur, there is a sauce that is sure to please everyone who has a sweet tooth. Their versatility is immense so you can serve them with a wide selection of different desserts to ring the changes. For sheer indulgence, serve Chocolate Sauce with Profiteroles, then next time drizzle it over your favourite ice cream or sorbet (sherbet). For a lighter, less calorie-laden treat, how about Maple Yogurt Sauce with Poached Pears, then perhaps serve the sauce with fresh strawberries for another occasion? If you are short of time, turn to Hazelnut Dip with Fruit Fondue – you can prepare it in minutes, and it looks temptingly pretty and tastes terrific. Equally, if you want to impress dinner party guests, you couldn't choose anything better than Calvados & Chocolate Sauce with Iced Pear Terrine. Finally, don't overlook the family favourites that please everyone. From Butterscotch Sauce with Waffles to Toffee Sauce with Hot Date Puddings, these are comforting and satisfying winter warmers.

Malted Chocolate & Banana Dip with Fresh Fruit

Chocolate and banana combine irresistibly in this rich dip, served with fresh fruit in season. For a creamier dip, stir in some lightly whipped cream just before serving.

SERVES 4

INGREDIENTS
50g/2oz plain (semisweet) chocolate
2 large ripe bananas
15ml/1 tbsp malt extract
mixed fresh fruit, such as strawberries, peaches and kiwi fruit, halved or sliced

1 Break the chocolate into pieces and place in a small, heatproof bowl. Stand the bowl over a pan of gently simmering water and stir the chocolate occasionally until it melts. Leave to cool slightly.

2 Break the bananas into pieces and process in a food processor or blender until finely chopped.

3 With the motor running, pour in the malt extract and continue processing the mixture until it is thick and frothy.

4 Drizzle in the chocolate in a steady stream and process until well blended. Serve immediately, with the prepared fruit alongside.

COOK'S TIP
This smooth dip can be prepared in advance and stored in the refrigerator until required.

Hazelnut Dip with Fruit Fondue

Any fruit that can be eaten raw can be served with this tasty dipping sauce.
Try to use fruits in a range of different colours for an attractive presentation.

SERVES 2

INGREDIENTS
selection of fresh fruits, such as satsumas, kiwi fruit, grapes, physalis and
  whole strawberries

FOR THE HAZELNUT DIP
50g/2oz/¼ cup soft cheese
150ml/¼ pint/⅔ cup hazelnut yogurt
5ml/1 tsp vanilla essence (extract)
5ml/1 tsp caster (superfine) sugar
50g/2oz/½ cup shelled hazelnuts, chopped

1 First prepare the fruits. Peel the satsumas and remove all traces of white pith, then separate into segments. Then peel the kiwi fruit and cut into wedges. Wash the grapes and peel back the papery casings on the physalis without removing them completely.

2 To make the dip, beat together the soft cheese, hazelnut yogurt, vanilla essence and sugar in a bowl with an electric mixer or a balloon whisk. Stir in three-quarters of the hazelnuts.

3 Spoon the dip into a glass serving dish set on a platter or into small pots set on individual plates and sprinkle the remaining hazelnuts on top. Arrange the prepared fruits around the dip and serve immediately.

Butterscotch Sauce with Waffles

This is a deliciously sweet sauce which will be loved by adults and children alike. It's not just fabulous with waffles, but delicious with plain ice cream and baked sponge puddings, and can even be poured over cake to make a speedy dessert.

SERVES 4–6

INGREDIENTS
1 pack ready-made waffles
vanilla ice cream, to serve

FOR THE BUTTERSCOTCH SAUCE
75g/3oz/6 tbsp butter
175g/6oz/³/4 cup dark muscovado (molasses) sugar
175ml/6fl oz/³/4 cup evaporated milk
50g/2oz/¹/3 cup hazelnuts

VARIATION
Substitute any nut for the hazelnuts. Pecans, for example, add a luxurious flavour. You could also add plump, juicy raisins and a dash of rum instead of the nuts.

1 Warm the waffles in a preheated oven, according to the packet instructions, while you make the butterscotch sauce.

2 Melt the butter and sugar in a heavy pan, stirring occasionally. Bring to the boil and boil for 2 minutes. Remove the pan from the heat and leave to cool for 5 minutes.

3 Heat the evaporated milk to just below boiling point, then gradually stir it into the sugar mixture. Return the pan to the heat and cook over a low heat for 2 minutes, stirring the sauce frequently.

4 Spread the hazelnuts on a baking sheet and toast under a hot grill (broiler) until golden brown. Tip on to a clean dishtowel and rub briskly with your hands to remove the skins.

5 Chop the nuts coarsely and stir into the sauce. Serve the sauce hot, poured over scoops of vanilla ice cream and the warm waffles.

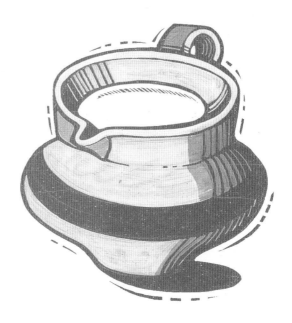

MAPLE & COINTREAU SYRUP WITH ORANGES

The maple syrup makes this one of the most delicious ways to eat an orange. For an alcohol-free version, simply omit the Cointreau or Grand Marnier.

SERVES 4

INGREDIENTS
melted butter, for brushing
4 medium oranges
crème fraîche, to serve

FOR THE MAPLE AND COINTREAU SYRUP
30ml/2 tbsp maple syrup
30ml/2 tbsp Cointreau or Grand Marnier liqueur
20ml/4 tsp butter

> COOK'S TIP
> *Check the label when buying maple syrup. Less expensive brands may be blended with corn syrup and are usually labelled maple-flavoured syrup. Pure maple syrup, although rather expensive, has an infinitely richer flavour.*

1 Preheat the oven to 200°C/400°F/Gas 6. Cut four double-thickness squares of foil, large enough to wrap each of the oranges. Brush the centre of each square of foil with plenty of melted butter.

2 Remove some shreds of orange rind for decoration. Blanch these in boiling water, drain, dry them and set them aside.

3 Peel all of the oranges, removing all traces of the white pith and catching the juice in a bowl.

4 Slice each of the oranges crossways into thick slices. Reassemble the slices and place each stack on a square of foil.

5 Tuck the foil up securely around the reassembled oranges to keep them in shape, leaving the foil parcels open at the top.

6 To make the syrup, mix together the reserved orange juice, maple syrup and liqueur, and spoon the mixture over the oranges.

7 Add a knob (pat) of butter to each parcel and close the foil at the top to seal in the juices. Place the parcels in the oven for 10–12 minutes, or until hot. (The parcels can also be cooked on a hot barbecue, if liked.) Serve with crème fraîche, topped with the reserved shreds of orange rind.

Real Custard with Castle Puddings

This traditional English pudding is served with one of the most traditional and popular sweet sauces – a really creamy vanilla custard.

SERVES 4

INGREDIENTS
about 45ml/3 tbsp berry jam
115g/4oz/½ cup butter
115g/4oz/generous ½ cup caster (superfine) sugar
2 eggs, beaten
few drops of vanilla essence (extract)
130g/4½oz/generous 1 cup self-raising (self-rising) flour

FOR THE REAL CUSTARD
4 eggs
25–30ml/1½ –2 tbsp sugar
450ml/¾ pint/scant 2 cups milk
few drops of vanilla essence (extract)

COOK'S TIPS
- *If you prefer, instead of baking the puddings, you can cover and steam them for 30–40 minutes.*
- *If you do not have dariole moulds, use small ramekin dishes.*
- *Make sure you buy real vanilla essence (extract) and not the artificial flavouring. You will need only a drop or two.*

1 Preheat the oven to 180°C/350°F/Gas 4. Butter four dariole moulds. Put about 10ml/2 tsp jam in the base of each mould.

2 Beat the butter and sugar together until light and fluffy, then gradually beat in the eggs, beating well after each addition and adding the vanilla essence towards the end.

3 Sift the flour and lightly fold it in with a metal spoon, then divide the mixture among the moulds.

4 Bake the puddings in the oven for about 20 minutes, until well risen and a light golden colour.

5 Meanwhile, make the custard. Whisk the eggs and sugar together. Bring the milk to the boil in a heavy pan, preferably non-stick, then gradually pour it on to the sweetened egg mixture, stirring constantly.

6 Return the milk and egg mixture to the pan and heat very gently, stirring, until the mixture thickens enough to coat the back of a spoon; do not boil. Stir in the vanilla essence. Cover the pan and remove from the heat.

7 Remove the moulds from the oven, leave to stand for a few minutes, then turn the puddings on to warmed plates and serve with the hot custard.

Toffee Sauce
with Hot Date Puddings

Always popular, this toffee sauce is a great standby for both hot and cold desserts. It is equally delicious served with poached apple or pear slices, spooned over vanilla or chocolate ice cream or drizzled over a hot steamed pudding.

SERVES 6

INGREDIENTS
50g/2oz/¼ cup butter, softened
75g/3oz/6 tbsp light muscovado (brown) sugar
2 eggs, beaten
115g/4oz/1 cup self-raising (self-rising) flour
2.5ml/½ tsp bicarbonate of soda (baking soda)
175g/6oz/generous 1 cup fresh dates, peeled, stoned (pitted) and chopped
75ml/5 tbsp boiling water
10ml/2 tsp coffee and chicory essence (extract)

FOR THE TOFFEE SAUCE
75g/3oz/6 tbsp light muscovado (brown) sugar
50g/2oz/¼ cup butter
60ml/4 tbsp double (heavy) cream
30ml/2 tbsp brandy

COOK'S TIP
It is preferable to peel the dates, as the skins can be rather tough: simply squeeze them between your thumb and forefinger and the skins will pop off.

1 Preheat the oven to 180°C/350°F/Gas 4. Place a baking sheet in the oven to heat up. Grease six individual pudding moulds or tins (pans).

2 Cream the butter and sugar together in a large mixing bowl until pale and fluffy. Gradually add the beaten eggs, a little at a time, beating thoroughly after each addition.

3 Sift the flour and bicarbonate of soda together and lightly fold into the creamed mixture until combined.

4 Put the dates in a heatproof bowl, pour over the boiling water and mash with a potato masher. Add the coffee and chicory essence, then stir the paste into the creamed mixture.

5 Spoon the mixture into the prepared moulds or tins. Place on the hot baking sheet and bake for 20 minutes.

6 To make the toffee sauce, put all the ingredients in a pan and heat gently, stirring until smooth.

7 Increase the heat and boil for 1 minute. Turn the warm puddings out on to individual dessert plates. Spoon a generous amount of sauce over each and serve immediately.

Calvados & Chocolate Sauce with Iced Pear Terrine

This is a sensational combination for a celebratory meal. However, the rich chocolate sauce would also complement vanilla ice cream for a simpler dessert.

SERVES 8

INGREDIENTS
1.3–1.6kg/3–3½lb ripe Williams pears
juice of 1 lemon
115g/4oz/generous ½ cup caster (superfine) sugar
10 whole cloves
julienne strips of orange rind, to decorate

FOR THE CALVADOS AND CHOCOLATE SAUCE
200g/7oz plain (semisweet) chocolate
60ml/4 tbsp hot strong black coffee
200ml/7fl oz/scant 1 cup double (heavy) cream
30ml/2 tbsp Calvados or brandy

> COOK'S TIP
> *This is a good dish to prepare in advance for a dinner party, as the terrine will store successfully for a month in the freezer, but remember to remove it in time to soften slightly before serving.*

1 Peel, core and slice the pears. Place in a pan with the lemon juice, sugar, cloves and 90ml/6 tbsp water. Cover and simmer for 10 minutes. Remove the cloves. Leave to cool.

2 Process the pears with their juice and pour the purée into a freezerproof bowl. Cover and freeze until firm.

3 Line a 900g/2lb loaf tin (pan) with clear film (plastic wrap). Let it overhang the sides. Remove the frozen purée from the freezer and spoon it into a food processor. Process until smooth. Pour into the tin, cover and freeze until firm.

4 To make the sauce, break the chocolate into a large, heatproof bowl. Place the bowl over a pan of simmering water and leave to melt.

5 Stir the coffee into the melted chocolate until smooth. Gradually stir in the cream and then the Calvados or brandy. Set aside.

6 About 20 minutes before serving, remove the tin from the freezer. Invert the terrine on to a plate, lift off the clear film and place the terrine in the refrigerator to soften slightly. Warm the sauce over hot water.

7 Place a slice of terrine on to each dessert plate and spoon over some of the sauce. Decorate with julienne strips of orange rind and serve immediately.

CHOCOLATE SAUCE WITH PROFITEROLES

A real treat if you're not counting calories and a sure-fire hit with all members of the family. This sauce is also good with scoops of vanilla ice cream.

SERVES 6

INGREDIENTS
65g/2½oz/9 tbsp plain (all-purpose) flour
50g/2oz/¼ cup butter
150ml/¼ pint/⅔ cup water
2 eggs, lightly beaten
150ml/¼ pint/⅔ cup whipping cream, whipped

FOR THE CHOCOLATE SAUCE
150ml/¼ pint/⅔ cup double (heavy) cream
50g/2oz/¼ cup butter
50g/2oz/¼ cup vanilla sugar
175g/6oz plain (semisweet) chocolate
30ml/2 tbsp brandy

> VARIATION
> *For White Chocolate and Orange Sauce, substitute 45ml/3 tbsp caster (superfine) sugar for the vanilla sugar, white chocolate for the plain (semisweet) and orange liqueur for the brandy. Add the finely grated rind of 1 orange to the bowl of cream, butter and sugar in step 1.*

1 Make the chocolate sauce. Heat the cream with the butter and vanilla sugar in a bowl over a pan of simmering water. Stir until smooth, then cool.

2 Break the chocolate into the cream mixture. Stir until it is melted and thoroughly combined.

3 Stir in the brandy, a little at a time, then set the sauce aside to cool to room temperature. Do not cover.

4 To make the profiteroles, preheat the oven to 200°C/400°F/Gas 6. Sift the flour on to a plate. Heat the butter and water in a pan and bring to the boil.

5 Remove the pan from the heat and tip in the flour all at once. Beat with a wooden spoon until smooth. Cool for 1–2 minutes, then gradually beat in enough egg to give a piping consistency. Beat well until glossy. Pipe small balls of the mixture on to dampened baking sheets.

6 Bake in the oven for 15–20 minutes, or until crisp. Make a slit in the sides to let the steam escape, and cool on a wire rack.

7 Fill a piping (pastry) bag with cream and pipe some into each profiterole. Pile them on to a plate and top with a little chocolate sauce. Serve the remaining chocolate sauce separately.

FUDGE SAUCE WITH SUNDAES

This rich, hot sauce is full of classic Mexican flavours – chocolate, cinnamon and vanilla. Definitely not one for dieters, it best kept for those special, indulgent days.

SERVES 4

INGREDIENTS
600ml/1 pint/2½ cups vanilla ice cream
600ml/1 pint/2½ cups coffee ice cream
2 large ripe bananas, sliced
whipped cream
toasted sliced almonds

FOR THE HOT FUDGE SAUCE
60ml/4 tbsp light muscovado (brown) sugar
115g/4oz/⅓ cup golden (light corn) syrup
45ml/3 tbsp strong black coffee
5ml/1 tsp ground cinnamon
150g/5oz dark (bittersweet) chocolate, broken into pieces
75ml/5 tbsp whipping cream
45ml/3 tbsp coffee liqueur (optional)

1 For the sauce, combine the sugar, syrup, coffee and cinnamon in a heavy pan. Boil the mixture, stirring constantly, for about 5 minutes.

2 Remove from the heat and stir in the chocolate. When melted and smooth, stir in the cream and liqueur, if using. Leave to cool to lukewarm.

3 Fill four sundae dishes with 1 scoop each of vanilla and coffee ice cream. Arrange the bananas on the top. Pour the warm sauce over the bananas. Top with a rosette of whipped cream. Sprinkle with the toasted almonds and serve.

Sabayon Sauce

Also known as zabaglione, this frothy sauce is very versatile and can be served cold alone with light dessert biscuits or hot over cake, fruit or even ice cream.

SERVES 4–6

INGREDIENTS
1 egg
2 egg yolks
75g/3oz/scant ½ cup caster (superfine) sugar
150ml/¼ pint/⅔ cup Marsala or other sweet white wine
finely grated rind and juice of 1 lemon
dessert biscuits (cookies), to serve

1 Put the egg, yolks and sugar into a medium, heatproof bowl and whisk until they are pale and thick.

2 Stand the bowl over a pan of hot, but not boiling, water. Gradually add the Marsala or white wine and lemon juice, a little at a time, whisking vigorously. Continue whisking until it is thick enough to leave a trail.

3 To serve the sabayon cold, place it over a bowl of iced water and continue whisking until chilled. Add the finely grated lemon rind and stir in. Pour into small glasses and serve immediately, with the dessert biscuits.

COOK'S TIP
A generous pinch of arrowroot whisked together with the egg yolks and sugar will prevent the sauce from collapsing too quickly.

MAPLE YOGURT SAUCE WITH POACHED PEARS

The sweet-sour taste of the maple syrup and yogurt will partner most poached fruit but is especially good with pears. Choose a firm but ripe pear, such as Conference.

SERVES 4

INGREDIENTS
4 firm pears
15ml/1 tbsp lemon juice
250ml/8fl oz/1 cup sweet white wine or (hard) cider
thinly pared rind of 1 lemon
1 cinnamon stick

FOR THE MAPLE YOGURT SAUCE
pear cooking liquid
30ml/2 tbsp maple syrup
2.5ml/½ tsp arrowroot
150g/5oz/⅔ cup Greek (US strained plain) yogurt

VARIATION
If you want to make this sauce for another dessert, substitute fruit juice for the pear cooking liquid in step 4.

1 Thinly peel the pears, leaving them whole and with the stalks intact. Brush them with lemon juice to prevent them from browning. Use a vegetable peeler or small knife to scoop out the core from the base of each pear.

2 Place the pears in a wide, heavy pan and pour the wine or cider over them, adding enough cold water almost to cover the pears.

3 Add the lemon rind and cinnamon stick and bring to the boil. Reduce the heat, cover the pan and simmer gently for 30–40 minutes, or until the pears are tender. Turn the pears occasionally so that they cook evenly. Lift out the pears carefully, draining them well.

4 To make the sauce, bring the liquid to the boil, and boil uncovered to reduce it to about 105ml/7 tbsp. Strain and add the maple syrup. Blend a little with the arrowroot. Return to the pan and cook, stirring, until thick. Remove from the heat and leave to cool.

5 Slice each cored pear about three-quarters of the way through, leaving the slices attached at the stem end. Fan out on serving plates.

6 Stir 30ml/2 tbsp of the cooled sauce into the yogurt and spoon it around the pears. Drizzle with the remaining syrup and serve immediately.

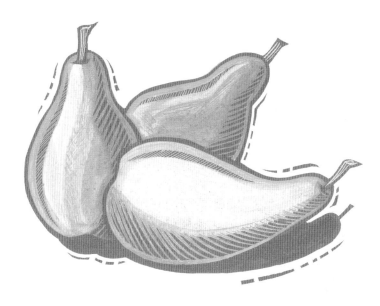

INDEX